Mountain
Miles

Mountain Miles

*A Memoir of Section Hiking
the Southern Appalachian Trail*

MARK CLEGG

Toplight

Jefferson, North Carolina

All photographs are by the author unless otherwise indicated.

ISBN (print) 978-1-4766-7722-4 ∞
ISBN (ebook) 978-1-4766-3679-5

LIBRARY OF CONGRESS AND BRITISH LIBRARY
CATALOGUING DATA ARE AVAILABLE

Front cover photograph: Mark Clegg on Blood Mountain,
April, 2013; background photograph: the Appalachian Trail
in Great Smoky Mountains National Park (© 2019 Shutterstock)

Printed in the United States of America

Toplight is an imprint of McFarland & Company, Inc., Publishers

*Box 611, Jefferson, North Carolina 28640
www.toplightbooks.com*

Table of Contents

Whan that Aprille with his shoures soote,
The droghte of March hath perced to the roote,
And bathed every veyne in swich licóur
Of which vertú engendred is the flour...
Thanne longen folk to goon on pilgrimages....
                              —Geoffrey Chaucer,
                    Prologue to *The Canterbury Tales*

Preface

When I decided in the last year to write this book detailing my section hikes on the southern part of the Appalachian Trail—from Springer Mountain, Georgia, to Damascus, Virginia—I had already read many "hiking books." I have enjoyed just about all of them.

My hiking book is different. It is not a technical backpacking book that is filled with detailed descriptions of gear or feats of extreme endurance and man against the elements machismo. Nor is it a story with a deep psychodrama backdrop. It is a slowly paced chronicle of a five-and-a-half-year journey broken down into nine different segments. I do try to give insights into the unique subculture of backcountry distance hiking. Hiking has never been an integral part of my lifestyle, and for that reason, I try to bring a perspective that is both fresh and curious. I met many, many interesting people along the way, and I hope I was fair and did them justice in my depictions of them.

I also attempt to delve deeply into the rich local history, culture, and biodiversity found along the southern portion of the Appalachian Trail and examine the social, economic, and environmental challenges along this ancient mountain range.

Finally, I weave several compelling family history stories into the story. All of these events took place very near today's Appalachian Trail, and I try to blend them into the narrative as seamlessly as possible. I have included numerous newspaper and book references to the records of my ancestors to ensure the reader that I have not used passed-down family legends or exaggerations in my accounts of them.

I have conducted a great deal of research for this book and cited all sources for facts not based on my own personal experience or knowledge.

All events represented in this book are true, with the exception of a few "trail names." My memory has unfortunately failed me in some instances, so I did have to make up a few (but not many) of the trail names mentioned in this book.

The black bear and the restaurant referenced in the dreams were real; the bear passed on and the restaurant closed decades ago.

Above all else, I have tried my best to deal with a region and a trail that are sacred in the eyes of many, myself included. My goal was to deal with these subjects as honestly, accurately, and affectionately as I could.

I am beholden to a number of people for their help in making this book possible. First and foremost, I would like to thank David J. Marmins, who encouraged me and passed on my initial draft to the publisher. I would also like to thank my father, George "Bud" Clegg, for instilling in me a strong interest and appreciation for the Appalachian Mountains. I am very grateful to my wife, Diane, who has held down the home front and provided shuttle service as my hikes gradually extended more northward and ever farther from home. My daughter, Tess, and son, George, have been constant sources of encouragement, as has my friend and neighbor Lisa Weldon, who well knows the pains associated with writing that first book. I would also like to thank my cousin David Wallace, who conducted a lot of the detailed family research on my great-grandfather, Etna Parks. Finally, I would like to thank Kendall Young of Wood Bat Brand for his patience and expertise in crafting the maps used in this book.

Introduction

On a clear day from the 28th floor of a skyscraper in downtown Atlanta, I can make out the 1,000- to 2,000-foot gray-green humps that Native Americans referred to as the monadnocks or "lonely mountains."[1] The name is appropriate because they are so isolated from other mountains, and thus are more conspicuous. These solitary peaks are named Lost, Pine, Arabia, Sweat, Sawnee, and Kennesaw mountains.

When the air quality is improved and light travels farther in the autumn, I can make out their more plentiful and tightly bunched cousins to the north and east, the Blue Ridge Mountains, and the very first real uphill hiking test on the northbound Appalachian Trail, at a distance of 53 miles, Sassafras Mountain.

I am one of the few residents of the Buckhead community of Atlanta to use public transportation to get to work each day. There are many reasons for this; first and foremost, I hate to drive, and time not spent on the road is time I can spend catching up on the news or reading a book. But it also affords me the opportunity to people-watch, to observe others, and get some idea of an event that may be occurring in the area that might be of interest.

Sports jerseys are, of course, dead giveaways that a game is being played that day or evening. Conventioneers also make it easy; they wear lanyards displaying who they are and why they are in town. The frazzled vacationers, loaded with too much luggage, are a signal that a long holiday weekend is approaching or ending.

Each March and April, for years, I would spot the backpackers starting to show up on the northbound train. They were usually young and carrying expensive and unblemished gear. Sometimes I would strike up a conversation with them, and invariably they would reveal they were

headed to the northernmost station on Atlanta's commuter rail system to meet up with a shuttle. From there they would catch their ride and head off to the start of the Appalachian Trail, just over an hour's drive away. They always had that bright shine that people on the verge of embarking on a new adventure share. I could tell they were eager to embrace the unknown. Their enthusiasm was always a bit contagious, even for an aging cynic like me, and I always held on to the hope that I, too, would give it a try.

Someday.

PART I

Someday Comes

SECTION HIKE 2

November 2–5 | Unicoi Gap, Georgia to Standing Indian Mountain, North Carolina

SECTION HIKE 1

April 22–26 | Springer Mountain to Unicoi Gap, Georgia

SECTION HIKE 1
Springer Mountain to Unicoi Gap, Georgia
April 22–26, 2013 (51 Miles)

Spring comes late in the Appalachian Mountains. Looking out from the crest of Springer Mountain in late April, across the Etowah River Valley and towards the Blue Ridge Mountains unfolding northward, oaks, tulip poplars, sycamores and hickories are still leafless, while Atlanta, less than eighty miles away, is already in full bloom. The rise in elevation of almost 3,000 feet from the Piedmont lowers the temperature a good 5–10 degrees and delays the onset of spring for weeks.

Springer Mountain is very near the southernmost extremity of the Blue Ridge Mountains; its close neighbor, Mount Oglethorpe, thirteen miles to the south, is the actual southwestern anchor of the Blue Ridge range and was formerly the starting point of the Appalachian Trail. In 1958, due to encroaching development, trail officials were forced to move the beginning of the trail from Mount Oglethorpe to Springer Mountain.

I took a deep breath of the clean, pine-scented mountain air and set out on the Appalachian Trail. It was 2013, and I was hoping to cover about 50 miles of "the AT" before getting off at Unicoi Gap near Helen, Georgia.

I was going to hike alone. I had discussed hiking with my cousin in California, but he and his wife had committed to other vacation plans. I was not worried about going solo on my first trip—I had read many books and articles about the AT, and I knew I would meet dozens of hikers along the way.

At the age of 54, this was my first big hiking and camping adventure in years. I had gone on a few two- or three-day trips in the Cohutta Wilderness in northwest Georgia in my 20s with my father and uncle, but I was otherwise inexperienced. I had read both Bill Bryson's and Cheryl Strayed's books on how they struggled as greenhorns learning the

Opposite: **Springer Mountain, Georgia to Standing Indian Mountain, North Carolina—88 miles. Map by Kendall Young, WoodBatBrand.com.**

intricacies of backcountry hiking, and I had every expectation that my experience would be equally trying.

I had mulled over the idea of hiking the AT for years, but my interest was really sparked when I found myself unemployed during the Great Recession; I met a man, about my age, in a job-networking group. He mentioned that he and his son were planning on hiking the 30 miles of the AT between Springer Mountain and Neel's Gap. The names were well known to me—Springer was just over an hour's drive from my home, and I knew it marked "Mile Zero," the starting point of the Appalachian Trail. I had also spent many times as a young boy fighting off motion sickness on the drive through Neel's Gap to visit my grandparents in their small mountain town of Young Harris in north Georgia. When cresting the top of the gap in the back seat of my family's station wagon and holding back the nausea, I would always look at the stone outfitters building next to the AT to see if I could spot any backpackers. The hikers always seemed to be an exotic group to me—even before the AT exploded in popularity, I was fascinated by anyone who would embark on an extended hike and forego the modern conveniences and comforts that are now so integral to our lives.

I was also intrigued by the physical test of hiking, alone and unafraid, through rugged mountain terrain. The romance of the trip also appealed to me—the idea of disappearing deep in to the backwoods for almost a week seemed to be the perfect antidote to my rather humdrum corporate daily life.

I had spent weeks preparing for the trip, including hiking my hilly neighborhood in Atlanta while carrying an old orange backpack from college that held 40 pounds of bricks. I read hiking blogs, talked to the staff at REI, studied weather patterns and pored over maps. Earlier in the month, I had talked to a group of hikers at Neel's Gap near Blairsville, Georgia, who had been forced to hike down the trail to a shelter in the middle of the night after a flash flood at near freezing temperatures filled their tents with icy water. I believed that I was prepared for whatever the trail might throw at me.

Most hikers elect to use the 8.8-mile approach trail that starts from Amicalola Falls (at 729 feet, the highest waterfall east of the Mississippi River), to reach Springer Mountain, the southern terminus of the Appalachian Trail, but I had been warned by several people that that particular stretch was brutal for hikers seeking to establish their trail legs—it has a jolting elevation gain of 2,000-feet over that 8.8 miles. As a novice backpacker, I did not want to wear myself out before the actual trail even began. Those who have "thru-hiked" the AT and every inch of its 2,181 miles are always quick to add, "plus the approach trail at Amicalola Falls."

I knew the area around Springer and Amicalola Falls very well. My grandparents had lived for years in Juno, a small foothills community a short drive away. My grandmother had taught school in the tiny nearby village of Nimblewill, and my grandfather, the son of a Civil War veteran, had farmed the area and later owned a general store. My mother, who had died at age 53 from ovarian cancer, was buried in the small cemetery at New Hope Baptist Church, only a 20-minute drive from Amicalola Falls.

After a full breakfast in Dahlonega, my father dropped me off at U.S. Forest Service Road 42, exactly .9 miles north of Springer Mountain. In order to start from Mile Zero, I hiked this short distance south to reach the official start of the AT. There were six or eight other hikers who had also elected to bypass the Amicalola Falls approach trail, and were, like me, excited by the start of the hike and were energetically moving up the dirt trail sunk two to three inches lower than the surrounding ground, beaten down by the tens of thousands of weighted down boots that had previously tromped by. That short distance of a little less than a mile to the top of Springer flew by in no time, and then, suddenly, the others and I were on the summit enjoying the mid-morning view.

There is an overlook near the peak of Springer Mountain where an unassuming bronze plaque with an oxidized, light green patina is embedded in granite rock. The plaque, made in 1934, is an art deco rendering of Benton McKaye, the visionary whose 1921 article called for the formation of the Appalachian Trail. People gathered around this plaque, took pictures, and signed the nearby hiker's log.

Heading north from the peak was an easy hike aided by a gentle slope and warming temperatures. My 1990s-style outside frame pack weighed 47 pounds for my planned five-day hike. On my first attempt at packing, the weight was 60 pounds, and I was gradually able to reduce it by 13 pounds by removing a hatchet, some books and heavier clothing.

With the naiveté of a true novice outdoorsman, I was still packed for almost every contingency and did not consider my pack weight to be overly burdensome. This was not a problem for the first five miles, as I passed the forest road again and continued past Stover Creek Shelter. I enjoyed a relaxing lunch at Three Forks, where three burbling creeks merged under a sun-splashed canopy of oaks.

The foolishness of my pack weight kicked in as I started the steady ascent up Hawk Mountain, my first true uphill test. The water breaks increased; as did my short stops to catch my breath during the climb. I passed the Hawk Mountain Shelter in mid-afternoon and made the decision to press onward, although this was my first day and I had already hiked over eight miles. I noticed that many of the hikers who had started that morning with me at Springer were setting up camp for the evening at the shelter.

The decision to continue hiking was also my first big mistake: up until this point, water sources had been plentiful, and I assumed this would be the case, basically, for the rest of the Appalachian Trail. I did not check the topographic map that showed water sources, marked by the squiggly blue water drop symbol. By the time I passed Hawk Mountain, I was almost out of water, and according to the map, would not find another source for six miles. I cursed my stupidity, and trudged onward, through a nasty series of steep switchback trails over Sassafras Mountain, hoping by some miracle that I would find a stream or creek that had not been marked on the map.

In the late afternoon, I stumbled into Cooper Gap, serenaded by swirling Army helicopters that trained at the nearby Frank Merrill Ranger Camp. There was a small camping area at the gap near the intersection of two forest roads, where two young hikers had already set up camp.

They were two young men from Florida in their early twenties who had quit their restaurant jobs in Naples to spend the next several months on the trail. The older of the two, Ansell, wore titanium barbell earrings and a two-day scruff of beard. He told me a stream was only a short distance away, down the forest road bordering the north side of the campsite.

I found the source about a quarter mile later, a concrete culvert with a small trickle of cold, clear water leading into a roadside ditch.

After filling my two-liter Camelbak water bladder (a hydration pack connected to a plastic hose and suction tube that allows the hiker to drink water, hands free), I headed back to camp, where Ansell and his roommate were inside their four-man tent, smoking weed. The tent was still enveloped in pungent smoke when a Dodge Ram truck pulled up with a local Dawson County license plate. The driver, dressed in a cowboy hat and jeans, handed Ansell a grocery sack in exchange for $20. This was my first encounter with a form of "trail magic"—the driver had come by earlier and taken their order of two steaks with potatoes. He also dropped off a load of firewood, free of charge.

Another hiker, a Filipino Muslim named Amir, walked in to our site, set up his prayer mat and knelt towards Mecca. He had read a book in the Philippines about the AT and decided to hike the entire trail. He was a "thru-hiker," one of thousands of hikers who set out each year to hike the entire AT in one journey. Eighty-seven percent of thru-hikers start their journey from Springer Mountain and head north. These hikers are known as NOBOs (northbound), and their southbound counterparts are known as SOBOs. Starting from Georgia instead of Maine has the obvious advantage of allowing for an earlier start—spring, and the warmer weather it usually brings, begins at least one month earlier in Georgia. Roughly 25 percent of thru-hikers complete the entire journey, which is almost 2,200 miles in length.[1] It takes the average hiker five to six months to complete a thru-hike, and the Maine portion of the trail leading to the northern terminus at Mount Katahdin usually shuts down for camping in mid to late October. This meant that the thru-hikers I met who were starting, like me, in late April, were not leaving themselves much margin for error if they wanted to complete the entire hike before the Maine trails shut down until the following spring.

I, by contrast, am what is known as a "section-hiker," a backpacker who contiguously hikes the trail in increments—in my case, in 40- to 75-mile chunks. My planned hike from Springer Mountain to Unicoi Gap was just over 50 miles, and it covered roughly two-thirds of the Georgia portion of the AT.

Amir trained for the journey by walking up and down the steps of his house, thousands of times. He had flown from Manila to Los Angeles, where he caught a connecting flight to Atlanta. After 21 hours in the air, he had arrived in Atlanta at 6 a.m. the previous morning, where a van picked him up at the airport and drove him to the approach trail at Amicalola Falls. He hiked the 8 miles of the approach trail before connecting to the AT at Springer Mountain and had camped at Stover Creek Falls the previous evening.

Amir had no family at home, and he was taking a six-month leave of absence from his job as an electrical engineer. I asked him what had drawn him to the trail. "The wilderness," he said, with a serene smile.

Amir cooked some noodles over a Jetboil, an isobutene/propane fuel cooker identical to the one I had bought at REI in Atlanta. He then locked his food in a bear canister, a plastic, airtight container that cuts off all food odors that might attract hungry bears. Finally, without a word to anyone, he went inside his tent, where he remained until the next morning.

Bears are usually well hidden but fairly plentiful in the woods that surround the trail. The last three to four miles before reaching Neel's Gap (about 20 miles away), the bear population becomes particularly heavy, and it is prohibited to camp in that area unless food is stored in a bear canister.

I used the more traditional method of "hanging a pack"—taking a long length of rope and tying a rock at one end. The trick is then to find a sturdy branch at least 15 feet off the ground, throw the rock-tied end of the rope over it, tie the loose end of the rope to a nylon food bag, hoist it at least ten feet above the ground, and finally, tie the other end around an adjacent tree trunk. Bears will not, apparently, figure out how to loosen or cut the rope tied around the tree.

With the water I had collected, I cooked some freeze-dried lasagna and sat on a log in the campsite, sharing my Wild Turkey with Ansell while he offered some of his pot on a night that grew ever chillier. It was the first time I had smoked marijuana in over 30 years, and it had a warm, calming effect after such a physically demanding day.

He and his roommate had brought a portable grill along, which they used to cook the steaks. Ansell took a plate in to his roommate, who ate his meal zipped inside the tent. I felt a little bit better about myself—as impractical as I originally had been on selection of heavy and unnecessary gear, I would have never considered taking a 7- to 10-pound grill on an extended hike.

Ansell had built a log cabin style fire, placing two logs parallel to each other, then placing two logs perpendicular, continuing to use this pattern to stack three levels up. This created a vortex airflow in the middle, and the logs gradually fell inward, creating almost a bonfire-sized blaze. It was not a windy evening, so fortunately I did not have to worry about embers getting picked up by an air current and landing on dry wood and creating a forest fire.

I learned that Ansell had become a restaurant manager after the crash of the Southwest Florida real estate market. He had, in his words, been a successful real estate broker before the wave of foreclosures swamped that local market. He was taking an unpaid leave of absence to hike the trail.

During the banking crisis several years earlier, I had worked with the FDIC on several failed banks in the swath of Southwest Florida where Ansell was from. From Naples to Sarasota, that region perhaps suffered more than any other area during the Great Recession. I had seen first-hand the life-changing blows that were dealt to thousands of homeowners and businesses in that stretch of Florida coast.

It had affected me—I lost my job at the beginning of the recession and was out of work for two years. I was lucky—I was able to "re-invent" myself with a new skill set that was, ironically enough, tied to investigating failed banks and resolving problem loans tied to the real estate crash.

One of the many reasons I took up hiking was that it was a cheap vacation. Gone were the visits to agriturismos in Tuscany and ski trips to Jackson, Wyoming. I was now steadily employed, but I was not making near the money I made prior to the Great Recession.

I asked Ansell how he had dealt with the changes in his life: "Shake and bake," was his response. I liked Ansell.

I was so tired I couldn't sleep. I tossed and turned on the hard ground inside my tent, as the occasional car headlights passed our intersection during the night. The night was also getting very cold, and I checked the temperature tag clipped on to my backpack. It was 34 degrees at 1:30 a.m.

When sleep finally arrived, it brought with it the recurring dream of the black bear from my childhood.

When I was a young boy, my uncle would take my cousin and me to the Black Bear Restaurant, a stone building made of brown, amber, and white rocks hauled from the creeks and rivers in the nearby mountain valleys. The restaurant was next to the state highway that leads northward from Gainesville, Georgia, to Helen, Cleveland, and Hiawassee. I have always thought of this spot as where the mountains began. It was here that the highway rose up, and the hot and humid hills gave way to the purple/green hues of Buckhorn Mountain and Mount Yonah, and then, on the distant northern horizon, Blood, Tray, and Bald mountains.

This was a 1960s diner that featured overcooked hamburgers prepared on a sizzling grill and French fries still soaked in grease. But I was young, and I didn't know the difference—burgers were still a good 40 years or so away from achieving gourmet status.

Flanking the restaurant to the left, perched next to a gorge, was a circus-style lion's cage that held a juvenile black bear. He was young and still frisky, his will and curiosity not yet beaten down by captivity. He wore that goofy, half smile that reminds me so much of Golden Retrievers—I never have known if they are smiling or if that is just the way their mouths are configured. He would pace the cage floor, strewn with hay, and lick food from my hands with his long, pink tongue. He would look at me with chestnut brown eyes and try to stick his snout through the iron bars to get a better angle at the sack of food I was holding. Sometimes he would let me stroke the top of his furry muzzle, and I would shriek with childhood delight.

❦

I woke up late the next morning, around 9:00 a.m. The sleep that finally came to me was fitful, and I felt groggy and weak. When I crawled out of my tent, I saw that Amir had already packed and left the campsite; Ansell and his friend were still inside their tent, which was once again wreathed in weed smoke. I stuck my head inside their tent and told them, "You know, this trail isn't going to hike itself." Ansell responded, "With the marvels of modern technology, it might soon." There were certainly sections from the previous day that I wish had had escalators.

After a bland breakfast of instant oatmeal and grits, I put on my pack and headed up Justus Mountain, through switchbacks trails bordered by trillium, columbine and wild ramp fields.

Ramps (Allium tricoccum), which had become a popular side dish in cutting-edge Atlanta restaurants, are wild onions that sprout up in the southern Appalachians in the early spring; the edible leaves taste best when picked before mid–May (warmer weather brings a more bitter taste to the plant). "Shunning sunshine and civilization, the ramp herolds spring in the rich, shaded coves near the mountain summits, sometimes bursting through the snow in their eagerness to be up and stinking."[2] They have large, tulip-like leaves, thin purplish stems, and small white bulbs. Ramps have an overpowering, garlic-like taste that lingers on the breath. Like many foods that have become popular, ramps used to carry a stigma—only poor people in the mountains who could not afford any better ate ramps.

The trail at the top of Justus Mountain followed an easy ridge line, which slowly meandered down the east side of the mountain to Justus Creek, where I made sure to fill up with three liters of water. Live and learn.

An assistant at REI in Atlanta who had hiked from Georgia to Maine told me that his rule of thumb for purifying water was whether or not it flowed from a pipe—many small springs on mountainsides have water trickles that flow through polyurethane pipes installed by trail volunteers. I used this very unscientific method to determine whether I would use iodine pills to cleanse the water from bacteria.

The temperature by 11:00 a.m. had warmed to the high 70s, a complete shift from the near freezing weather I had battled the night before. Ansell and his friend passed me, and he offered a smile and a "Shake and Bake!"

Early that afternoon, I saw the first person leave the trail, a woman I had met briefly at Springer Mountain. By that time, we had hiked about 16 miles in over a day and a half, and she decided to call her ride to pick her up at Gooch Gap. She had simply hit the wall and could go no step further. No amount of water, food, or coaxing was going to change her mind. The white shuttle van crept up the gap, picked her up, and she was gone.

I had similar feelings on the approach to Woody Gap, about four miles farther along the trail. The climb was not so difficult, really nothing more than a series of ascending ridge lines, but fatigue caused me to miscalculate distance and speed—I thought every time I turned on a switchback I would see or hear the whoosh of cars and trucks speeding over Georgia Highway 60 through Woody Gap. This, I learned, was the hiker's mirage. The "green tunnel" of trees limits sight, so the mind begins to wildly calculate remaining time and distance, usually with undue optimism. As the day's final destination gets closer, arrival time expectancy increases, which defies the laws of physics unless a hiker is speeding up. And I, most certainly, was not speeding up my hike as I approached day's end.

Luckily, there was a privy at Woody Gap, which I used. Reinvigorated, I decided to push on and camp at the top of Big Cedar Mountain, a 3,700-foot peak that rises over Georgia Highway 60 just on the east side of the gap. This would jumpstart me for the next day's hike over Blood Mountain in to Neel's Gap, where there was a hiker's hostel.

True to its name, Big Cedar Mountain's summit was covered with cedar trees, which is rather unusual for the southern Appalachians. I set up my tent on a bare space next to a campfire pit surrounded by a ring of stones and close to the ledge overlooking the valley to the south.

A tall hiker with curly black hair with the trail name "Log Splitter" approached my campsite. He had hiked 18 miles from Stover Creek on just his second day on the trail. Impressed by his accomplishment, I invited him to pitch his tent in the one available spot across the fire from me.

Log Splitter had recently graduated from a small liberal arts college in Tennessee named Lincoln Memorial. He had been the mascot for their athletic teams, the Log Splitters, which earned him his trail moniker. It was an hour before dusk, and I had created a nice, roaring blaze of a campfire. Temperatures were plummeting, and for the second straight night were expected to fall below freezing. The cedar wood from the fire created a melody of loud, popping sounds that periodically sent sparks flying beyond the ring of stones.

Log Splitter was a thru-hiker, and he planned to finish in Maine in August, despite the fact that he had started in late April. Four months to complete the over 2,000-mile journey was ambitious, but he seemed to have the long legs and stamina to fulfill his goal. He was not planning on leaving the trail for a break until Fontana Dam, more than 100 miles away.

Shortly before nightfall, Log Splitter wanted to turn in, and he asked me to put out the fire. I was learning "trail hours"—you sleep when it is dark, you hike when it is light.

Before I crawled into my tent, I went to the ledge overlooking Yahoola Valley, bathed in an early spring shimmer of light green. The southern edge of the valley yielded to the brick buildings, houses, and the twinkling lights of the college town of Dahlonega.

My great-great-great grandfather, Benjamin Parks, Jr., had discovered gold near modern-day Dahlonega in 1828, kicking off what was then the biggest gold rush in the history of the United States. In a scene reminiscent of the opening of the old TV show *The Beverly Hillbillies,* Benjamin Parks had been out hunting on a late October morning when he stumbled across a huge ingot of gold near the Chestatee River.

The Reverend Robert O'Barr, the pastor of the Baptist church Parks attended in Yellow Creek, owned the land where Parks had found the gold. Parks convinced his pastor to lease the land to him for mining rights—the preacher thought that Parks had lost his mind, and there was no possibility of any gold on the land. Once he realized his mistake, he tried to buy the lease back from Parks, who refused. O'Barr's frustration gradually grew to the point that he sold the land to John C. Calhoun, who eventually became the seventh vice president of the United States.

As part of the sale, Parks also agreed to sell the lease to Calhoun— it is unclear why he sold it— perhaps Parks thought that nearly all the ore had been depleted from the 239 acres of land formerly owned by O'Barr. After the sale, when gold in what came to be called the "Calhoun Mine"[3] continued to prove plentiful, it was Parks's turn to be upset: "I was inclined to be as mad at him as O'Barr had been with me. But that is the peculiarity of gold mining. You will go day after day exhausting your means and your strength until you give it up. Then, the first man who touches the spot finds the gold the first opening he makes."

Calhoun picked Thomas G. Clemson, his son-in-law and a mining engineer, to operate the mine. Money made from the mine was later used to help start Clemson College (later University). There is some dispute about how rich the veins were from the Calhoun Mine, but according to Parks, 24,000 pennyweights were taken out in the first month alone.[4]

According to Parks, "The news got abroad, and such excitement you never saw. It seemed within a few days as if the whole world must have heard about it, for men came from every state I had ever heard of. They came afoot, on horseback and in wagons, acting more like crazy men than anything else. All the way from where Dahlonega now stands to Nuckolsville (Auraria) there were men panning out of the branches and making holes in the hillside. It was an exciting time!"[5] In 1828, communication from a remote area like Georgia to the wider world was very slow. But, since it was gold that was discovered, the news spread like wildfire.

Benjamin Parks had made his discovery in late October 1828, and by 1829, the "29ers" had already swarmed into the valleys, ridges, creekbeds and riverbeds of northeast Georgia in search of gold that was purer than "Spanish doubloons." It was, in the words of Thomas Clemson, so pure that "a mere glance of the eye is frequently sufficient to fix its value. The gold from the Chestatee River has a smooth, clean, glossy appearance, something like flax seed."[6]

The town of Nuckolsville, just west of Dahlonega, had its name changed by John C. Calhoun to Auraria, a derivative of the Latin word for gold, aurum. Today it is a ghost town, but in 1833, it had "one hundred family dwellings, eighteen or twenty stores, twelve or fifteen law offices, and four or five taverns."[7] One pint of whiskey could be obtained in an Auraria saloon for 3½ grains of gold (about .07 oz.).[8]

Chances to make a fortune were limited in early 19th century America—opportunities to invest in stocks, bonds, real estate, or factories were not available, thus making gold one of the few avenues of wealth creation. And gold in the Dahlonega area was easy to find in the first few years—it was in the streams and on the ground.[9]

Inevitably, the invasion of speculators and miners in to the mountain counties of northeast Georgia created tension with the semi-autonomous Cherokee Nation. The Cherokees' eastern border abutted modern day Lumpkin County (then part of Hall and Habersham counties), the area where Parks had stumbled across that first gold nugget.

The State of Georgia had long advocated for removal of the Cherokees and had gradually chipped away at their rights. Federal treaties in the early 19th century had led to the formation of the Cherokee Nation, but Georgia laws were subsequently passed that established that the Cherokee Nation's Constitution was inconsistent with the rights of

Georgia, and the state government had the right to claim title to Cherokee lands on terms at its pleasure.

The federal treaties signed in the early 19th century had resulted in the Cherokees losing about half of their territory—they agreed to shrink their nation to north Georgia and adjacent lands in western North Carolina and eastern Tennessee. At the time that gold was discovered, the white population of Georgia had reached almost 500,000, and the Cherokees numbered only 8,000—it was only a matter of time before the white settlers overran their lands, but gold was the spark that lit the fire for their forced removal.[10]

Before it ended and the 29ers moved on to the richer gold fields of California, over 6,000 miners had swarmed into northeast Georgia. Many settled in the region, and this was one of the contributing factors to the 1838 Trail of Tears, when an estimated 16,000 Cherokees were forced from their homes in Tennessee, Alabama, Georgia and North Carolina and forced to embark on the 1,000-mile trek to reservations in Oklahoma—an estimated 6,000, many of whom were women and children, died along the march.

Years later, Benjamin Parks was interviewed late in his life by *The Atlanta Constitution*, and he expressed regret over the "Great Intrusion" caused by the 29ers. When Parks and his family had moved from Rutherford County, North Carolina, to the Dahlonega area when he was a child they had many Cherokee neighbors and were welcomed among them. Parks remembered a special meal prepared by his Cherokee friends called conee-banee, probably made from the traditional "three sisters" of squash, corn, and beans.

He also claimed that he fell in love with the daughter of a Cherokee chief: "she was a stunner—as pretty a woman as I ever saw, her eyes I can remember yet." She shared his love, but, in the words of Parks, "I was a white and could not marry a woman from another race. I could never have brought her over to my folks, and as a consequence, I would have been forced to go with hers. Our children would have had no nation, so I did not marry her; but dear me, how beautiful she was!" Parks never saw his princess again when she vanished during the Trail of Tears. The Cherokees, he said, "would have gotten on all right if they had been left alone. Those were good times," he said, as his sad eyes wandered in their gaze towards the tall treetops.[11] In old age he still had

Sarah Parks and Benjamin Parks, Jr., sometime in the late 19th century (Georgia Archives, Vanishing Georgia Collection, image lum219-84).

a sincere sense of loss over the sad fate of the Cherokees and the role his discovery might have played in their expulsion from their homeland.

Benjamin was a bit of a ham (he also claimed to have killed two deer from one shot from his five-feet, ten-inch rifle named "Old Susie"), and no one knows for sure whether he was truly the first white settler to discover gold in Georgia. There were many other claimants, and Parks's story has inconsistencies on dates and the amount of gold that was actually made from the Calhoun mine. His claim, more than anything else, might have been solidified by the fact that he lived long enough to make his assertion to the reporter from the *Atlanta Constitution* in 1894: "I turned up the first nuggets ever found about here. Other men will claim it—men will claim anything—but dog-my-cats if I ain't the one, sure enough."[12]

Parks and his wife Sarah had eleven children, and he remained spry into his nineties, when he amused local children doing handstands. He enjoyed riding his mule, Becky, to the school in Dahlonega where he would entertain the young students with tricks and stories of the Gold Rush. He died after falling off Becky at the age of 92 in 1895.[13]

❧✳❧

I had a more restful night of sleep. Winds from the Yahoola Valley flew up the side of Big Cedar Mountain and made a mournful, wailing sound. My tent rattled from the wind gusts all night long, but the ghostly cacophony was somehow peaceful and helped lull me into a dreamless slumber.

When I got out of my tent the next morning, Log Splitter had already packed up and was cinching up his pack. He was headed to Neel's Gap, my destination, and he would be getting an hour's head start.

I enjoyed a leisurely breakfast while sitting on a felled log that bordered the camping area. I pulled out my Lumberjack all-utility knife (which weighed over a pound and was one of the least practical items I had packed for the trip) to cut some moleskin as a bandage for my blistered foot. I was sitting with my left leg crossed over my right knee while trying to cut through the moleskin. I had to apply more force than I expected, and when the blade finally cut through the material, it continued its arc until it sank into the ball of my left foot.

As always after an injury, there is a 10–15 second period of stunned disbelief that the event actually occurred. But blood was pouring from the wound, and I finally took action by using two large gauze pads that immediately soaked up the gushing blood. I used two more fresh pads to cover the inch-long cut and bound it with medical tape wrapped around my entire foot.

My options were to hike back down Big Cedar Mountain and flag a ride to the hospital or continue on my hike. I convinced myself that all foot wounds look worse than they actually are and put my socks and boots on.

At this point, I realized I had made another major mistake. My metal hiking poles were gone. I ran through a quick mental checklist and realized I had left them at the privy I had used the previous afternoon at Woody Gap. I was not going to go back down to look for them, so I grabbed a long stick of cedar to use as a cane and started my descent down the mountain.

My goal was to make it to Neel's Gap, a distance of 10 miles. The major hurdle was Blood Mountain, at 4,458 feet the sixth highest mountain in Georgia, and the tallest peak until the trail reached North Carolina, almost 50 miles distant.

About halfway down my descent from Big Cedar Mountain, I stopped to get water at a nearby spring. A father and son duo from Miami, whom I had met earlier, walked by me. The father, a retired Marine who was taking his 20-something son on the thru-hike to Maine, was using my hiking poles. I mentioned this to him and he asked me if I wanted them back. "Ummm, yeah, please." I gave him my cedar cane, and he and his son continued down the trail at a rapid clip.

I soon met up with Dean, a Milwaukee cop who was taking a six-month leave of absence to hike the trail. His trail name was "Retina" because he was attempting to hike the trail with a detached retina. He had a wicked, self-deprecatory sense of humor that made him fun to be around. He related a story from Hawk Mountain Shelter, where an amorous Brazilian couple decided to memorialize the beginning of their thru hike with a romantic coupling inside their two-person sleeping bag. This cleared out the rest of the shelter except for Retina, who was stubborn because it was "his shelter, too."

While starting the long ascent up Blood Mountain, we met a trail volunteer (these are experienced local outdoorsmen and women who "adopt" certain stretches of the trail where they offer assistance and advice to hikers). The 50-ish volunteer was a "Triple Crowner"—he had thru-hiked the AT, Pacific Crest and Continental Divide trails. That added up to almost 8,000 miles of hiking, or about one-third the circumference of our planet. So, I listened to what he had to say.

"A bad storm is coming from the west, and it is going to hit mid-afternoon and last through the evening. You may want to rent a cabin at Neel's Gap." Sure enough, a glance over my shoulder revealed that clouds approaching from that direction were heavy and gray. Retina and I agreed to get a two-bedroom cabin and split the $60 cost.

He further suggested that we take a side trail that went around the mountain in order to avoid the steep descent off Blood Mountain's granite-faced eastern side. Over the course of my life, I had passed through Neel's Gap by car hundreds of times while driving by Blood Mountain on Highway 19. There was no way I was going to hike around Blood Mountain.

Despite its relative height at this early stage of the AT, the hike up Blood Mountain from the west is not too strenuous, with mostly easy-to-manage switchback trails. At 4,000 feet, I encountered what would become familiar signs that I was approaching mountain summits: rhododendron tunnels, the cool rush of sub–Alpine air, and the invigorating Christmas tree aroma of firs.

At the top of Blood Mountain, the sturdy Depression-era Civilian Conservation Corps shelter made of local stone was billowing clouds of ganja smoke. Inside were two French Canadian hikers who had bused down from Quebec City to hike the trail and had arranged a comfortable camp inside the structure, shielded from both wind and rain.

The rain came down as I started my descent from Blood Mountain, heavy and suffused with the metallic smell of ozone. That, combined with the now black clouds that were scurrying over my head to the east, left no doubt that this rain was going to last for a while. The AT on the upper east face of Blood Mountain consists of a path that winds its way down granite rock angling downward at 45 degrees for 800 feet before it finally levels out. The slippery rocks, combined with the drenching rain and a poorly marked trail (the white paint "blazes" marking the AT were scarce) made this the most treacherous stretch of trail yet.

Ponchos are never impermeable to rain, I discovered, and I was soon soaked to the skin. I skidded and slid down a good portion of the trail until it leveled out near Byron Herbert Reece State Park. From there, I could hear the whoosh of traffic and spray of water from semis and cars rushing down from Neel's Gap on U.S. Highway 19. The AT runs parallel to this highway for about a quarter mile before it faces Walasi-Yi, a rambling, Civilian Conservation Corps stone building that now houses Mountain Crossings, an outfitter and a hostel that had a dozen or so bunks (first come, first serve) at $15 a night. The building was originally a dance hall, inn and restaurant and was placed on the National Register of Historic Places in 1979.[14]

I spotted Log Splitter, who had arrived three hours earlier than I had. He was bunking down in the hostel, as was the retired Marine and his son. Ansell and his friend had arrived early but wasted too much time and by the time they decided to pay for bunks, there were no more available. So they were forced to stay outside in the cold and rain, where presumably their ample supply of pot would provide some comfort.

I bought a frozen Red Baron pepperoni pizza and four quarts of Gatorade before walking the short distance to Blood Mountain Cabins. Along the way, I passed under the trees where successful thru-hikers had had their boots hung from branches, similar to gang members slinging a pair of tied together shoes over a telephone wire to mark territory. I found out my room number, knocked on the door, and Retina let me in. He had showered and changed in to comfortable clothes and was watching a movie, *The Legend of Bagger Vance*. This was a bit of a jolt—30 minutes ago I had been struggling down Blood Mountain in a pouring rain, now I was in a warm, dry place with satellite television.

Retina had already claimed the downstairs bedroom, and the cabin was an A-frame, so I went upstairs and dropped my gear in my bedroom. Before showering, the moment of truth arrived with my foot wound. I carefully peeled off my woolen sock, which stuck to the ball of my foot with dried black blood. I cringed as I pulled the bandage off, fearing the worst. It was not as bad as I feared—an inch-long hook shaped wound that already seemed to be scabbing up.

I scrubbed off three days and 30 miles worth of sweat, dirt, and blood. My body was bruised and there were abrasions on my shoulders due to friction with the pack straps. I emptied out all my garbage, dressed, and went back downstairs.

Prolonged hiking and camping stir my primitive carnivore cravings—after a few days of jerky, fruit bars and oatmeal, protein-laced treats swam in my head—namely, cheeseburgers. A beer wouldn't be out of place, either. But a pizza would have to do on this evening, and I wolfed it down in 15 minutes. I drank three liters of Gatorade and watched the movie as the rain continued to pour.

Retina was writing a hiker's blog, and he asked me about Blood Mountain and how it had gotten that name. It felt good sharing that bit of local Cherokee lore that I had learned years ago with someone who lived almost a thousand miles away.

Where the southern Blue Ridge Mountains meet the upper Piedmont marked the informal territorial line between two great native tribes, the Cherokee and the Creek.

The Cherokee names for places in the northeast Georgia mountains have a haunting beauty: Walasi-Yi (Home of the Great Frog), Choestoe (Land of the Dancing Rabbits), Chestatee (Fire Light Place), Amicalola (Tumbling Waters) and Dahlonega (yellow or gold), just to name a few.

Blood Mountain derived its name from a battle between the Cherokees and Creeks in an area of Union County between Blood Mountain and Slaughter Gap. As legend has it, the battle was so vicious that the mountain "ran with blood," hence the name. The Cherokee were victorious, and this may have marked the last major incursion of Creeks into Cherokee land.

Blood Mountain was an especially sacred place for the Cherokee. They believed in the Nun'ne'bi or "People Who Live Anywhere." Blood Mountain was one of the three major places where this mystical race of spirit folk lived.

These spirit people only revealed themselves to humans during times of need. The Cherokees believed that after gold miners overran the area, the Nun'ne'bi left the sacred mountain. It is said, though, that the drumming of the Nun'ne'bi can sometimes still be heard deep in the woods. The sound is mistaken by those who hear it as trees bending in the wind or birds pecking at ancient oaks, but it is the Nun'ne'bi paying tribute to the earth and Creator.[15]

Morning brought the return of brilliant sunshine. I went by the front office and picked up my clean laundry. Retina and I had both dropped off our dirty clothes at the front desk—for our $60, we also got free laundry.

I walked the short distance to Mountain Crossings, bought a few items and set off on the trail. Adjacent to Mountain Crossings is a stone arch, the only man-made structure hikers pass beneath on the entire Appalachian Trail.

I talked with a few hikers who had spent a miserable night outside during the cold rain and congratulated myself on the decision to bunk at Blood Mountain Cabins. I was refreshed and invigorated from two showers and a restful night of sleep.

The former Marine and his son, the pair who had returned my hiking poles, were sitting in the porch area of Mountain Crossings. They had started their hike with nothing more than heavy ponchos to protect them from the cold and rain, despite the fact that they slept in hammocks, not tents. Every night since they started had seen temperatures nudge down to freezing, which they had not bargained for. The father called his wife in Miami and asked her to buy used sleeping bags and a tent for shipment to Walasi-Yi—he refused to pay "outfitter prices" for his gear.

Anecdotally, at Neel's Gap, 30 miles in to the AT, an estimated 20–30 percent of thru-hikers quit the Trail.[16] Some do not finish the 8.8-mile approach trail to Springer Mountain, never making it to "Mile Zero."

The reasons people who have spent months planning and blogging about their upcoming thru-hike quit the AT so early in the hike are myriad—they get injured; the weight of their packs becomes unbearable; they wildly miscalculate the physical demands of trying to hike 10–12 miles a day in rough terrain in inclement weather. Many thru-hikers who start out in March or April, like the former Marine and his son, do not properly plan for cold weather in Georgia, when temperatures in the mountains still drop below freezing in the early to mid-spring. The psychological demands of an extended thru-hike are enormous. Nothing in life has prepared most people in the United States for the challenge of regularly sleeping outdoors next to strangers, eating repetitive, tasteless and unappetizing food, getting soaking wet, and trudging through mountains while carrying 30–45 pounds on their backs.

It is easy to buy into a romanticized version of hiking the AT, and the actual experience hits some unsuspecting novice hikers like a sledge-hammer. The reality is that the AT very rarely consists of a 70-degree sunny day with a light, soothing breeze and a gentle downhill trail. And when they realize that it is not going to work out for them, it can be traumatic. They have spent months talking about their upcoming hike with friends and family, sent packages to be picked up at waypoints along the trail, and blocked out 5–6 months of their lives for this grand adventure. It is understandable that they feel an overwhelming sense of shame and disappointment once they realize that their dreams of hiking the entire trail have been shattered.

The legendary and greatly missed former owner of Mountain Crossings, Winton Porter, used all his persuasive powers to try and bolster wavering thru-hikers at Neel's Gap:

> "I tell them, 'Here are the people who are going to help you. Their names are Lumpy, Flying Pork Chop, Dartman and Cornbread (store assistants),'" says Porter. "After a warm shower, a nice bunk, a great view, I talk to them. I spend 50 percent of my time talking people out of things. They tell me, 'I need a new backpack.' I say, 'Well the backpack I can work with, it's the sleeping bag that's killing you…. I'm a back-ologist, a shoe-ologist, a psychologist, a sociologist and a plumber.'"[17]

The process that Porter and his assistants used to reduce pack weight was called "the Shakedown," and the discards (which have included a machete, a coffee grinder, a hardback copy of *War and Peace*, a snorkel and mask, and other useless weight) were boxed up and mailed home. Porter said UPS trucks pick up about 9,000 pounds of unnecessary gear at Mountain Crossings every year.[18]

A pair of 2009 thru-hikers, Georganna and Logan Seamon, bought Mountain Crossings from Porter in 2014. They have met different hikers who have brought along such curiosities as a cello with an amplifier, a pet fox, and an eagle. Georganna counsels wavering hikers headed north to abide by the "Three Day Rule"—give the AT another three days, and something good will happen; maybe something as simple as a beautiful sunset or a hamburger.

After leaving Walasi-Yi, the hike toward Cowrock Mountain offered several brilliant views to the north. With May fast approaching, the leaves were still mostly bare on the gently swaying tulip polars, oaks, and beeches. Mountain laurel and wild hostas bordered the path. The trill of wood thrushes, always active in the early morning, provided a welcomed musical accompaniment that took me back to my days as a boy in the woods.

I met Caveman at the summit of Cowrock. Caveman was a heavy-set, balding man in his thirties from rural Indiana. His right arm was withered and in a sling—he had injured it in a warehouse accident several years before. He was living on long-term disability insurance, but the injury had not stopped him from hiking most of the Appalachian Trail the previous year. He made it all the way to New England where, in his words, "he fucked around too long in New Hampshire" and had to get off in October due to weather conditions. Baxter State Park in Maine, which is the last approach area at the end of the trail to Mt. Katahdin, typically shuts down for campers in mid-autumn.

Caveman was a chain-smoker, but he moved quickly. A lot of hikers smoked and, like Caveman, had less than lean physiques, but that did not slow them down. Since he had already hiked almost 2,000 miles of the trail, he had attracted a following of three or four thru-hikers who relied on his knowledge and experience.

Caveman also always had a bag of pot, which was not uncommon on the AT. Carrying a supply of marijuana is referred to as "green blazing." It added nothing to pack weight, and it offered an easy way to unwind in the evening after a 12-, 14-, or 16-mile hike. In Caveman's case, however, smoking pot offered a way of coping with the actual hike. He and others would hike the trail while high, which astounded me—the trail can be confusing at times, with side trails that veer off, and there are stories of hikers getting lost for days. I had always heard about one backpacker who had taken a wrong turn at Blood Mountain and ended up in Tallulah Gorge, 20 miles south of the AT. More tragically, there was the case of "Inchworm," a 66-year-old woman who died in Maine after getting lost. While attempting to find her way back to civilization, she kept a log for 26 days before dying, and her body was found two years later, just two miles from the AT.[19]

The white blazes on trees marking the trail can be inconsistently placed, and if I did not see one for a quarter mile, my thoughts immediately jumped to the possibility that I had taken a wrong turn. It is very easy to get into a rhythm and get confused when an old logging road converges with the trail or a rocky area is poorly marked. In short, a weed induced haze and the paranoia that might ensue were not something that would enhance my experience.

Caveman left his weed near the top of the gorge on the trail descending down to Tesnatee Gap. He and a couple of his entourage had stopped and smoked on a large rock. Caveman had then hiked down the steep trail to the gap, leaving his friends behind. They realized his mistake, and began shouting "Caveman!" that reverberated at least a mile away, which is where I first began to hear it. The logistics of reuniting Caveman with his pot were discussed—he was going to camp at Deep Gap that evening, the same place I was planning on pitching my tent. After briefly discussing the possibility that I would be the mule, his friends ultimately decided to drop it off to him during their night hike to Blue Mountain Shelter.

It was during the steep ascent up the other side of the gap, a steep 500-foot climb, that I really began to slow down and take mini-breaks every 50 feet or so. In preparation for my trip, I had spent months hiking my neighborhood in Atlanta using an old backpack filled with forty pounds of bricks. Nothing, though, serves as adequate physical preparation for hiking the AT. In my case, shortness of breath and elevated blood pressure were really slowing me down. This was worrisome, because I noticed that other hikers were not having the same trouble.

After finally reaching the top of Tesnatee Gap, it was still another five-mile hike to Deep Gap over rolling hillocks, called "stamps," in north Georgia. These stamps usually had elevation gains of 250 to 500 feet, but since they are shorter than mountains, trails take a more direct approach, sometimes a straight line over the top instead of the switchbacks used for the higher elevation gains.

I finally spotted Deep Gap in the early evening at the top of a long switchback trail leading into a welcoming little glen bisected by a bubbling creek. While hiking down the trail, I spotted dozens of tents and hammocks strung out in the campsites that bordered the shelter. It was a perfect set-up—lots of campers and a water source, but plenty of space for privacy and quiet for a light sleeper like me.

For many thru-hikers, shelters are the only way to bunk for the evening. They will plan their day's hike based on when they will arrive at a certain shelter, and if it is full, they may hike the 8–10 miles to the next shelter to avoid camping alone in many of the small, cleared areas right off the trail.

I never saw the attraction of shelters, which were three sided structures with tin roofs and wooden planking for flooring. Mice smell food in packs and will go to great lengths to get to it, including tightroping across wire and chewing through backpacks. In order to keep their teeth sharp, rodents have to chew on hard surfaces, and canvas packs are ideal for that purpose. I have heard many stories from hikers who have been woken from deep sleep by mice scurrying across their faces.

Depending on whether the structure is double decked or not, shelters can comfortably sleep six to 12 people. During times of rain and heavy hiking traffic such as the early spring, more will squeeze in, meaning that strangers are stretched out with their faces inches away from each other. When this many people are grouped together, the inevitable nocturnal noises of snoring, farting, and constant shifting in sleeping bags will keep a light sleeper like me up for most of the night.

I spotted Caveman and gave him the happy news that his weed would soon be arriving. He was one of the early arrivals who had claimed his spot in the shelter

Retina was near me, and his tent had a pronounced sag to it. This did not go unnoticed by Retina, who made a string of self-deprecating comments about his camping abilities.

I met Bob from New Orleans, a deep-voiced, pony-tailed thru-hiker who hung a hammock in the spot next to mine. Bob had outdone me with his initial pack weight, starting the approach trail at Amicalola Falls with 60 pounds, including half a dozen cans of weighty Campbell's soup. One learns quickly on the AT, and less than one week later, Bob was able to laugh at his newbie ignorance.

I sat on a log bordering my camping area and followed, through a series of text messages with my wife, my eighth grade son's middle school baseball championship game. They lost in the last inning.

It was a beautiful, cold and windless night, perfect for camping. Our cove was bathed in full moonlight. It was what the Native Americans termed a "Pink Moon," an April full moon, so called because the early spring is when the pink-hued ground cover named phlox is in full bloom. Even by going to bed as soon as the sun dipped over the western ridge, I was lucky to sleep maybe six or seven hours. The muffled tones of other campers talking and unzipping their tents and bags will prevent me from dozing off. I always struggle with finding a comfortable spot on the tent floor or trying to find the optimal spot for resting my head on a makeshift pillow of a sleeping bag cover stuffed with clothes. Even with a 10–12-mile hike from the previous day under my belt, I still needed earplugs to muffle the ambient noise and relax enough to get any measure of rest.

༺✵༻

The next morning was clear and bracingly cold; many campers had already quietly departed when I began my now familiar ritual of sorting and repacking my gear.

Before I left the camping area, Caveman asked me how I slept. "Ten hours of lying on my back, six hours of sleep," was my response. He smiled and responded, "Yeah, that is about right." It made me feel a little better to know that seasoned campers like Caveman also had trouble sleeping outdoors.

I felt even better about myself a little bit later—someone discovered that a hiker who had gotten an early start that morning had left his food pack hanging from the bear cable. Caveman knew whom it belonged to and put it in his pack; he would eventually catch up with the hiker and return it to him. It was also another example of hikers looking out for each other on the AT.

It really is easy to make mistakes like that on the trail. Almost no one is prepared for the physical grind and lack of sleep. Keeping up with a hundred different items that should find their way in to a pack each morning is also a new experience. I liken it to the first day of traveling abroad—I'm tired from jet lag, disoriented, unsure of where I should be going, and suddenly in charge of keeping up with a bunch of luggage.

The day's hike, which was only about eight miles to Unicoi Gap, started with a pleasant five miles over dusty old logging trails. Descending at a steep angle can be as strenuous as a tough climb, but this was a gentle path, with a slight breeze and no threat of rain.

I had lunch at Chattahoochee Gap before my final climb of the trip, over the boulders of Raven Cliffs and Blue Mountain down to Unicoi Gap, where my father would be picking me up.

The source of the Chattahoochee River, which formed Lake Lanier and supplies water and hydroelectric power for Atlanta, is about 300 feet off the trail. It is nothing more than a small hole trickling water off of a ravine. Visibly, the trickle never became a meaningful flow as it made its way down the mountainside to the valley below before it started its journey through north Georgia on its way to the Gulf of Mexico. Bob from New Orleans and several other thru-hikers stopped to rest at the sign pointing to the source of the river. I told them that it was worth the effort to hike down to it. But when I told them the distance, they shrugged their shoulders, hoisted their packs, and headed back up the AT.

Almost every hiker maintains a different pace, and I would talk to numerous people over the course of a day, typically just a snippet of conversation. These short encounters are invaluable, however, for picking up news on upcoming weather, bear sightings, the degree of difficulty immediately ahead, and other important information on the vagaries of the trail.

These encounters are also interesting from a tortoise and hare standpoint. The person that I speak to briefly may zoom ahead of me, but I may catch up with him or her several times up the trail. "Everyone has a different hike," so the saying goes, and the pace of the hike is strangely not dependent on age, body type or training. There are a lot of heavy-set hikers (Caveman, for instance) on the trail, and they, by their own admission, have not spent much time on the treadmill before stepping foot on Springer Mountain. Determination and single-mindedness seem to be the best ingredients for successful, extended hiking trips. Many thru-hikers give up early in the trip when they cannot mentally accept the cruel math that lies in front of them. They end up continually re-calculating the remaining miles to Maine, which will make the goal seem insurmountable. Focusing just on the next few days, the next week, and breaking the trip up in the mind into small increments seems to be a much less stressful strategy.

It is a melancholy feeling when the summit of the last mountain is reached and the descent down to the gap means the end of the hike. In my case, my father was picking me up at Unicoi Gap at Georgia Highway 17. The highway can always be heard well before it is seen, sometimes as early as 5–6 miles before it becomes visible. The steady hum of cars and trucks can reverberate for miles if there is no ambient noise in between. The north Georgia poet, Byron Herbert Reece described this bewildering clash where civilization invaded his mountain sanctuary:

> A pace or two beyond my door
> Are highways racing east and west.
> I hear their busy traffic roar,
> Fleet tourists bound on far behests
> And monstrous mastodons of freight
> Passing in droves before my gate.[20]

I spotted Caveman, who needed to restock his supply of cigarettes and was hitching a ride to Helen, a former lumber town that had turned into a tourist attraction in the 1970s by converting itself into a faux Bavarian village. I had mentioned Helen earlier to Retina, thinking a Milwaukee German like him might enjoy it. He seemed to like the idea and asked that we give him a lift to town if he were unable to hitch a ride—we knew that he would arrive at the highway before me. He obviously was successful, because there was no trace of him when I crossed the road.

My father picked me up in a parking area off Highway 17, and as we drove southward to Dahlonega, my emotions were mixed. I was pleased that I had managed to spend almost a week on the trail without getting lost or dying, or even seriously injuring myself. I was not an experienced outdoorsman, so there was that bit of accomplishment that I could hang my hat on. But I also felt almost guilty that I was leaving those like Retina and Caveman behind. I had completed 50 miles of the trail, just over two percent of the total distance of the AT. They, on the other hand, were still out there making the hour-by-hour decisions on how far to hike for the day, when to get off the trail due to bad weather, when to replenish supplies, and how to tend to injuries. I felt both a little jealous and a little relieved.

SECTION HIKE 2
Unicoi Gap, Georgia, to Standing Indian Mountain, North Carolina
November 2–5, 2013 (40 Miles)

When I picked up the trail again at Unicoi Gap, it was early November 2013. My plan was to hike the 40 or so miles to Standing Indian Mountain in North Carolina before starting a new job back in Atlanta. This trip was a spur of the moment decision; I had quit my job the week before and was starting a new one in mid–November.

November has always been my favorite time of the year. In Atlanta, it is the time of seasonal transition, when summer's hold on the land is finally, irretrievably, broken. In the mountains, autumn arrives earlier— the first frosts dust the mountaintops in mid–October, two or three weeks after the equinox, sometimes coinciding with the emergence of the Hunter's Moon.

I had upgraded my gear from my previous trip, replacing my over-sized 1990s outside frame backpack with a sleek new model from REI that featured heavily padded shoulder and hip straps and more pockets than I could possibly ever use. I also replaced the ancient sleeping bag, which was so large I had been forced to strap it to the outside of the old pack. I also had bought several light, synthetic fabric shirts and better rain gear, which further reduced my load. With various other adjustments, I was headed into this section hike with 38 pounds of weight, versus 47 on my previous trip.

The skies were gray, and the temperatures were in the low 50s, befitting a typical mid-autumn day in the north Georgia mountains. The trail started with two moderately difficult hikes over Rocky and then Tray Mountains. Past Tray, the path ran parallel to Blue Hole Falls, where I used to swim as a kid. We would camp in the area next to the creek above the falls. There, we would fry the rainbow trout that we had caught earlier in the day, coated in cornmeal batter, in an iron skillet held over a campfire. During one outing, my father was at the top of the

45-foot falls, looking for a flat surface to dive from into the deep, cold pool of water at the bottom. There was a section of the lower falls that jutted out, and divers had to push out and dive in an arc to avoid the rocks on the way down. As he planted his feet and shifted forward in preparation for the dive, he slipped on a slick, moss-covered stone and tumbled awkwardly headfirst over the falls before splashing into the water below. On the way down, he grazed his head on a protruding rock and when he finally emerged from the surface of the water after what seemed like an eternity, his head was covered with blood. It was traumatic for me as a boy, and I still remember the anguished screams from my mother when he finally bobbed up, bloody and probably briefly unconscious. We walked back to the car, a distance of several miles, with my father's head wrapped in a towel. The wound was tended to in a hospital in Hiawassee and required 25 stiches to close.

He was not the only one injured (or killed) by daredevilry at Blue Hole, and today there is a large log placed against the falls to discourage people from jumping from the top.

The trail is quieter and more serene in the autumn, with much less traffic than in the spring. While leaves are late to fall in autumn in north Georgia, there were enough to cover the trail, in some instances, up to the top of the sunken trail edges.

A pleasant, level portion of the AT called the Swag of the Blue Ridge leads to the foot of Kelly's Knob, which features the longest and steepest grade of the Georgia portion of the AT. I had learned to save the tough uphill hikes for early in the morning, so I hung my bear pack and pitched a tent at the foot of the Knob.

There are advantages to camping in gaps instead of ridges or summits. On top of ridges, campers are more exposed to the elements—wind gets funneled up valleys and reaches its peak crescendo of noise and highest velocity at the top of the mountain. There is also less tree cover on top of mountains, so campers are more likely to get pummeled with rain. Water sources are also easier to find at lower elevations.

On the other hand, gaps tend to be eerie, dark and quiet places. Hoot owls come out at dusk and provide a mournful serenade. I always somehow feel more exposed in gaps, because my tent is just off the trail and easily visible to passersby. My childhood dread of night and darkness comes back to a certain extent when alone in a gap. It is not a terrifying fear; it is just a bit unnerving to be outside in complete darkness. Campfires help deal with the uneasy seclusion and are a source of light and warmth in the all-enveloping darkness.

The next morning, my campsite was shrouded in a cool mist, which gradually burned off as the sun rose over Kelly's Knob. Still a novice to packing, it usually took me three or more attempts to get my backpack in the order needed. Inevitably, I would put something on the bottom that I would need immediately, like a map or food, and have to take everything out and re-pack.

Kelly's Knob was every bit as difficult as advertised, with a 500-feet rise in a half mile. At the summit is a rocky outcrop that overlooks the Tesnatee Valley. The slate gray skies from the previous day were replaced by a brilliant sapphire blue color, interrupted by a few airplane vapor trails.

I continued to encounter just the occasional hiker, almost all of them headed south—thru-hikers who started in Maine and were wrapping up their trek with the finish line of Springer Mountain only 60 miles away.

Thru-hikers in the latter stages of their journey are especially single-minded. They can smell the finish line, and it is not unusual for them to hike 35 miles in a day—I was typically hiking about one third of that distance. They don't spend much time talking to hikers passing by, maybe just a quick exchange of information. Thru-hikers generally fall into two categories—young and recently graduated from college or discharged from the military, and the older, late 50s/early 60s hikers who have recently retired. Many of the young men have long beards that have been expertly sculpted over the course of their trek.

The percentage of women hikers is steadily growing, and they are treated as equals on the trail—almost 30 percent of thru-hikers who complete the entire Georgia to Maine journey and become members of the "2,000 Mile Club" are female.[21]

Many of the younger thru-hikers travel in packs of three or four that meet up at pre-ordained locations in the evening. They look out for each other—as they inevitably spread out over the course of day, they will ask hikers that they pass if they have seen "John/Sue." Anyone who deals with the day-to-day strain of the trail quickly gains respect. For this reason, women can largely travel alone or with male hikers they meet along the trail and not fear for their safety.

There are of course, tragic exceptions, including the horrible abduction and murder of a recently graduated 24-year-old University of Georgia woman, Meredith Emerson, on a section of the trail near Blood Mountain in early 2008. Out for a day hike with her dog, she was attacked, kidnapped and murdered two days later by a psychopathic serial killer who was later arrested one mile from my house in Atlanta, planning his next murder at an area mall.[22]

Perhaps the most frequent question I get from people who are unfamiliar with the trail is whether or not I carry a gun for protection. I do not—I don't own a gun, and for the most part, it would be impractical on the AT. A gun would add additional weight, and unless it is strapped on a holster, it is most likely to be somewhere in the pack that is not easily accessible in a time of need.

A sense of trust and community permeates the entire AT culture. Hikers will leave packs unattended to get water, which can be as far as a quarter mile off the trail. If a hiker is short of food, water, or a key piece of equipment, others will gladly offer what they have. I once had a headlamp that malfunctioned; another hiker gave me his spare, and he refused any money for it.

Thru-hikers will typically eat Snickers and other chocolate and energy bars during the day and cook ramen noodles at night. Instead of paying for healthier (but more expensive) options at outfitters, they will instead look for the closest Dollar General store when they are in a town. Everything is geared to economy of motion and eliminating delays. Thru-hikers near to their goal have conquered the physical pain and mental hardships and become machines, undaunted by tough climbs or harsh weather.

The Georgia section of the AT (and much of North Carolina) has some of the most secluded areas of the trail until Maine. Other than the state highways that cross the AT every 10–15 miles, signs of civilization, like electrical transmission towers, fenced-in cow pastures, and nearby homes, are absent. This is somewhat surprising to many, who expect more amenities on the trail in Georgia, maybe because of its close proximity to Atlanta. A northbound hiker on the AT does not physically cross a town until Hot Springs, North Carolina, more than 270 miles from Springer Mountain.

The 78 miles of trail in Georgia are similar to a roller coaster—a series of climbs up to 4,000 feet, followed by descents in to gaps of about 3,000 feet. The mountains never get too high or the gaps too low, but it is nonetheless daunting for an inexperienced hiker trying to establish "trail legs."

I headed down into Dick's Creek Gap and ascended the trail to Little Bald Knob. The trail crisscrossed Dick's Creek, where Retina had slipped and fallen on some rocks the previous spring, breaking two ribs. He managed another 20 miles north before leaving the trail and flying home to Milwaukee.

The only sound was the steady rattle of dead leaves getting kicked by my hiking boots and the intermittent roar of distant rifle shots—this was the middle of deer hunting season. Fall brings stillness and solemnity upon the land—the steady symphony of bird songs that provide a backdrop to spring hikes is gone. There was one heart-attack-inducing flutter of wild turkeys startled by my presence, but other than that, silence.

It was November 3, the first Sunday after the Day of the Dead on November 1. One hundred miles away, my neighborhood church was hosting, as it did the first Sunday in every November, a chamber orchestra that performed Mozart's *Requiem Mass.* It was a production that I always tried to attend—at the end of the performance, a bell pealed for each member of the church who had passed away in the previous year—one long toll after each name was announced. I played the Lacrimosa over and over in my mind while I walked:

> Full of tears will be that day
> When from the ashes shall arise
> The guilty man to be judged;
> Therefore spare him, O God,
> Merciful Lord Jesus,
> Grant them eternal rest. Amen.

My grandfather used to call November the "hog-killing season," because families in north Georgia used to slaughter and salt their hogs in mid-autumn to provide a ready food source over the approaching winter. That same sense of somber finality, an impending end, hovers over the AT in November.

The descent into Plum Orchard Gap was completed by late dusk. I had the shelter to myself and set up my sleeping bag on the second level. I was almost certain that no other hikers would be looking for a place at the shelter—I had passed less than ten hikers the entire day.

Plum Orchard Shelter was quiet, except for the sounds of the hoot owl, which started as soon as the sun fell over the ridge. It was a new moon evening miles from civilization, so the sky was not obscured by either lunar or terrestrial light and brilliantly lit by thousands of stars—a "Sternenzelt," or canopy of stars. The stunning celestial array was humbling, and feeling unsettled, I went to bed after taking several sips from my flask of the Muscadine grape–infused moonshine my cousin from Dawson County had made and sold to me in a Mason jar for $50.

Henry Etna Parks, "Etny," my great grandfather, was a moonshiner and the richest man in Dawson County. Although he was nearly six feet tall, his nickname was High Pockets, perhaps because he pulled his pants up well above his waist. He had a thin frame but a large paunch belly, so he might have pulled his pants up to hide that protrusion. Brown-haired with piercing blue eyes, he was a well-respected businessman in Dawson County during the 1920s. He owned a 300-acre farm in the Shoal Creek area with a two-story house where he lived with his wife, Ola, and their nine children. Etny also owned eight tenant houses, a corn mill, car garage, and a large pasture where people would pay rent to graze their cattle. He was a savvy businessman—he pulled out his deposits from a nearby Gainesville bank right before it failed, and he bought the first car ever owned in Dawson County.

My grandmother, his third child, remembers driving with him in his car when he told her he made "$10,000 in the last week." He always favored her, and bought her nice clothes, which was a source of envy with her schoolmates. She once wore a beautiful sailor-style blue dress to school and heard a girl remark, "I'd have a pretty dress too, if my daddy sold moonshine."

In the 1920s, Dawson County was a sparsely populated area about 50 miles northeast of Atlanta. It felt cut off from the outside world—state Highway 400, which linked Dawsonville (the county seat) to Atlanta and helped spur development, was not completed until the 1970s. Dawson County's hilly terrain did not allow for large-scale farming, but with its tucked away hills and plentiful creeks, it was perfect for making moonshine.

Given the inaccessibility of the region and the inherited talents of the local residents for making hooch that was passed down through generations from the original Scots-Irish settlers, Dawson County became the hub of the north Georgia moonshine trade that supplied Atlanta during Prohibition. Dating back to when their ancestors still lived in Ulster, the Scots-Irish were people who "would live where they please, own a gun, and could distill and drink his corn whiskey without interference."[23] By the mid–1700s, plumes of bluish smoke clouds poured from hundreds of stills all along the Appalachian chain. "Where there's smoke, there's bound to be whiskey," was the favorite expression of the time.[24]

It is estimated that at its peak in the 1930s, Dawson County provided Atlanta with 50,000 gallons of bootleg whiskey a week.[25] Skilled local drivers drove the whiskey to market in Atlanta along the legendary Highway 9, known as "Thunder Road." As a child, I was often told the tale of one driver who was ticketed for speeding while hauling whiskey to Atlanta. Supposedly, the driver paid the policeman twice the ticketed amount because he "didn't have time to get stopped again" on his return trip to Dawsonville.

Etny was so successful with his moonshine because he offered quality—he was able to maintain that high quality because he controlled all elements of his product: he grew the corn, turned it into mash and distilled it, and he also distributed the bottled whiskey. In the 1920s, there were major dangers from drinking contraband whiskey, including lead poisoning from the soldered pipe joints of the still. Moonshine was often condensed in radiators from junk cars or trucks, which contain a great deal of lead solder.[26] Other moonshiners took shortcuts by using methyl, or wood alcohol, which was cheaper but could also be fatal.

Etny Parks had financially supported his friend Will Orr's candidacy for sheriff of Dawson County and drove him to campaign events. The two remained political allies and close friends until Parks decided to play a practical joke. One day, Orr was crossing the street in Dawsonville, lost in his thoughts. Parks was backing up his Dodge and approached Orr quickly, slamming on his brakes at the last second. This not only frightened Orr, but even worse, it publicly humiliated him. No apology was forthcoming from Parks, and the two became, from that point onward, bitter enemies.

My great-grandfather had embarrassed a proud man, and in the Scots-Irish culture of the hill country, this slight would not be forgotten.

I have seen many examples of the Scots-Irish temper flaring up in my lifetime, so it is not difficult for me to imagine the impact this must have had on Orr almost a century ago. The rage can explode and then dissipate quickly—I have been on the receiving end of threats of violence followed quickly by offers to get together for dinner or a beer. As part of my cultural inheritance, I have also struggled to control my own temper, which has detonated over the years over slight provocations; it has only been in the past decade that I stopped "seeing red" when I experienced a real or imagined slight. It will never be known if Orr's anger might have been assuaged by some act of public remorse by Parks, some sort of admission that he had been in the wrong, or if scores would have to be settled at some point no matter what after Orr's honor had been impugned.

The enmity between the two former friends escalated with insults and accusations of illegal behavior. Parks had various court charges brought against him, including driving without a license and illegal possession of firearms. According to Parks's daughter and my great-aunt, Clara, Orr would appear at the family's home and cuss Etny "like the devil. They had the most fusses. My daddy would be on the porch and here he would come. We'd run to the bushes. We'd run behind the house way down there in the grape vines. It would scare us to death."

The feud culminated on July 7, 1924. Orr came to Parks's downtown garage and mill store, supposedly looking for an escapee from the local jail. Once again, the two men had a heated argument, and this time, Orr pulled out his pistol, accusing Etny of hiding the escapee on his property. Parks, in the presence of two employees, ordered Orr out of his store.

Charley Swafford, who was at the scene, recalled later at trial: "I had an idea that Orr was hunting Parks with his pistol. He looked mad. I don't know that I ever saw a man look much madder than Orr did at the time. He and Parks both are mad looking men to me."[27]

Orr cursed Parks, calling him a son of a bitch, and drew his gun from his holster. Parks asked him to leave, telling him he wanted no trouble. Orr was finally persuaded by Swafford to leave the store. Leaving by the front entrance, Orr soon returned through the rear door, with his pistol drawn. Parks had been weighing corncobs in scales and moved across the room, in the direction of his car, as Orr came towards him. Parks reached in the car, pulled out a pistol and fired three times, hitting Orr each time, twice in the back. Orr died instantly.

The Parks family lived in a house opposite the store, and decades later, Clara (his daughter) reminisced:

> Will Orr came in the store just a cussing and had his gun out and said he was looking for this [escapee]. My daddy said, "You look all you want to, but don't you come back in here again." So he went out the front door, and came down and went in the back door. And my daddy was by his car over there and he saw him and he shot him. I heard it. It went pop, pop, pop! I was ten years old. That was 1924 ... I was making sand cakes ... it had rained the night before a bit.

Etna Parks (courtesy Dawson County Historical and Genealogical Society).

Fearing that he would be the victim of a lynch mob, Parks got into his car and drove. Word soon spread, and the governor of Georgia, Clifford Walker, set a reward of $500 for Parks's capture. Dawson County offered an additional award. Two days after the killing, Parks turned himself in to the Lumpkin County Sheriff in Dahlonega. According to *The Gainesville News*, "He seemed badly frightened, having heard news that posses with dogs and guns were after him."[28]

Parks was tried for murder in 1925, and after a hung jury, he was found guilty of the lesser charge of voluntary manslaughter. The judge and jury took into account the long-standing feud between these former friends when delivering the verdict, which was a sentence of seven years in prison. Parks was sent to a state prison near Blairsville, deep in the mountains about 30 miles north of Dawsonville. A friendly warden allowed Parks to set up house in a cabin in the forest, where he lived with a woman named Pearl. Later, Parks confided that he enjoyed his stint under confinement.

After he was released, Parks rejoined his family in Dawsonville, where he lived until dying from cancer just shy of his 63rd birthday in 1944.

A bright, chilly morning greeted me. I would be finishing the Georgia portion of the trail that day, continuing on into North Carolina, where I planned on camping at the foot of Standing Indian Mountain.

I passed several taciturn southbound (SOBO) hikers and climbed As Knob. From there, it was ridge hiking to Bly Gap, which marked the border between Georgia and North Carolina.

On my final approach to Bly Gap, I came across an excited beagle with a tag and a stamped phone number. He obviously belonged to someone, and I called his owner from my cell phone. About half an hour later, a man appeared on horseback, sauntering up the trail. The dog recognized his owner and the horse instantly. After a brief greeting and thanks, the three of them headed back down the trail. How this man on horseback arrived to such an isolated area of the AT so quickly has always been a mystery to me.

There is a small wooden sign bolted on to a tulip poplar marked "NC/GA" at Bly Gap. Previous hikers had stacked a small cairn of rocks on top of it as tokens of their memories or accomplishments. I noticed

Border sign at the Georgia/North Carolina state line.

this many times along the trail, and it reminded me of the small stones placed on top of tombstones in old Jewish cemeteries, in respect of the memory of the deceased.

For SOBOs, this sign is a welcome indication that their journey is almost over, only 78 miles to Springer Mountain. For northbound hikers, it is more of a grim reminder that they have finished one state and have 13 more in front of them.

The trail takes a sharp right turn at Bly Gap as it crosses into North Carolina, and overlooking a windswept ridge staring southward is a gnarled oak tree shaped like a moose, standing sentinel almost as if to serve as protection against Georgia. This crooked, ancient oak is one of the best-known landmarks on the AT. On a cold, windy day in November, this mystical and foreboding beacon was a stark reminder of the fact that the wheel was turning, slowly but inexorably towards the solstice, and yet another year would soon be gone.

As I looked south over acres and acres of forest towards my home state, I was reminded of the traditional ballads written by the Georgia mountain poet, Byron Herbert Reece that focused heavily on the change of seasons:

> At autumn things are all at odds:
> From their immortal seeds
> Fall to decay their temporary pods;
> And over the clairvoyant clods
> The blight of winter breeds,
> And the world so beautiful.[29]

Reece was an award-winning poet and novelist in the 1940s and 1950s, but despite the acclaim he received for his poetry (he was nominated for a Pulitzer Prize, won two Guggenheim Awards and was the writer-in-residence at both UCLA and Emory University) he was never financially secure, and he could never focus strictly on his writing; he also had to tend to his family's small farm in the shadow of Blood Mountain. He suffered from both depression and tuberculosis (contracted through taking care of his ill parents), which was worsened by heavy drinking. My grandfather, Dr. Charles R. Clegg—who was president of the small Methodist school nearby, Young Harris College—was criticized by some for hiring him, despite his illness, as a part-time faculty member in that school's English department.[30]

The iconic oak at Bly Gap, North Carolina.

One June evening in 1958, unable to bear the dark clouds of disease and depression any longer, Reece graded a stack of his students' final exam papers, put them on a neat stack in a drawer in his desk, placed a Mozart record that played "Piano Sonata in D" on his turntable, and took his life with a gunshot to the chest at the age of 40.[31]

North Carolina does not waste any time welcoming northbound hikers in the form of a 700-foot elevation gain over the next mile, ending on the summit of Courthouse Bald, which at 4,700 feet, almost matched the highest peak in Georgia. At the top, I threw off my pack and sprawled on a mossy patch, taking a long break. The typical ailments of hikers—back, knees, feet—were not causing me any trouble, but an elevated heart rate was forcing me to take frequent mini-breaks on uphill climbs, in some instances, every 100 feet or so.

Upon crossing the border into North Carolina, the Chattahoochee National Forest ends and the Nantahala National Forest begins. The terrain changes dramatically—gone are the more linear, roller-coaster-like ascents going up to 4,000 feet and back down to 3,000. They are replaced by steep climbs up to 5,500 feet followed by steep plunges into gorges of less than 2,000 feet.

After about two days of hiking and eating jerky, fruit bars, dehydrated foods and instant grits, my body once again began to crave protein. As usual, many of my daydreaming moments while hiking were consumed with beer and cheeseburgers. The other form of daydreaming was involuntarily turning my brain into a jukebox. Usually, songs had walking themes—"Walking in Memphis," "Walk on By," "Walk Don't Run." Of course, I could not get rid of these songs and they were constantly replayed in my head.

I sat on a log and ate lunch just off the trail near Muskrat Creek Shelter. I was learning to never look on the other side of a log that lies just off the trail. People relieve themselves, and the uncovered residue, mainly toilet paper, remains for months. Everyone who has hiked any length of the trail has had to defecate in the woods, but many do not go to any effort to cover droppings by digging a "cat hole" with a small trowel. As the AT grows in popularity, unfortunate signs of this and other types of trash, including discarded gear, are all too prevalent.

The hikers who desecrate the areas along the trail are a small minority, and I have never witnessed anyone leaving trash behind. Ansell and his friend had left their grill at the campsite at Cooper Gap back in Georgia, but this was equipment that could become a fixture, something that other hikers could use.

Discarded dehydrated food packages are difficult to burn and they remain in campfire pits for months. Cigarette butts and empty cooking fuel canisters litter areas around shelters. Day hikers will leave empty beer cans along the trail.

In perhaps the most dramatic change due to human activity that could be coming to the AT, officials in Maine are considering rerouting the end of the AT at Mount Katahdin due to damage caused by hikers and campers at surrounding Baxter State Park.[32]

"Pack It Out" and "Leave No Trace" are strict canons on the trail—hikers should take out all trash they accumulate. Most of the ones who do leave garbage behind must be alone at the time they do so; otherwise they would risk being shamed by other hikers. There are also many inspiring stories like the two thru-hikers who picked up and carried out over a thousand pounds of trash between Georgia and Maine.[33]

To their credit, trail volunteers perform a very underrated service of removing tons of trash annually from the trail. I know several volunteers on the Georgia section of the AT, and they have "adopted" a mile of trail. They periodically get emails from the Georgia Appalachian Trail Club informing them that their section needs to be cleared of fallen trees, and they get reminders if they are not prompt enough in following up.

There are 31 different volunteer organizations for the different sections along the trail, all with varying numbers of volunteers and resources. It is astounding that so many people are willing to spend their free time hauling saws and shovels to clear fallen trees on remote mountain trails and pick up the litter that careless backpackers leave behind. The work is particularly strenuous in some backcountry sections where chainsaws are not allowed. The AT continues to explode in popularity—since the trail opened in 1936, there have been almost 20,000 people who completed thru hikes, two-thirds of which were accomplished since the year 2000.[34] This, combined with increased traffic from section and day hikers, is creating an unsightly strain on the trail.

In a late afternoon framed by a dying golden light, I descended the valley that would lead me to the foot of Standing Indian Mountain. I pitched my tent at Deep Gap campground just above a creek. There was a paved road next to the camping area that led to the state highway about five miles away. Periodically, pickup trucks with hunters would park in the camping area or depart after a day hunting game.

I had hoped to find water, but the creek was dry except for some wet leaves that gave off a musky odor of decay. This was my last night on the trail, and after several futile attempts to start a campfire, I turned in for the evening. It was a grim and depressing place to spend an evening. I had yet another fitful night of sleep punctuated by strange dreams.

❧✗❧

Few things are more difficult than pulling myself out of a sleeping bag on a freezing morning. I delayed climbing out of my tent until 8:30, and I wasn't on the trail until almost 10. This day was supposed to be a short hike up to Standing Indian Mountain. At the summit, I planned to take a side trail off the north side of the mountain, hike the four miles down it, and meet up with my father at a parking lot in a campground.

Standing Indian Mountain, at 5,499 feet, is the highest mountain on the northbound section of the Appalachian Trail until it crosses into Tennessee and the Great Smoky Mountains National Park, about 70 miles distant. In the Cherokee language, Standing Indian is known as Yunwitsuli-nunyi, which translates to "where the man stood." According to Cherokee mythology, a hideous, winged, Grendel-like monster lived on the mountain and would swoop down into the surrounding valleys and steal Cherokee children.

One warrior discovered the lair of the monster and prayed to the Great Spirit for his destruction. The prayer was answered in the form of thunder and lightning that killed the monster. But it also terrified the warrior, who turned to run. For his cowardice, he was turned to stone by the Great Spirit, hence the name, Standing Indian.[35]

The trail up the mountain was a series of easy switchbacks. I felt great. The hiking was easy; the weather was early November picture perfect, with a bright sun, chill temperatures in the low 50s and a slight breeze. I filled my Camelbak with water at a rocky, bubbling creek near the Standing Indian Shelter and took a couple of selfies, which I texted to my daughter, a sophomore in college.

By late morning, I reached the telltale signs that I was nearing the top—a rhododendron tunnel, a blast of spruce fragrance, and a soothing sub–Alpine breeze.

There are only ever subtle hints that a summit is near in the Appalachian Mountains. Unlike the Rockies or the Alps, there are no tree lines in the Appalachians where vegetation suddenly ends and stone commences for the rest of the journey to the summit, making the top easily visible.

I lunched on the top of the mountain, spotted the blue blaze on a tree marking a side trail, and then began my descent down the Lower Ridge Trail. The trail was sparingly hiked and hard to follow—leaves completely covered sections of it, and I was forced to rely largely on the blue blazes that were painted on trees every 200 feet or so to make my way down the side trail.

A rhododendron tunnel on the AT.

I was on time to meet my father at the scheduled two o'clock pickup time when the trail disappeared. I immediately became disoriented and mistakenly started back up the trail I had just walked down. To be alone and lost in the woods is terrifying—it is not a gradual feeling, it is sudden, and sheer panic sets in.

When heading back up the trail I ignored several clear indications that I was hiking back up the mountain, back up the same path that I had previously descended. I even passed a downed Nantahala National Forest sign that I had noticed during my earlier descent. I rationalized it as an additional fallen sign, not the one I had so recently spotted. I re-traced my hike for two miles until I passed a ridge corner and spotted the silhouette of Standing Indian—irrevocable proof that I was hiking in the wrong direction, back up the trail. I ran and even sprinted back down the trail, hoping to make up for some of the lost time I had created by my stupid mistake.

I was out of water and still fearful that I was lost when I made it back to the point of my original misstep. This time, I was able to find a blue blazed tree farther downhill, which showed the continuation of the trail. Completely dehydrated and with a racing heart, I moved at a fast clip, wanting more than anything to be rid of this mountain and hike.

Toward the base of the mountain, the trail widened and became easily visible, and I finally knew that I was on the right track. I exited the trail at 3 p.m., an hour late, and spotted my father. I was so dehydrated that I drank three quarts of Gatorade on the drive home without having to urinate.

I realized more than ever how unforgiving mountains could be for even minor lapses in concentration. I had seen it with other hikers, who, tired by a long day of hiking, tripped over roots or slipped on wet mossy rocks and fell, hurting themselves. I resolved to never let my mind drift like that again on the trail. I also resolved to never take a side trail again during the autumn.

PART II

HYOH
(Hike Your Own Hike)

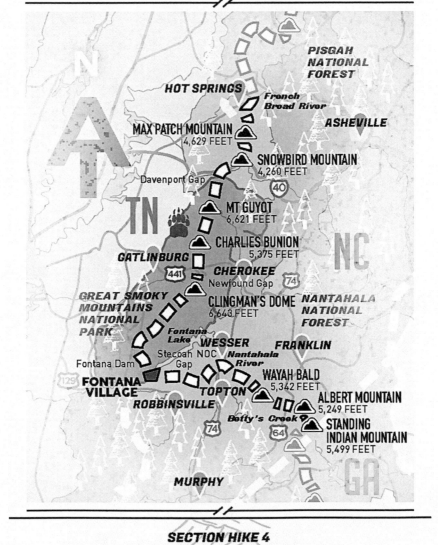

SECTION HIKE 3
Standing Indian Mountain
to Wayah Gap, North Carolina
October 11–13, 2014 (30 Miles)

Demands at work prevented me from resuming my journey in the spring of 2014, as I had originally hoped. As autumn approached, I decided on an 80-mile hike from Standing Indian Mountain to Fontana Dam, the gateway to the Great Smoky Mountains National Park. While this would easily be the longest hike I had attempted, I felt like I needed to make up lost ground from skipping the spring hike.

October is typically the driest period in the southern Appalachians. Water sources that are so plentiful in the spring from the abundant rains dry up in the early autumn.

This year was different. A series of storms off the Baja Peninsula of Mexico had spawned heavy rain and even cyclones across the Midwest and into the southeast.

With the responsibilities of work and home, I had to plan my trips in specific intervals, weather be damned. I spent the week before this trip studying local weather forecasts in the Franklin, North Carolina, area hoping for a break in the weather to give me more favorable conditions.

As the week prior to my hike progressed, the rain moved like a right uppercut, in thick bands from the Gulf of Mexico, through the northeast. I spent an early Saturday morning at my father's house in Dahlonega, before finally deciding that the rain would at least temporarily cease by late morning. I was dropped off at Deep Gap at the foot of Standing Indian Mountain, so I retraced my hike up the switchback trails before reaching the top in early afternoon.

The skies were threatening, with ominous ashen clouds moving in from the southwest. As I descended the eastern side of Standing Indian, the rain arrived. It pounded the mountain in thick pellets, making the already wet trail even more treacherous.

Opposite: **Standing Indian Mountain, North Carolina to Hot Springs, North Carolina—189 mile. Map by Kendall Young, WoodBatBrand.com.**

By the time I reached Beech Gap at the foot of Standing Indian, the heavy rain forced me to put on my poncho and take shelter under a huge Fraser magnolia tree. The wide sweep of its branches kept me dry during the downpour.

After a half hour, the rain subsided, and I hiked the three miles to Carter Gap Shelter, which was situated on a pleasant overlook with a spectacular south-facing view of Georgia. Unfortunately, a fidgety old man, his three sons, and their dogs had overrun the small shelter. Although it was only mid-afternoon, they made it clear that they planned on staying the night at the shelter. Trail etiquette suggests that people take priority over dogs on shelters along the AT, but I was not going to mention this uncomfortable fact. Instead, I ate my lunch, packed back up and headed up the trail.

I was noticed by a stray dog with a GPS collar, which followed me for three miles down the trail. I was unsure if he was lost or his GPS signal had quit working, but he was headed in the same direction with a sense of purpose.

Just to the west of the Betty Creek Gap was a pleasant camping area bisected by its namesake, a good-sized stream named Betty's Creek, and a gravel parking lot. I found an unoccupied spot bordering the creek and set up my tent.

There were several clusters of campers in the area, including a Boy Scout troop, a group of college men and one young couple.

I realized after opening my pouch of dehydrated beef stroganoff that I had left my eating utensils at home. I frantically searched and re-searched my pack, to no avail. I then asked the other hikers if they had a spare spoon or fork, but no one did. I was forced to improvise with two unused tent spikes that I employed as makeshift chopsticks.

I had just turned in when I heard a commotion outside—the young couple had found the stray dog with a GPS collar, fed it, and called the owner. The owner arrived and loudly and gratefully reclaimed his dog. He and the dog passed inches from my head inside the tent—someone popping in like that from the outside world seemed like an intruder, and made me realize I had developed a certain wariness towards those who appear on the trail without the commonality of the hiking experience.

I dozed off and slept comfortably, as comfortable a sleep as I have ever had outdoors, when I heard six or eight heavy thuds hit the domed nylon roof of my tent. I tried to shrug it off at first, as either my imagination or small tree debris that had improbably fallen. The thuds were followed by dozens more drops in the next minute as the heavens opened up.

When stuck inside a tent during a pounding rain, sleep is impossible. Lightning that sent flashes of bright light through the camping area soon joined the rain. I cursed myself for spiking my two metal hiking poles in an upright position just outside my tent, thinking that I had put a bulls-eye on myself with lightning in the immediate area. I unzipped my tent flap, pulled in my dirty hiking boots, lay back, and waited.

Like the sound of rain, creeping wetness inside a tent is something that at first creates a state of denial. Once acceptance sets in though, there is little to do, other than try to sleep on your side to limit the amount of material that absorbs the water.

I was soon wet, and miserable, and unable to sleep another minute that night.

❧❦❧

When I opened my tent flap at about 8:30 the next morning, the rain was still coming down, although not quite as heavy as it was earlier. I surveyed the camping area and saw puddles of water an inch or so deep. I guessed we had experienced a flash flood the previous evening with two or three inches of rain.

Groggy with lack of sleep, I ate another tasteless breakfast of grits and oatmeal, packed my wet gear and set out on the creek trail to rejoin the AT. Missing was my poncho, which I now realized that I left at Carter Gap Shelter during my lunch the day before. I did not worry too much about it, because my gear was now soaked. My goal for the day was to make it to Winding Stair Gap, about 12 miles away. Early in the hike I would have to climb the notoriously difficult Albert Mountain.

I set off on the creek trail that would reconnect me to the AT. I saw the sign after about a quarter mile and swung to the right.

After about two miles of hiking, I passed the Boy Scout troop I had seen the night before at Betty's Creek. I asked the leader how much longer it would be until we reached Albert Mountain. He gave me a quizzical look and told me that we all were hiking towards Standing Indian. I instantly realized my mistake—I had taken a right at the juncture of Betty's Creek Trail and the AT when I should have taken a left.

Due to lack of sleep the night before, I had made another error that would cost me an additional two hours of time and added at least four more miles of unnecessary hiking—"bonus mileage" as it is referred to on the AT. I wheeled around and set forth toward the north and Albert Mountain.

At 5,249 feet in height, Albert Mountain climbs about 500 feet in less than three-tenths of a mile at about a 60-degree angle. On a map, the mountain resembles a two-dimensional equilateral triangle. The dirt trail gives way to exposed granite, which during rainy conditions becomes slippery and dangerous. The granite surface on the uphill climb is generally flat, with no jutting rocks or tree roots to use as rungs for foot or hand support.

Although the rain had virtually stopped, trickles of water continued to flow down the trail. I slipped and fell backwards, skinning the palms of my hands. A heavy fog obscured the summit, making distance impossible to calculate. I inched upward, slipped again, fell back about five feet until my foot could find a hold and scraped my chin. I thought about Retina, who had somehow managed to climb Albert Mountain with two broken ribs. The physician he visited, who examined him later in Franklin, did not believe him when he told her he had scaled the mountain with his injury.

After a dozen fitful starts and stops, I reached the summit of Albert Mountain around noon. As I was standing near the metal fire tower on an exposed bald looking out towards the Little Tennessee River Valley, the heavens opened up. I had no choice but to collect my gear and sprint for tree cover on the northern trail descending the mountain. Thankfully, the descent was easier to navigate, although water continued to pour down the trail.

The rest of the day was followed by luminous sunshine interrupted by spurts of heavy rain. Thick dark clouds continued to roll across the northeast, and every hiker I passed spoke of more rains to come.

As I approached Rock Gap, there was a small shelter to the left of the trail. Shelters on the North Carolina portion of the trail thus far were unimpressive—this one was little more than a shack, and as I soon learned, had no source of water. A couple of hikers named Jeff and Ricky, from Pompano Beach, Florida, were already set up in the shelter, drying out their sleeping bags and tents on nearby tree branches.

They were section hiking southward, with the goal of reaching Unicoi Gap in Georgia in three or four days. Weather was probably going to not allow that to happen—the forecast was calling for continued heavy rains.

I debated whether to try and spend the night next to these two strangers inside the cramped and dark shelter. I made a light-hearted comment about "hoping that nobody snores." Ricky immediately responded, "I'm a bad snorer." I pressed him, thinking he was either joking or trying to get me to move on to clear out more space. "Oh yeah, it is really bad."

With the prospect of sleeping next to a loud snorer on a rainy night in a dingy shelter, I decided to walk down to the road at the gap and try to hitchhike my way into Franklin, which was the closest town. After 30 minutes of sticking my thumb out and having at least 20 cars drive by without stopping, I called a local cab. A guy named Larry answered ("Lahr-eee," as he called himself) and said he would be by to pick me up. For $45, Larry agreed to drop me off at the Hampton Inn in Franklin.

It is always a shock to re-enter civilization, even after just two or three days on the trail. The lobby of the Hampton Inn was festive, decorated for the autumn with scarecrows, dried cornstalks, and pumpkins. A gaggle of motorcyclists was staying there—Harley enthusiasts are all over the southern Appalachians, traveling in flying wedges down state highways; these motorcyclists, despite their best efforts, are never intimidating—they reminded me of retired orthodontists in their black t-shirts and jeans with chain wallets.

After checking in to my room and hanging my wet tent and sleeping bag over the shower curtain rod, I walked down the hill to a Taco Bell. The air was thick with humidity, and the rumble of thunder could be heard from the west.

I gorged on bean burritos and tacos and went back to my room. I turned on the TV and watched the Weather Channel, which showed massive green bands of rain moving through the area the next day.

The southern portion of the AT includes areas, such as western North Carolina, that receive the heaviest rainfall in the eastern United

States, and there is enormous variation in precipitation depending on elevation and geographical positioning relative to mountain ranges. For instance, Lake Toxaway (92 inches of average annual rainfall) and Asheville (37 inches) are only 50 miles apart, but Lake Toxaway lies at the foot of the Blue Ridge Mountains and is not shielded from moisture. By contrast, Asheville is nestled in the French Broad River basin and is protected from moist winds by the Balsam and Smoky Mountains. As a result, Asheville is actually the driest city in the state of North Carolina.[1]

There is always a fine line between dealing with the weather on a prolonged hike and packing it in if conditions become too taxing. The AT from north Georgia to southwestern Virginia is in a temperate rainforest that receives heavy precipitation, and rain is part of the experience. Rain, in addition to making hikers uncomfortable, nourishes the verdant forests and supplies the gushing waterfalls and fast-flowing rivers of the region.

The planning that goes into a section hike typically includes fixed timelines due to the demands of work and family. This precludes adjusting a trip based on optimal weather conditions.

I can endure a moderate amount of rainfall—I have only been on one section hike where there was no rain—but hiking in the midst of a prolonged inundation is, for me, neither an ego trip nor some sort of contrived personal battle against the elements. If weather is making me miserable and there is no break in sight, I get off the trail.

❧❧❧

The next morning, I woke up early and saw that the Weather Channel was predicting a brief break in the rain for the day, followed by at least one more day of heavy showers. I called my father and asked him to pick me up at Wayah Gap, which would allow me to start from where I left off the previous day and complete, hopefully, a ten-mile hike before getting off the trail.

Lahr-ee picked me up at 9 a.m., and we drove in a light rain towards Wayah Gap. He turned up the radio each time there was an update on an Ebola virus case, which was creating quite a scare that month.

Near the gap, I saw Jeff and Ricky with thumbs out, trying to catch rides. They had clearly spent a wet, rainy night in the ramshackle shelter at Rock Gap, and I chuckled inwardly at their misery—somehow I doubted that Ricky had spent a blissful night of uninterrupted sleep, snoring loud enough to wake the dead.

I ascended Winding Stair Gap in a misty drizzle over a soaked and treacherous trail. The AT in the southern Appalachians is seldom a smooth, level, hard-packed dirt path—it is usually an obstacle course of tree roots, protruding and loose rocks, and after heavy rains, standing water. After prolonged storms, deep puddles accumulate in the depressed portions of the trail, forcing hikers to temporarily step off the path to get on dry ground.

For every section hike, there has been at least one instance where I tripped and fell. These falls happen during downhill portions of the trail, and I usually tumbled headfirst—luckily, with no severe injuries. The heel of my hiking boot would catch a root, and the force of a sudden stop would send me plunging forward. Many hikers have had their trips aborted over just one unguarded moment where they don't spot a muddy, leaf-covered patch or choose the wrong rock when fording a narrow creek. I always think of Retina breaking ribs less than one hundred miles into his thru-hike because of a fall.

The many volunteer groups along the trail generally do a great job of clearing fallen trees and branches directly on the AT. But many of the obstructed spots are in remote areas, and dicey, makeshift detours are common.

The cool, fog shrouded mist—what is called dragon's breath in Wales—was soothing, and it felt like an amble along the Monterey Peninsula on the Pacific coast. I passed several SOBO thru-hikers who confirmed the return of the heavy rains the next day—they were planning on riding out the storm in a Franklin hotel—and I silently congratulated myself on the decision to end my hike early.

After heavy rain, mushrooms spring up like daisies in the southern Appalachians. The dampness and temperate climate are ideal for fungi, and unbelievably, only about 2,300 of the estimated 20,000 species of mushrooms believed to exist in the area have been identified.[2] I have passed rows of chicken of the woods, hedgehog, lobster and chanterelle mushrooms along the trail. After returning from my hikes, I always regretted not bringing back mushrooms, ramps, sassafras root and other mountain delicacies.

The more than 100 different native species of trees in the southern

Appalachians have provided humans with hundreds of industrial uses and medicinal cures. Many of the medicinal uses were passed down from the Cherokees, such as poultices for sores from the leaves of tulip poplars, the boiled bark of hickory for arthritic pain, and pine used as antiseptics and antioxidants.[3]

Almost since the beginning of white settlement in the region, the abundant resources of the southern Appalachians have been extracted and exploited—gold and other precious metals, lumber, coal, and, most recently because of fracking, natural gas.

Signs of erosion from the gold rush of 1829 are still visible in Dahlonega today—miners would divert water from streams and use powerful water cannons to strip the hillsides of trees and soil to more easily get to the gold just below the surface.

Before the advent of conservation and the establishment of the national park system that protected millions of acres of forest land, it was common for lumber companies to clear cut entire mountains and convert the felled trees into pulp, resin, and tar. Today, many portions of the AT were formerly old lumber roads.

The 233-acre Vogel State Park in Georgia near Blood Mountain, which I have visited and enjoyed my entire life, is a hemlock and oak forest that was formerly used as a farm for the extraction of natural tannins for the leather tanning business. Once a synthetic substitute was discovered in 1927, the Wisconsin industrialists who owned the property donated it to the state.

One of the oddest examples of man-made desecration in the southern Appalachians is 3,420-foot Bell Mountain, near Young Harris, Georgia, where my grandparents lived. In the early 1960s, several investors from nearby Murphy, North Carolina, decided, apparently without conducting much research, that the mountain contained vast amounts of silica that could be used for industrial purposes.[4] In order to get to the imagined lodes of quartz rock (the project never became commercially viable and was soon shut down), they dynamited the middle portion of the top of the mountain, creating a large, wedge-shaped crevice that can still be seen for miles. My uncle used to tease me and tell me that is where Paul Bunyan placed his axe when he sat down and had a sandwich. It has become a bizarre type of tourist attraction, and the slagheap at the top has attracted graffiti artists.

From my perspective, invasive insects are currently inflicting the most damage along the AT. Their names sound like they could be the benign mascots for minor league baseball teams—emerald ash borers, Asian long horned beetles, gypsy moths and hemlock wooly adelgids—but their destructive work is evident all along the southern Appalachians. At overlooks, on the side of the trails, and at campsites, the dead hulks of destroyed trees are ever present. In some camping areas, a dead tree may be the only option for hanging a bear pack—but once the rope is draped over a branch, it gives way and comes crashing to the ground.

This was Columbus Day weekend, so I ran into several day hikers, including some college students hiking while drinking beer.

I wound my way through forests just starting to shed their amber and blood red leaves as I climbed Siler Bald. I completed my hike in the mid-afternoon, at Wayah Gap at Highway 69, where my father picked me up. It was an altogether disappointing trip—I completed only about 30 miles of the planned 80-mile journey, but I consoled myself over the fact that I tried to hike during a freakish tropical storm that passed over the southern Appalachians in October. Still, I felt some of the regretful twinges that thru-hikers experience when they exit the trail early.

I was solemn and quiet during the long drive through the Nantahala National Forest, interspersed with small farms where harvested alfalfa hay had been rolled in to giant wheels in the fields, and the yards of the modest houses were festooned with jack o'lanterns and scarecrows.

SECTION HIKE 4
Wayah Gap to Fontana Dam, North Carolina
April 25–29, 2015 (51 Miles)

At the beginning of spring in 2015, I saw a small gap opening up in my work schedule, and the plans for my fourth section hike crystallized.

On a Saturday morning in late April 2015, it was raining at Wayah Gap while the sun was shining. It was also blustery, which made for a confusing weather mix—my rain gear would be put on and taken off multiple times over the course of the day.

This planned segment of 51 miles picked up where I had left off the previous autumn. I started where the AT crossed Highway 69 and would end up at Fontana Dam. My wife and I had gotten up early and driven for three-and-a-half hours to the drop-off point.

It was about a 3.5-mile hike up to Wayah Bald, which has an elevation of 5,342 feet. At the top is an old Civilian Conservation Corps (CCC) stone tower built in the 1930s. At that point in the day, the sky was clear, and I had an unobstructed view of Georgia to the south and the Smoky Mountains to the north.

The CCC built structures mainly of stone, and they have held up remarkably well over the years. My grandfather was a CCC education director during the Depression—he attended classes at Clemson during the day and taught at the nearby CCC facilities at night—and he always spoke reverently about how they took unemployed men, mainly from urban areas, and taught them to perform remarkable feats of engineering and aesthetic beauty.

During its short existence in the 1930s more than three million men worked at the CCC. Some of the specific accomplishments of the Corps included 3,470 fire towers erected, 97,000 miles of fire roads built, 4,235,000 man-days devoted to fighting fires, and more than three billion trees planted. Five hundred camps were under the direction of the Soil Conservation Service, performing erosion control. Erosion was ultimately contained on more than 20 million acres.[5]

The AT is dotted with the handiwork of the CCC, with fire towers, ranger stations and other stone buildings such as Walasi-Yi at Neel's Gap in Georgia. The CCC also worked on the scenic Blue Ridge Parkway, which cuts through the AT in Virginia.

At the top of Wayah Bald, I met Gentleman Jim. Jim was a previous thru-hiker—he had completed the entire trail from Springer to Maine in the late 1990s. He was a retired engineer living in Massachusetts, and he had worked for years on Boston's "Big Dig" project, which lasted for years and ultimately resulted (after billions in cost overruns) in the completion of a tunnel being built under the Boston Waterfront that relieved surface traffic in the downtown area.

Gentleman Jim was a short, stocky, bandy-legged man of medium height. He resembled *The Flintstones* cartoon character Barney Rubble. He wore a General Pershing, World War I–style wide-brimmed hat, and walked without hiking poles with a pronounced gait, shifting from side to side while moving forward.

Jim's memory had faded a bit from his previous journey, and the severity of the hiking (coupled, no doubt, with the addition of 20 years of age) had surprised him and made him already decide to get off the AT in Connecticut.

In addition to the AT, Jim had also hiked half of the Pacific Crest Trail (PCT). Gentleman Jim spun one yarn after another about his previous hikes. He talked about a woman he met on the PCT who was exhausted and could go no farther. They were 50 miles or so from the next sign of civilization, so Jim, in the desert, walked her pack five miles and then would walk back, pick up his pack, and with the woman, return to where her pack had been dropped off. In other words, for every five miles he advanced, he was actually hiking 15 miles. When they reached a place where she could call home and ask to be picked up, Jim continued his journey up the trail.

Jim had several interesting sayings. My favorite was, "After the Smokies, the whiners are all gone," meaning that if a hiker managed the 70 rugged miles through the Great Smoky Mountains National Park, he or she was probably going to make it all the way to Maine. He also was fond of saying, "No rain, no pain, no Maine," which was a twist on the Friedrich Nietzsche quote, "That which does not kill us makes us stronger."

Jim was also one of the few hikers that maintained a slower pace than me, so I passed him an hour or so after our conversation.

I ran into Stinky Shirt and Granny as I started my ascent up Wesser Bald, where I planned to camp near the 4,627-foot summit. Stinky Shirt was a 20-something millennial with black curly hair and a huge smile. Once I got within 15 feet of her, I instantly understood how she acquired her trail name. Granny was retired and lived in Brevard, North Carolina. She was outfitted like Cheryl Strayed in *Wild,* with an oversized pack, a sweatshirt, and a huge plastic whistle she wore around her neck. She was originally going to thru-hike, but, by her own admission, she was the slowest hiker on the AT and now planned to get off at Harper's Ferry, West Virginia, the midpoint of the trail.

I made it to the top of Wesser Bald in the late afternoon. All the spots in the shelter (more like a hovel—North Carolina was maintaining its reputation for poor shelters) were taken, as were all the desirable camping spots. I finally chose a relatively smooth patch of ground that sloped downward at 5–10 degrees. I knew I was taking a big chance with the possibility of the downhill flow if a rainstorm hit, but I had no other option.

Gentleman Jim sauntered in about an hour after I arrived, and took the adjacent spot, which was situated at an even worse downhill angle.

I met Bluto, a young hiker from Odessa, Texas, who worked the West Texas oil fields and had decided to thru-hike after he lost his job due to the recent crash in oil prices. He said he acquired his nickname due to his insatiable desire for hamburgers. I did not have the heart to tell him that the Popeye character that loved hamburgers was Wimpy, not Bluto. I guessed someone else would break the news of his error to him at some point on his trek.

Straggling hikers continued to drift into the shelter area at dusk, and the only remaining spots were on the bald area of the summit. I was lucky—if I had arrived an hour later, I would have had to join them on the wind-swept ridge.

One thru-hiker ambled in, heavily favoring one leg. He had badly twisted an ankle, and it was clear that he was going to need medical care at the next state highway, 11 miles below in Wesser. He declined all offers of assistance and made his way to the ridge to pitch his tent.

Sunset arrived at about 8 p.m., and I crawled into my tent, zipped up the flaps, and drifted off to sleep. I woke up around 11 p.m. to the sound of thunder. I had left my dirty hiking books just outside the tent entrance, so I unzipped the flaps, pulled them in, and waited for the inevitable deluge of rain that would naturally flow down the mountain, leaving me soaked.

I was fortunate. This storm dropped a brief shower, and amid howling winds, moved on to the east. Once I was convinced that the worst had passed, I relaxed and managed to enjoy a relatively undisturbed sleep.

❧❦❧

The next morning brought brilliant rays of sunshine, which slanted through the white pines, hemlocks, and oaks that bordered the camping area. The hikers forced to camp on the ridge walked down to the shelter area to get water and told us, not surprisingly, that they had slept very little because of the winds that shrieked up the valley all night long.

I had longish gray hair at the time, and a full silver beard. While packing for the trip, at the last minute I had stuffed an old, red woven ski cap into my pack before leaving Atlanta. Granny volunteered that I looked like Santa Claus, which I chuckled at. For the sake of trail peace, I kept several obvious comebacks to myself.

I planned on hiking to Wesser that day, better known as Nantahala Outdoor Center, or "NOC" (pronounced like "knock"). I had already booked a bed in a hiker hostel for about $20, and planned to get a good meal and a nice evening's rest before continuing my hike to Fontana Dam.

Half of the day was spent "ridge running," managing the easy dips between Wesser Bald, and the "Jump-Off," where I would start the deep descent down to NOC. Along the way, I passed Gentleman Jim, and we discussed lodging for the evening. I felt in the mood for an upgrade over the hostel, so we agreed to split the cost and share a room in a local motel, provided there was a vacancy. The next day, Jim was taking a "zero day" in Wesser—zero day being a term used by thru-hikers for a day off the AT spent washing clothes, picking up supplies, and relaxing from the rigors of the trail.

The Jump-Off starts at a rocky outcropping at about 4,300 feet, and over four miles drops 2,600 feet to a gorge carved by the Nantahala River. The first mile of the Jump-Off drops 800 feet and the AT very closely hugs the north side of the mountain, with no tree line tunnel that hikers on the AT are accustomed to—hikers are not shielded from a plunge off the mountainside on their left hand side as they carefully navigate the granite and scrub tree pathway downward.

I started my descent by rounding the first corner around a huge boulder when I spotted a young woman relieving herself just off the trail. I had learned by this point not to make a scene—I did not make coughing noises or loudly clear my throat—I just backed up, waited a respectable interval, and then proceeded down the path. I nodded and wished her a "good hike" as I passed her on the trail.

There were several hairpin turns on the hike down, and I was forced to slide down several sections, holding on to tree roots for support. The view was stunning. NOC, four miles below, was visible, as was the churning Nantahala River, which bisected the small village of Wesser. Nantahala means "Land of the Noonday Sun," in Cherokee; there are areas in the national forest that bears its name that only receive light when the sun is directly overhead in the middle of the day.[6]

As I made the final downhill approach to NOC, it began to rain. I was beginning to think that I was destined to spend every day on the AT getting wet, when I spotted Stinky Shirt up the trail, about a hundred feet ahead of me. She was singing, to herself and the world, "You Are My Sunshine," with a huge smile on her face. I felt renewed by this performance—she had no idea I was around—and I decided, at least temporarily, to stop worrying about the weather so much.

When I arrived in Wesser, it was late afternoon and the sun had reappeared. There was a gas station/convenience store next to the highway, and the man behind the counter was able to make my reservation at a motel, just across the Nantahala River, which could be crossed via a footbridge. I told him to be on the lookout for Gentleman Jim and to direct him to our room. I slung my backpack over my shoulders, stepped back outside, and crossed U.S. Highway 74.

On September 28, 1922, in Murphy, North Carolina, my great-grandparents decided to take a sightseeing drive along this very same road. The day before, my great-grandfather and Methodist minister Mark Bynum Clegg and his wife Louise had celebrated the birthday of Charles, my grandfather, who had just turned 16. Louise and Mark decided to drive, with their youngest child, three-year-old Ruth, along the newly completed Highway 74, to Topton, about 20 miles away, and enjoy the mountain vistas. Mark drove the Model T, while Louise sat in the passenger seat, holding Ruth.

Mark was born in Chatham County, North Carolina, just south of Durham. His ancestors left Yorkshire in England in the late 17th century and arrived on the Delmarva Peninsula, near modern day Accomack, Virginia. His family, attracted by the rich farmland, gradually moved southward and inland, settling in central North Carolina in what is modern-day Chatham County.

Mark, like many in his family, was a Methodist minister. He graduated with a degree in theology from Trinity College (later Duke University) and was selected to serve the Western District of North Carolina for the Methodist church. After stints in Henrietta and Caroleen in Rutherford County, he took over as minister for the church in Murphy, a small town nestled in the Blue Ridge Mountains just across the border from Georgia. With his leadership, a beautiful domed Byzantine-style church—with three semi-circular sets of stairs leading to three arched doorways, flanked by four Doric columns—was built in the downtown. His name still appears to this day, chiseled on the cornerstone of the church.

Louise was a descendant of German immigrants who had settled in Shelby, North Carolina, and was a "most attractive, blue-eyed, curly haired woman, with the sweetest of dispositions."[7] Her father, Lemuel, was an officer in the Confederate Army at Pickett's Charge during the Battle of Gettysburg and later served as a state senator in North Carolina.

Mark and Louise had endured more than their fair share of tragedy. They lost their daughter Irma, from fever, just after her first birthday in 1914. Their 11-year-old son Paul drowned in 1919 while swimming at a family picnic. That same year saw the passing of one-year-old Mark Bynum, Jr., and three-year-old Baxter. But this late September day in 1922 promised to be a good one. It was the first week of fall, and the morning beckoned with that early autumnal chill and airiness.

They had lunch together in Topton, and Mark later remarked that it seemed to be "one of the happiest days of Louise's life."[8] They drove northward on Highway 74, past Wesser, before deciding to drive home to Murphy.

Just south of Topton, there is a sharp turnoff to the right onto Highway 129. After crossing a bridge, the road veers sharply upward as it begins to wind its way back to higher elevations as it continues northward in the direction of Robbinsville. Just a few hundred feet past the turnoff is an overlook that commanded a brilliant view of the valley below. In 1922, this was an unobstructed view because the sides of the ravine had been clear-cut by a lumber company. Today, that ravine is covered in new-growth forest, making it hard to imagine how it may have looked like almost a century ago. At the bottom of the ravine, running parallel to Highway 74 is a railroad track. Louise suggested that the view was too beautiful to pass by and suggested they pull over to enjoy it.[9]

For some reason, Mark decided to back in to the overlook, perhaps because they had just driven past it, and Louise had made the suggestion to pull over as a spur of the moment decision.

After walking along the overlook to soak in the view, Louise and Ruth got back into the car. Mark remained outside—in the early 1920s, Model Ts were started by a hand crank, which was located just below the hood of the automobile. He cranked the car in one quick clockwise motion, and the Model T, with his wife and daughter inside, plunged over the cliff and down into the ravine below. When he had parked the car, Mark did not shift into neutral—he had left the car's gears in reverse.

As the car crashed over the precipice and down 90 feet into the railway bed, Ruth was flung from the vehicle. Later it was speculated that her mother threw her out in order to try and save her. Mark and a farmer working in a nearby field searched for his wife and daughter. Ruth was miraculously found at the bottom of the ravine, walking around dazed, bleeding, and crying. Louise was discovered grievously injured and unconscious underneath the wreckage.

A special train was commandeered from the Carolina and Georgia Railroad, and the mother and daughter were loaded on to a railcar and brought to the hospital in Murphy. A huge crowd gathered at the small hospital, as word had quickly spread about the accident.[10]

At age 43, Louise was declared dead at 9 p.m. The cause of death, according to her death certificate, was a "crushed pelvis and profound shock." After spending days in the hospital, Ruth recovered fully.

Almost a year to the date after the death of Louise, on October 4, 1923, Mark was remarried to Alzada "Lily" Roberts, an Asheville artist, in the old Langren Hotel in Asheville.[11] Soon afterwards, my grandfather, Charles, was sent off to boarding school at Young Harris Academy, just across the border in Georgia.

Mark and Lily left Murphy shortly after their marriage, and he assumed ministerial duties at the Methodist church in Lake Junaluska. He later became pastor of the small church in Biltmore, just outside Asheville, and he passed away in 1947 at age 73. His obituary stated that after he had retired as a minister, he spent time as a "spiritual leader," counseling area youth. Mark was also mentioned as a minister who confronted the theme of science versus religion—he postulated that there was no inherent conflict between the two.[12]

He and his wife are buried at the foot of a beautiful hemlock tree in Riverside Cemetery in Asheville, not far from the grave of that city's most famous son, Thomas Wolfe.

Ruth, who miraculously survived the crash, grew up and became a nurse and the mother of four daughters before passing away at the age of 88 in 2009.

⚜

After arriving in my room in Wesser, I showered and laid down on one of the two twin beds. About an hour later, Gentleman Jim walked in with his bandy-legged gait, carrying a twelve-pack of Budweiser, with no other drinks. This was a bit strange—the first thing hikers normally seek after getting off the trail is some sort of energy drink like Powerade or Gatorade (followed typically by beer). But Jim had eliminated the first step of rehydration with water or an energy drink and cracked open a Bud as he sat on the edge of his bed.

"Zero day tomorrow," Jim reminded me, as he took a deep swig of his beer. "Mind if I borrow your phone?" I thought that it was odd that a thru-hiker, especially one who was retired on Cape Cod, to ask to use another person's handheld. Cell phones are indispensable on the trail; they are used for phone calls, texts, weather updates and, more recently, as sources for topographic maps through the Guthook app. But I handed him my phone, and he called his wife in Massachusetts, gave her a brief update on his status, and then hung up.

We decided to have dinner at the restaurant overlooking the Nantahala, called River's End. I ordered a local craft beer, a Nantahala Brewing Company IPA, and wolfed down a veggie burger with fries. Jim ordered several Budweisers, and the next hour was a stream of consciousness outpouring of Jim's experiences and views on hiking.

Jim had cancelled his membership to the PCT because it had publicized its connection with Cheryl Strayed and her book and movie, *Wild*. He was angry because, like Bill Bryson and his famous book on the AT, Strayed had only hiked about half the PCT, and the movie had made no mention of that fact.

He had chosen his trail name because it put women he met on the trail at ease (he had a point here—picking Spike or Wildman as a trail name would have the opposite effect). Jim thought hiking poles were for sissies. The Mountain Harbour Bed and Breakfast in the Roan Highlands, 250 miles to the north, had the best pancakes on the trail. He was getting off the trail in Connecticut, because he had hiked the AT in its entirety 20 years previously, and he "had nothing to prove."

His most interesting story related to the end of his thru-hike in 1999 when he was in Maine and Tropical Storm Floyd struck in mid–September. He did not leave his tent for two days, and when he finally emerged, the river in front of his campsite was so high that it was not fordable. He walked parallel to the stream until he reached a pond with an old-fashioned dinner bell attached to a pole. He rang the bell, and someone paddled across the pond in a canoe, picked him up, and took him to his house where he enjoyed a delicious chicken dinner.

Most tellingly, Jim volunteered that he "was not an alcoholic"—he had spent the previous evening camping without anything to drink and "hadn't missed it."

We made our way back to the motel at dusk, and Jim popped open another Budweiser and resumed his position sitting on the side of his bed. I was dead tired and turned in. I was soon able to drift off to sleep, despite the fact Jim was still up with the lights on. I woke up once in the middle of the night, and Jim had not moved as he talked to himself, sipped beer, and stared straight ahead.

❧❦❧

I woke up at dawn the next morning and gingerly walked out on the deck of our room and cooked grits and oatmeal with my Jetboil. After showering, I silently packed up and noticed that all the beer cans were empty and in the trash can. Jim mumbled "zero day" in his sleep, and I carefully shut the door so as not to wake him.

I walked back over the footbridge to the outfitter located on the opposite side of the river. They were closed for another hour, so I was not able to pick up the few supplies I wanted. NOC was already a beehive of activity, with staff loading trucks with rafts and kayaks—Olympic kayaking hopefuls have trained on the Nantahala for years, and tourists now flock to the region for whitewater and zip-lining excursions. I enjoyed rafting in whitewater, but I had avoided canoeing or kayaking since my adolescence. When I was 14, I was caught in a hydraulic on the Upper Chattahoochee River (a hydraulic occurs after a drop-off, when swift water flows in a circular motion from the riverbed to the surface, creating a sideways whirlpool that can easily entrap and drown a person). My father and I had misjudged our approach to some shoals, and the canoe went over the rapids, back first. I was flung from the front of the canoe into a hydraulic, and my father had to pull me out by my hair.

When passing back over the footbridge to get back on the trail, I spotted Bluto down below at a picnic table, writing his trail blog. He was getting an early start on his zero day.

I was faced with having to regain all the elevation I had lost the previous day when descending from the Jump-Off. Starting at about 1,700 feet in Wesser, I would be climbing back up to 5,042 feet to reach the summit of Cheoah Bald. This is known as one of the toughest hikes on the AT, and it is highlighted by the "Jump-Up" at 4,000 feet, which bends upward at almost a 60-degree angle over rock cliffs until it finally begins to level out at 4,700 feet.

I was getting an early start and was on the trail before 8 a.m. I always liked the feeling of an early start when energy levels are at their highest and temperatures are at their coolest.

Early in the hike, near Wright Gap, I passed a bronze plaque embedded on top of a cairn of flat rocks. The memorial was in honor of Wade Sutton, a forest ranger who died near that spot fighting a massive fire in the Nantahala National Forest in 1968. Hikers had dropped off dozens of tokens of respect on top of the plaque, which had oxidized over the years and turned a light green. Coins, the orange plastic tops of cooking fuel canisters, small wooden crosses and other items were placed on top of the memorial.

The first three miles out of Wesser rise at a steady incline until about 3,500 feet. At that point, the gradient increases dramatically, with the start of the "Jump-Up." I suffered from green tunnel syndrome, believing that I was nearing the top when actually I was still hundreds of feet away. I had started taking medication for high blood pressure several months prior to this section hike, but once again, my heart was racing, and I had to take dozens of short mini-breaks during the ascent.

I finally reached the mountain summit around noon, where I sprawled out on a clearing near the edge. I lay flat on my back, staring at the sky, breathing like a fish pulled out of the water and tossed on the pier. After talking with a volunteer crew clearing dead trees off the trail, I realized that I had not reached the top of Cheoah Bald, but was instead on Swim Bald, Cheoah's sister peak connected by a saddleback. After a short lunch, I resumed my climb up to Cheoah.

As I struggled to the real summit, I had that internal debate once again on the why? Why was I doing this? The physical exertion was enormous, especially for someone like me closing in on age 60. The hardships of exposure to the elements, not being able to bathe, viewing food as nothing more than an opportunity to replenish energy, worrying about water sources—there were a lot of items on the negative side of the ledger to warrant finding a new way to spend my vacation time.

There is also the chance of an accident, perhaps even a deadly one, particularly since I hiked alone. Nature will mete out punishment, even to those who are prepared. My father suffered frostbite near Blood Mountain one March when a Nor'easter blew in and dropped temperatures by 30 degrees in a few hours. I met a thru-hiker who had to be airlifted out of the Smokies in April due to hypothermia. It is easy to trip or slip and fall, break bones or sustain bad cuts. In extremely rare circumstances, there is the possibility of a snakebite or bear attack.

What was the draw? There is certainly the "getting away from it all" aspect. The idea of strapping on a pack and traveling to a relatively undisturbed part of the country and trying to hike 10, 12, 14 miles a day, is completely alien to my normal daily existence, with its easy access to every modern convenience. And, even with advances in technology that allow for pretty much constant connection, hikers are isolated on the trail, particularly in the more remote regions of the AT like the southern Appalachians and Maine. Cell access is usually limited to mountain summits and areas near state highways. Water can be a constant challenge, particularly during the dry months of autumn.

On the other hand, there is also the chance to build camaraderie and a sense of community with strangers that is harder and harder to do in today's society. As a hiker, you are immediately accepted into a subculture, no matter your race, gender, economic status, educational attainment, etc. It is, in a sense, like a modern Canterbury Tales, with people meeting each other, traveling towards a common destination, and sharing entertaining stories.

There is also ego gratification. It feels *good* to get back and tell friends and colleagues that I hiked 50, 60, or 70 miles on the AT. Many people have a sense of awe about the accomplishment and say they would like to join me on my next journey.

It is also a way to connect with my father, who has hiked 200–300 miles of the AT. Even after many trips on the AT, I am still only an average outdoorsman at best, and he has passed on many useful tips to me over the years. I had also learned a lot from his mistakes, which are inevitable for anyone who spends a great deal of time alone in the woods.

Finally, the challenge of climbing mountains is a powerful motivation. It is, I believe, part of our DNA to see a mountain and want to conquer it. I remember sitting in a Dahlonega winery in January one year with my wife and daughter, looking at Justus and Sassafras mountains. I felt a warm glow (aided by the Cabernet Franc) knowing that I, probably alone among all the other customers, had struggled and sweated and made my way over those imposing peaks. From time to time, I will pull out a creased and soiled old trail map and smile inwardly as I retrace my steps.

After reaching the top of Cheoah Bald, I weighed my options. It was almost six miles to Stecoah Gap and Highway 143, a distance I probably was not going to cover—I had already hiked a very arduous seven miles, and I knew my energy would be ebbing quickly once I resumed my hike. Furthermore, there was only one source of water over the six-mile hike to Stecoah—a small spring at the northern base of Cheoah Bald. From there, I could refill my water supply and set up camp in Simp Gap, about three miles from Stecoah Gap.

The creek at the bottom of Cheoah was a leaf-covered pool of water, with one small trickle flowing over moss-covered rocks. This was always worrisome—a swift-flowing creek reduces impurities and the bacteria they may contain, and this water was stagnant, with insects buzzing over it.

Unlike many hikers, I did not use a full-blown water purification kit with its pumps and contraptions. Instead, I continued to rely on iodine tablets to purify water, which always turned my drinking water (and urine) into a light orange hue. Fecal coliform contamination of water, usually from bears, can be a serious matter—later on the AT, I met two SOBOs who had to spend a week in a motel with extreme diarrhea in Tennessee after coming down with this water-borne bacteria.

As I set up camp for the evening, several hikers passed by and asked me a few questions about water and distance, and they ultimately continued on their journey to Stecoah Gap. I was going to be spending this evening alone.

After a long day of hiking, I liked to unwind with a few pulls from Muscadine grape moonshine that my cousin had made in Dawsonville. I brought a small half-pint plastic container, and usually sipped on about one ounce per evening. That, along, with a few tokes of weed, calmed my nerves as darkness descended in another eerie gap, the hoot owl announced his presence, and I dozed off into a deep sleep.

I got off to an early start the next morning, easily managing the last couple of hillocks before descending a series of switchbacks bordered by dew-flecked white trillium and lavender dwarf irises. Along the way, there was another instance of "trail magic." A stranger had left a Styrofoam cooler full of popsicles. I grabbed an orange flavored one, sucked it down, and continued down the trail. At the parking area adjacent to Highway 143, which crossed Stecoah Gap, there was an elderly man with a truck bed filled with apples and bananas—more trail magic. I thanked him for the apple and crossed the busy highway.

On the opposite side of 143, there was a ridgeline that rose parallel to the highway. I began climbing it and noticed for the first time how quickly the sights and sounds of traffic disappeared as I gained elevation.

I knew Jacob's Ladder would be coming up soon—a hiker I had met the previous day had warned me about it. When looking at my trail map, it resembled Kelly's Knob, back in Georgia—about a 700-foot elevation gain in a little less than a mile at a steep, 50- or 60-degree angle. The difference was the trail—Jacob's Ladder was a "goat path," straight up the mountain. I was not mentally or physically prepared for this—in trail lore, Jacob's Ladder was not particularly legendary like Albert Mountain or the Jump-Up. But both my body and expectations were conditioned for switchback trails that lengthen the hike but lessen the exertion by leveling out the angle during the climb. I was, in short, a huffing and puffing mess as I trudged slowly up the mountain.

Dwarf iris flower along the AT.

When I finally reached the top, a long flat top that extends for about one-quarter mile, Bluto came hiking up the trail. This was astonishing, because he had taken a zero day the day before, and he was passing me at midday. This meant that he would have covered the distance from NOC, about 15 miles away, in three or four hours. It turned out he got bored during his zero day and started back up the trail in the mid-afternoon, camping at Sassafras Gap Shelter, about six miles from NOC. In AT lingo, his planned zero day had turned in to a "nero" (near zero) day. I asked him what he thought about Jacob's Ladder, and he responded, "What is Jacob's Ladder?" In stark contrast to me, the experience of climbing it had obviously left him unfazed. That summer, I followed Bluto's trail blog and learned, unsurprisingly, that he had completed the "Four State Challenge," crossing the borders of West Virginia, Virginia, Maryland and Pennsylvania (43 miles) in one 24-hour period.

I arrived at Cable Gap Shelter at dusk. Unlike most of the other shelters in the Nantahala National Forest, this one was tidy and spacious and even featured bear cables for hanging packs. It was, of course, already fully occupied, which did not matter to me—there were plenty of available spots for camping adjacent to the creek that bordered the eastern edge of the shelter area.

I pitched a tent on a perfect spot covered with pine needles and light sand that was a short walk to the creek and my water supply. It was also a couple of hundred feet from the shelter, which would help dissipate the inevitable noise that would be coming from it as evening approached.

Next to me was a young man from Providence, Rhode Island, named Matt. He was finishing up his last section hike of the AT—he had flown to Charlotte several days earlier, bused to Hot Springs, North Carolina, and was covering that 270-mile segment to the southern terminus of the AT in two weeks.

Matt, like me, did not assume a trail name. I was too self-conscious to give myself an unflattering nickname like "Lost Again" or "He Who Breathes Heavily While Engaged in Steep Hikes." Matt, unlike me, was probably just too cool for it. He worked in the telecom business back home, was a huge Red Sox fan and a vegetarian. He had a long black mane of hair and was lithe and tanned. He moved like a panther over the mountains, covering 25–30 miles a day. He was meeting up with his girlfriend in Georgia and they were going to hike the final portion to Springer Mountain together.

As the sun set on the cove, we talked about a number of topics, including section hiking versus thru-hiking. We agreed that we both enjoyed civilization too much to consider a thru-hike. Watching baseball, drinking beer, and reading a good book in the comfort of home were all activities we gladly would give up for a week or two, but beyond that, the dirt and grind of the AT would become tiresome.

I handed Matt a couple of sticks of vegetarian jerky and gave him my phone number in case he needed an emergency contact in Georgia. When I got up early the next morning, he was gone.

It was about a seven-mile hike to Fontana Dam, where I would be leaving the trail. It was a relatively innocuous hike—I caught several glimpses of sapphire blue Fontana Lake on ridgelines as I covered the last few miles of the AT in the Nantahala National Forest.

The "Fontana Hilton," as it is affectionately known, is a shelter located on a paved side road—the main road it connects to leads directly over Fontana Dam. The "Hilton" has luxury accommodations by AT standards—it is situated directly on the lake on the north side of the dam. The interior has tiered bunks, most of them filled by sleeping hikers. The area adjacent to the shelter has a wooden deck that overlooks the lake with a fire pit in the middle. Although it was late April, it was a bit chilly, and a young woman was trying to get a fire going. A couple of hundred feet away from the shelter, towards the main road leading to the dam, were showers and bathrooms.

Given the availability of running water, showers, and functioning modern-day toilets, many hikers linger for several days at the Hilton. The nearby Fontana Village, a rustic resort several miles away, is also a major resupply point for hikers awaiting packages either pre-sent by themselves to themselves or mailed by friends or family, timed to arrive hopefully before the hikers reached the area. There were several hikers who took the shuttle bus each day to the Village to see if their packages had arrived. Since most of the young hikers were on a limited budget, they were at the mercy of mail delivery and would sometimes wait two or three days at the Hilton anxiously awaiting the money and supplies tucked inside the boxes.

I had called earlier in the day to book a room at Fontana Village. I caught a ride from a local woman who drove a shuttle to the Village, and we chatted along the way. The Village, which was built in the 1940s to provide lodging to the workers building the nearby dam, was a major employer in Graham County, a sparsely populated area across the Little Tennessee River from the Great Smoky Mountains National Forest and the state of Tennessee. From the lake, I had already spotted the dark, 6,000-foot peaks of the Smokies looming across the water.

The van driver had a classic southern Appalachian accent, where short a's become long i's (gas became "gice") and long i's became short a's (rice became "rahs"). The French spoken in Quebec reflects many of the characteristics of the provincial French spoken by the settlers who settled that region in the 17th century. Similarly, the English spoken in the southern Appalachians still echoes many of the attributes of language spoken by the early white settlers from Britain. Words such as nary, yonder, tetchy, nigh, betwixt, and fetch were used by Shakespeare, and pert, atwix, and smidgen date back to Geoffrey Chaucer.

Normalizing irregular verbs in the past tense is also a throwback to Elizabethan English. "Knowed" instead of knew, "throwed" instead of threw, and "choosed," instead of chose. The use of double nouns such as "preacher-man" and "church-house" also has its origins in the every-day English spoken hundreds of years ago. Double-barreled pronouns are also prevalent in Appalachia. Few people say "y'all" in the mountains—that is lowland vernacular—when using the third person plural, it is "you-uns" in many parts of Appalachia.[13]

We talked about Graham County, which is nestled in the south-western extremity of North Carolina and, with less than 10,000 residents, is the third least populated out of the state's 100 counties. Economic opportunities are few and diminishing further with the loss of manu-facturers that had kept generations of local families employed. Leisure and hospitality related jobs with Fontana Village and the nearby lake created by the damming of the Little Tennessee River in the 1940s rep-resent some of the only employment opportunities in the area.

Fontana Dam is one of the United States' least known but hugely impressive engineering feats. It is the highest dam east of the Mississippi River, and it was built in less than two years during World War II. The downriver city of Alcoa, Tennessee, needed hydroelectric power to run the aluminum plants utilized for manufacturing military aircraft. Even today, Graham County is difficult to reach with modern roads. It is hard to imagine how imposing it must have been to haul heavy equipment and materials across the southern Appalachians in the 1940s.

An unfortunate side effect of the hurried construction of the dam was the forced relocation of 1,300 residents in the valley that was flooded to create the reservoir. These residents, many of whom were elderly, had multi-generational ties to their homes, and they were offered no compensation as part of their removal. Those who refused had their land condemned and taken.

The federal government did promise to build a 32-mile road around the lake, to give residents access to their 28 ancestral cemeteries on the mountainsides. However, only six miles of this road were ever completed, a stretch that dead-ends in the North Carolina portion of the Great Smoky Mountains National Park. Local residents derisively refer to it as the "Road to Nowhere."[14]

The lobby of Fontana Village appears to have been refurbished in the 1980s or 1990s, and it gives off a somewhat dated Rocky Mountain ski lodge appearance. Black and white photographs detailing the Village's World War II history dotted the paneled walls. The lobby was a beehive of activity as both hikers and Mini Cooper conventioneers were checking in—Mini Cooper enthusiasts, it seems, congregate at Fontana Village every April.

Fontana Village also received and held mail for thru-hikers, so there was almost a constant stream of hikers approaching the front desk to check the status of their packages. Many, when learning the news that their package had not arrived that day, went back outside to await the shuttle and a return to the Fontana Hilton. They would get up the next morning and repeat the exercise again, their thru-hikes delayed and at the mercy of the U.S. Postal Service.

One disappointed young female thru-hiker loudly announced that she was quitting the trail because she was fed up with the hold-up in her mail. She was handing out items she would no longer need, like granola bars and jerky. Apparently this was a common occurrence—there was a barrel set up in the gift shop for other hikers who had already left the trail to deposit their unneeded goods for anyone else to take. It was full.

I checked in to my room, which definitely had a rustic feel and probably had not changed much since my parents honeymooned at the resort in October 1957.

On a hot summer's day in August 1957, my father graduated from Emory University in Atlanta. His mother attended the ceremony, and later went with him back to the fraternity house to help clean out his room. They drove the slow mountain roads back to their home in Young Harris, Georgia, and stopped late in the afternoon at the tiny post office in town. My father opened a government-stamped letter that contained the terse official notice that he had been drafted into the U.S. Army. He called his girlfriend, my mother, back in Gainesville, Georgia, and told her the news. "I'm not waiting," was her response, so they became formally engaged that evening. Graduating from college, getting drafted by the Army and getting engaged to your future wife all in one day is something we still laugh about.

They were married that October. My father was 21 and my mother, 17. Thirteen months later, I was born in a military hospital in Nuremberg, Germany.

I walked around the perimeter of the Village and discovered a combination gas station and bar called the Pit Stop, run by local Cherokees. In addition to offering normal convenience store goods, it also served hot dogs, cheese nachos and alcohol from a small bar area with a half dozen barstools.

There were three thru-hikers doing Fireball shots at the counter—Hero, Big Brown and Florida Girl. Hero got his name from hiking 20 hours consecutively, arriving at a shelter at 4 a.m. Big Brown was an effusive Mexican American and was not bothered by his politically incorrect trail name. Florida Girl was an African American young woman from Tampa who had already decided to leave the trail in Gatlinburg, Tennessee, due to money issues.

Many young thru-hikers are strapped for cash, and they make their way up the trail between package pickups through a series of bartering arrangements (agreeing to wash dishes at a hostel in exchange for free lodging, for instance) and the kindness of strangers. It is not cheap to hike the Appalachian Trail—the average thru-hiker spends $5,500, not including the initial outlay for gear.[15] For this reason, I felt bad when they insisted on buying me a shot while I nursed my Nantahala IPA. But this sense of community, even by those who have little, is prevalent on the AT. I offered them the remaining food in my pack as a form of payback.

The next morning the lobby of the resort was filled with hikers preparing to move on into the Smokies. Many of them were lined up at the one public access computer, ordering and printing out their $20 permits, the amount the National Park charges hikers for the right to pass through the 70 miles of the AT that cut through the park.

I had arrived at Fontana Dam ahead of schedule and considered the possibility of continuing for a day or two into the Smokies. But there is only one road that goes through the park, at Newfound Gap, 40 miles up the trail. The Smokies would have to wait until my next trip.

My wife picked me up at the Village in mid-morning, and as we drove back to Atlanta, a parade of Mini Coopers zoomed by in the opposite direction, headed to the convention at Fontana Village.

As we proceeded southward, I knew I would be back in the autumn—the dark mountains on the other side of the dam beckoned.

SECTION HIKE 5
Fontana Dam, North Carolina, to Newfound Gap, Tennessee
October 23–26, 2015 (40 Miles)

The Cherokees called the Smoky Mountains Shaconage (Sha-Kon-O-Hey), "Land of the Blue Smoke." The hazy, mystical mist that we associate with the Smokies comes from the organic compounds emitted by the area's intense vegetation—the vapor molecules from the millions of plants, bushes, and trees scatter blue light, giving the area its name.

The combination of elevation, inaccessibility, and temperate climate conditions make the 800 square miles of the Smoky Mountains the most biodiverse national park in the United States.

It was only in 1998 that the National Park Service began to try and catalogue all the different species of plants, fungi, and animals that exist within the Smokies. To date, 19,000 different species have been identified, and scientists believe that an additional 80–90,000 may exist.[16]

The National Park Service carefully guards this biological richness and its fragility—hikers have to pay a $20 impact fee to pass through the Smokies, and they must camp in designated shelter areas; veering off the trail to explore is strictly prohibited.

When planning my trip, I called a park ranger and was told that unless a shelter structure was full, I could not camp in the adjacent areas. To hike the 70 miles of the AT through the Smokies, I also had to state that I was a thru-hiker if I wanted to stay in a shelter. I bit my lip and told a white lie—after all, section hikes are just thru-hikes that take a little longer.

Once again, my work schedule was extremely hectic leading up to the hike. I did manage to search weather conditions, and for the most part, it looked like the week of the hike would bring beautiful, Indian-summer type conditions, with highs during the day in the 70s, dipping down to the 40s at night—Goldilocks weather.

Although I grew up in the southeast, I had never visited the Smoky Mountains. I have always been in awe of them, these fog-shrouded, ancient and impenetrable beasts of mountains.

The trail through the Smokies passes over three mountains that exceed 6,000 feet in elevation, including Clingman's Dome, which at 6,643 feet is the highest peak on the Appalachian Trail.

I had enough respect for the Smokies to not try and attempt the entire 70-mile journey in one trip. Instead, I planned on getting picked up at Newfound Gap after a four-day hike.

⊰❊⊱

Fontana Dam on that late October day was like a soft water color illustration from an A.A. Milne book—a gentle array of azure skies, amber leaves on the mountain slopes and sapphire blue lake water.

The Appalachian Trail crosses directly over the top of the dam, extending a half-mile on a two-lane road (the only time the AT crosses a dam). It felt odd seeing the "AT" logo painted on concrete instead of on the side of an oak. On the left, looking south, was the concrete dam, sloping down 481 feet to the churning Little Tennessee River. On the right was Fontana Lake, held back now for over 70 years by the World War II–era dam.

My wife walked with me over the dam until we reached the far side and saw the sign and the turn-off to the Great Smoky Mountains National Park. We said our goodbyes and I headed up the road that would start the ascent to the first peak in the Smokies, Shuckstack Mountain. Fontana Dam is at an elevation of only 1,775 feet, and Shuckstack tops out at over 4,000 feet, so I was poised for an immediate challenge.

This point marked a new beginning in every sense—I had left the Nantahala National Forest, left North Carolina, and left a familiar Appalachian wooded area for a denser, more primeval forest. The change is subtle but almost immediately noticeable—the hues are darker and shadows more frequent in the Smokies; the animals and birds are more prevalent. I had the sense that I was entering their sanctuary, not plowing through a trail where they were an exotic side attraction. A thousand eyes were watching me, it seemed.

As always, I had a lot of energy when starting out a new section hike, and I managed the switchbacks up Shuckstack with relative ease.

Along the way, I met a group of three young men from a church group in South Carolina that were headed the ten miles to Mollie's Ridge, the same designated camping area where I was planning on spending the evening. In addition to their packs, each hiker was carrying, by hand, a gallon jug of water. I chuckled inwardly, thinking that that was something I might have done as a beginner.

The hike up Shuckstack was four miles, and I reached the top, at the foot of a fire tower, in the early afternoon. I had lunch there with several other hikers. Two young women from Clayton, Georgia, had struggled mightily with the hike up the mountain, and one, in tears, said she could not go any further. She had a medical condition that had flared up, and she was having an anxiety attack. Her girlfriend comforted her and told her it was okay; they lived a short distance away and could always try again. I offered my condolences to them and wished them the best as they headed back down the trail to Fontana.

A hiker named Dave was also at the top of Shuckstack. Dave was a transplanted Texan who had followed his girlfriend to Boone, North Carolina, where she was studying for her masters at Appalachian State University.

Dave, like the hikers from the church group I had passed earlier, was a newbie. He wore a heavy cotton sweatshirt and blue jeans with a long Buck knife strapped on his belt, encased in a leather sheath. I tried a gentle jab with him, telling him the knife would do him no good in the Smokies—it would not stop a bear, only piss him off. That brought a slight smile to his face.

About a mile after leaving Shuckstack, winding my way up to the top of Doe Knob, I passed a hiker headed south who told me that, just up the trail, there was a fat eastern diamondback rattlesnake sunning himself in the middle of the trail. The snake, the hiker said, had an elongated midsection, probably from digesting a small rodent. I was on high alert as I rounded every corner and stepped on top of every log the crossed the trail (my father had taught me long ago that while walking in the woods, never step over a log, step on top of it—an unseen snake may be on the other side). I never saw the rattlesnake—he had slithered off after enjoying his post-meal nap.

I was climbing out of Ekaneetlee Gap when I caught up with Dave and a group of Texans he had met earlier on the trail. They were all stopped and hushed, staring into the woods to the left of the trail. "Bear," Dave whispered to me. He pointed to the left side of the trail, where 150 feet away, in a sun-splashed patch of forest, a juvenile black bear was frolicking on its back, oblivious to our presence. The group of us stood together in awed silence, watching the bear as he enjoyed that brilliant autumn afternoon.

After we snapped pictures, Dave asked what we should do. "Hike up the trail," I responded. One of the Texans had read that bears don't like it when hikers clang their aluminum hiking poles together, so we did that while the bear continued to ignore us, and we finally continued up the trail.

Black bears are estimated to number 1,600 in the Smoky Mountains National Park, and park rangers have closed sections of the park when they have become aggressive and refuse to back away from humans. They are much more docile than their predatory counterparts in the west, the grizzly bears, but there are isolated incidents of black bear attacks. Just earlier that summer, in June, a 200-pound black bear had attacked a 16-year-old boy sleeping in his hammock on the edge of the park. He and his father, who were finishing a four-day hike, had even hung a bear pack on a cable in their camping area. The boy survived after being airlifted to a hospital in Asheville.[17]

In May of 2016 near the Spence Field Shelter in the Smokies, a black bear attacked a 49-year-old man named Bradley Veeder while he was asleep in his tent, biting him on the leg and returning several times before being driven off by loud shouts. This camper had hung his food pack at the nearby shelter, but the bear had picked up a scent that piqued his curiosity he ended up destroying Veeder's tent, backpack, water filter and books. Veeder survived with a leg injury that required treatment.[18]

A friend of mine was once nearly victimized by a curious bear that invaded his campsite. He was not injured, but the bear climbed on top of him while he played dead and nuzzled him. He claimed that his only thought was not of imminent death; he was focused instead on stifling the strong urge to vomit due to the rank breath of the bear.

The likelihood of a black bear attack is extremely remote on the Appalachian Trail. When attacks do occur, they tend to be sensationalized, similar to shark attacks on ocean shorelines. And, when the rare attack does occur, they are seldom fatal. The victims of these attacks were all experienced campers who had taken the necessary precautions. All the attacks occurred in the springtime, when the bears had emerged from hibernation and were probably in desperate need of sustenance before the berries that they depend on as a food source had begun to ripen.

Although their appearance can be fearsome, black bears lead a fragile existence in the Smokies. Their main food sources are berries, roots, and other vegetation, and in extreme weather conditions such as drought or abnormally warm springs that drive the bears out of hibernation early, they will starve.

This particular autumn, the acorn supply was severely diminished due to drought conditions. Bears rely heavily on acorns to build fat reserves before they go in to hibernation, and the local non-profit group, Appalachian Bear Rescue, trapped and nursed back to health multiple malnourished, injured, and orphaned bear cubs.[19] "Nuisance" bears that invade campgrounds or neighboring populated areas often are forced into foraging for food when their normal sources of nutrition are disrupted. This makes them dangerous and can also make them susceptible to gunshot wounds and injuries caused by automobiles. Unless prompted by hunger, black bears in the area typically do not travel great distances. The bears previously tagged during the massive fires in East Tennessee in November 2016 hardly moved from their familiar turf.[20]

I arrived at Mollie's Ridge Shelter in the early evening, with an hour of daylight still remaining. I walked in at the same time as the three church members from South Carolina, still carrying their gallon plastic jugs of water.

I had heard that the shelters in the Smokies were luxurious by AT standards, and Mollie's Shelter was no exception. It is a long, tin-roofed structure supported by two flat-rock walls, with the rocks expertly stacked to provide support without any mortar. The far wall contained a fireplace and a chimney that jutted several feet above the roof.

The roof covers a picnic table that is separated from the double-decked bunk area by the other rock wall. Every shelter space was taken, so I could pitch my tent in an adjacent camping area without any sense of guilt.

The small spring next to the shelter ran dry after one hiker filled his container. Luckily, I had re-supplied earlier and would be able to cook and drink with what I had on hand—the other hikers split their water between themselves so that no one would suffer from thirst.

All shelters in the Smokies have steel bear cables with hooks to hang packs. Bright red, yellow, and blue food packs hung from the cables 20 feet off the ground like Japanese lanterns.

Several SOBO thru-hikers were staying at the shelter. Beatrice, a young French woman, carried a light pack and wore a pretty designer scarf while she sipped Calvados on one of the logs placed around the fire. If anyone would somehow look elegant on a thru-hike, it would be a French woman.

I asked one of the thru-hikers, a 30ish Pennsylvanian named Mike, what he would do once he reached his goal at Springer Mountain. "Get on a plane and go home," he responded dryly.

Everyone, like clockwork, retired to their sleeping bags once the last beam of light fell over the mountains. I own a flock of chickens, and hikers always remind me of my fowl when they mimic their light/dark Circadian rhythms of down at dusk, up at dawn.

As I walked the short distance to my tent, my headlamp beam caught a red fox, scampering across the path. I enjoyed a little weed before climbing into my tent for the night and nestling into my sleeping bag and drifting off into a fitful sleep.

The black bear in the cage appeared in my dreams that evening. I was a young adult, and the bear was approaching his middle age. Black bears can live up to 30 years in the wild, but the hopelessness and boredom of life in the cage had caused him to age prematurely. He teeth were yellow, and his long nails had never been trimmed. Touches of silver were starting to appear on his long muzzle, and he was missing patches of fur on his thick black coat.

It was a hot, summer day, and he ignored the flies that buzzed noisily around his head. The mountains in the distance were barely visible, covered by a thick summer haze.

He was no longer pacing in his filthy cage—he had resigned himself to eternal captivity and did not eagerly approach me when I held two iron bars and peered in at him. He raised his head, and when he realized I had no food, retreated to his corner, where he gazed briefly at me before lying down on his side and shutting his eyes.

❧❦❧

I woke up early, snug in my sleeping bag. The slight autumn chill and the rays of sunshine reflecting off the ceiling of my tent were favorable signs that a great day of hiking laid ahead.

The thru-hikers were long gone by the time I emerged from my tent, and the church group were packing up and heading back to Fontana Dam. Dave, with his Buck knife secured to the sheath on his belt, was heading up the trail.

Unlike most shelters, which are at the top of mountains or on gentle ridges leading down to coves, Mollie's Ridge featured an immediate 300-foot vertical hike to Devil's Tater Patch, which reaches 4,800 feet. This is followed by a descent into Little Abrams Gap and a short hike up to the next shelter, Russell Field. The Smokies group shelters closer together than what is typical in the AT due to the prohibition on camping in non-designated areas, and this shelter was only 3.3 miles distant from the one at Mollie's Ridge.

I walked into the shelter area around 10 a.m. to replenish my water supply and met three young Russian men grouped around the fire pit, cooking a meat stew over a black pot while sipping Jack Daniels from a bottle. They lived in Chicago and had bussed 16 hours to get to the Smokies. I offered them a "krasiviya pagoda sevodnya" (nice weather today), which was about all the Russian I could muster up from having studied it almost forty years ago in college.

As I continued up the trail to Spence Field and Rocky Top, a herd of white-tailed deer, led by an eight-point buck, thundered across the trail about one hundred feet ahead of me. I had learned by then to tell the difference between pellet-shaped deer poop and the more sinister, potato-shaped blobs of bear scat. Both animals were apparently on the move nearby, as evidenced by their multiple droppings along the trail.

The trail up to 5,441-foot Rocky Top Mountain was a bare goat path, which left me exposed to the midday sun. I took multiple mini-breaks during the climb, wheezing from shortness of breath. When I reached the top, I sprawled out on the turf summit and enjoyed an unobstructed view of the cobalt waters of Fontana Lake to the east as two red-tailed hawks swooped and danced in their mating ritual high in the air currents.

I pulled myself up to eat lunch, and the three Russians came by, beaming and waving. Everyone has a different hike, I reminded myself. I stood up, dusted myself off, and headed to Derrick Knob, the next shelter, which was three miles away.

Terrain maps can be deceiving because they do not always capture the nuances of grade or degree of difficulty. The three miles on the map looked easy, but owing more to fatigue than anything else, I struggled, and my "hiker's mirage" once again kicked in. I knew that the shelter was always just over the next ridgeline, and my 12-mile hike for the day would finally be completed. I met up with Kurt, a German hiker living in the Atlanta area, and his father, who had traveled from Karlsruhe in Germany to experience the AT. Kurt was similarly frustrated with the invisible shelter, and we both began to worry that we had passed it—sometimes the signs for the turn-off to the shelters are poorly marked, so it is possible to walk by and not see them.

Finally, on the approach to another ridgeline, Derrick Knob appeared on the left, the final rays of the sun spilling through the leaves and glinting off its tin roof.

Derrick Knob was another brilliantly constructed shelter. Like Mollie's Ridge Shelter, it had a fireplace and chimney built on the far wall to the east, but the two picnic tables were placed out front, covered by the cantilevered roof.

Kurt's father was busy sweeping off dust from the bunk area with the shelter-supplied broom. Dave was already in his sleeping bag, and it appeared that the rest of the group, including the Texans, had already eaten and were preparing for bed.

I pitched my tent about 30 feet from the chimney-bordered side of the shelter and cooked some dehydrated lasagna by pouring boiling water into the food pouch and sealing it for ten minutes. It was only after eating for five minutes and poking around in the bottom of the pouch that I realized I had cooked the lasagna with the preservative food packet still in the container. Luckily, it did not open, and I was not poisoned with chemicals. After cleaning up, I went to bed, thankful that I had not ingested toxins.

At about 3 a.m., I was awoken by a loud "k-k-k-k-kuh KA!" That night, like most on the AT when I camped near a shelter, I was wearing earplugs to block ambient human noise. But the snoring was so bad, in this instance, that it traveled the 30 feet to my tent, penetrated my earplugs, and woke me up. I felt sorry for the poor guys in the shelter, where the noise must have been eardrum shattering. And then I got pissed off—someone who snores that badly must be aware of it, and why is he inflicting it on other campers packed tightly in a common sleeping area? The more I thought about it, the angrier I got, and I became even more sensitive to the noise until I finally drifted off at about 5 a.m.

✺

When I woke up around 7 a.m., I walked over to the shelter and spoke to Kurt about the snorer. Not only had he kept most of the occupants up most of the evening, but he had also set his alarm for 5:30 a.m. to get an early start on his hike, and he was not too quiet about packing up his gear. As is the case in most activities, it only takes one person to wreck what should be a pleasant experience for others. Kurt, to his credit, was able to laugh about it. "It was more of a yell than a snore," he said, which was a pretty accurate.

It was another beautiful day, and I was in a quandary because of the national park's shelter rules in the Smokies. I was 22 miles into the Smokies, and Newfound Gap, where my father would be picking me up the next day at 3 p.m., was 18 miles away. Clingman's Dome, at 6,643 feet, was eight miles away, and the last shelter before Clingman's, Double

Spring Gap, was at the foot of the mountain. The next shelter after Double Spring was on the other side of Newfound Gap, so I had to stay at Double Spring Gap shelter that evening and then get up very early the next morning to hike the remaining 12 miles to Newfound Gap in order to make it by the appointed pick-up time. To complicate matters further, rain was expected to arrive this evening and last throughout the next day. This sort of mathematical word problem is typical of hiking, as time, distance, weather and terrain have to be considered when making decisions about the daily trek.

The seven-mile hike to Double Spring was difficult, as the ridge line slowly shifted above 5,000 feet on the approach to Clingman's Dome. In Buckeye Gap near Proctor Creek, a chestnut-colored beaver, sitting on his back legs, eyed me curiously before doing its strange hop across the trail in to the woods beyond.

It is easy to understand why the Smoky Mountains were sacred ground to the Cherokee—they teem with animals, and one of the legends of the tribe held that deep within the mountains, an enchanted lake existed that was not visible to humans, and it abounded with birds, fish, reptiles, and animals who drank its water.

One legend says a Cherokee man was able to see this lake after days of fasting and prayer. In exchange for seeing the lake, the young man had to make a solemn vow to never hunt there. But when his trance ends, the young man marks the spot where he had had his vision with a pile of rocks. The next winter is terrible, and it brings the tribe close to starvation. The man, desperate to feed his family, returns to the rock pile and enters Atagahi to hunt game. He shoots a bear with a bow, the bear tells the young man he has betrayed them; a slew of bears then attacks and kills the man. After the long winter ends, the Cherokee find the young's man's lifeless body but can find no tracks or signs of bears. From that point onward, Atagahi was closed to humans, but legend claims that the mist rising from the mystical lake can sometimes still be seen from the top of Clingman's Dome.[21]

I arrived at the shelter around 2 p.m. Even at that early hour, there was, at 5,525 feet, a crisp chillness in the air. I joined the three Texans on a wood-foraging expedition to build a blaze inside the shelter's fireplace. In shelters, the "easy wood" in the immediate vicinity has usually all been gathered, so we went deep into the forest to amass our supply.

We came back with our arms full, the haul including an old shelter sign that had been tossed into the woods.

Kurt's father was fastidiously sweeping the bunk platform while Dave sat on a picnic table bench with a sick look on his face. The hike had killed his appetite, and he had hardly eaten in the past several days. He had decided to get off the trail at Newfound Gap rather than complete the entire 70 miles of the AT in the Smokies.

We gathered by the edge of the stone fireplace and talked about our plans. The rains were expected to arrive in the early morning and last throughout the next day, so we agreed that we needed to get an early start, in the darkness, at around 7 a.m. One hiker called his wife and asked her to pick him up on the top of Clingman's in the mid-morning. Kurt and his father had similarly arranged for a shuttle pick-up in the visitor's parking lot area of Clingman's.

The Texans had flown to Atlanta and taken a rental car to Fontana Village. They were also contemplating getting off the trail at Newfound Gap.

We talked about the recently completed, record-setting thru hike of Heather Anderson, who had, a month earlier, completed the Maine-to-Georgia hike in 54 days, averaging 40 miles per day. Unlike previous speed hikers, Anderson had hiked alone, without a supporting crew.[22]

Someone periodically announced college football scores, accompanied by either happy cheers or groans of dismay.

Several hikers passed by, including one wiry gray-headed, southbound Vermonter, who was completing a thru-hike he had had to abort 30 years earlier. He asked if there was room in the shelter, and one of the Texans misunderstood him, thinking he had asked, "Where is the next shelter?"

"Siler's Bald Shelter is about two miles down the trail," responded the Texan. "That is not what I asked," snapped the Vermonter as he marched off down the trail. I had to chuckle inwardly at the matter-of-fact bluntness of New Englanders.

As dusk approached, I pitched my tent in thick turf grass on the other side of the trail from the shelter. I strapped on my headlamp and realized that it no longer worked, despite my having inserted new batteries before the trip. I went back in the shelter and asked if I could borrow someone's headlamp. One of the Texans had a spare that he gave me; I offered payment, but he refused. I passed around my small plastic flask of Dawson County moonshine, and several guys took small sips, grimacing while screwing the top back on.

As I gathered my gear and went to my tent, my little patch was bathed in the shimmering light of a brilliant hunter's moon. Storm clouds scudded past the moon, but I soon drifted off to deep, restful sleep.

I woke up a 6:30 a.m. and opened my tent flap. The grass was slick with rainwater; the storm had passed by in the night without disturbing my sleep. The thick heath grass had absorbed the heavy rain and probably kept my tent from flooding.

It was not raining as I rolled up my tent and sleeping bag and went inside the shelter to get my pack, which I had hung on a wooden peg. Everyone laughed when I told them I had slept through the storm; apparently, they had been woken by the light and sound show that accompanied the heavy rain that had fallen in the early morning.

By 7 a.m. I was on the trail, the light from my headlamp bouncing off trees and the path, thick with fir needles. Early in the 1,000-foot ascent of Clingman's, the Christmas tree scent of Fraser firs and red spruce filled my nostrils. My eyes gradually adjusted to the darkness, and I could make out dark hemlocks and cream-colored beeches and a ground covered by thick, avocado-colored moss.

Unfortunately, the damage caused by adelgids was also on display; the forlorn and bare dead husks of firs ravaged by the invasive insect dotted the forest. As I climbed higher and the rain started, knobby krummholz, bent by years of wind, reached out their arms in supplication to the sky like Joshua trees.

I took a wrong turn near the summit and walked down a side path that dipped to the visitor parking area below. About 400 feet down the path, I could see the cars parked in the area, realized my mistake and reversed back up the path. I passed Kurt and his father, who were meeting their shuttle below. I shook their hands, wished them an "Alles Gute," and turned to the right at the top of the path and back on the AT.

The AT skirts the futuristic, flying-saucer-shaped viewing tower at the top of Clingman's Dome. In addition to being the highest peak along the AT, Clingman's is the third highest mountain in the Appalachian chain, so I walked across the 375-foot-long concrete runway leading to the tower, hoping to capture some picturesque views. Unfortunately, the rain and mist had created a dense fog that made it impossible to see more than a hundred feet.

At the summit, I still had almost a ten-mile hike to the parking area at Newfound Gap where my father would be picking me up at 3. I had five hours to get there, so I moved quickly down the switchbacks on the northern face of Clingman's, meeting up with Juan, one of the Texans, as I stopped for lunch at Collins Gap.

Mount Collins, at 6,168 feet, was not billed as a difficult hike, but it had several steep gradient stretches that sent my blood pressure soaring.

Juan and I walked quietly—I had finally met someone who kept my exact same pace. We passed through Luftee Gap and the trail hooked left to run parallel to Highway 74 for almost a mile. Along the side of the trail were several mammoth oaks that had fallen, with their extensive root systems facing the trail. The storm that had toppled them must have been recent; the leaves that still clung to the branches were not yet completely dead.

We emerged onto Highway 74 at 2:30, and crossed Newfound Gap to the parking lot on the other side. The rest of the group, including Dave, had already arrived. My father was on track to arrive a bit early, so I did not have long to wait. I offered Dave a ride to Cherokee, North Carolina, which was the easternmost point on our drive before we swung to the south, back to Georgia. That would shorten the distance his girlfriend had to drive from Boone to pick him up.

We met Jen, a nurse originally from South Carolina who now lived in Columbus, Ohio, who had driven down to see the leaves and "eat some Chick-Fil-A." She passed out some trail magic in the form of ice-cold Sam Adams Oktoberfest beers.

In the rain and fog of the parking lot, we exchanged contact information on slips of paper, well knowing that we would never meet again. My father pulled into the parking lot and flashed his headlights.

As we drove through Cherokee with Dave in the back cab of my father's pickup truck, I noticed how little that town had changed in the 50 years since I had last visited as a small boy. I still have the snapshot of my sister and I when we visited Cherokee in the early 1960s, when I was not yet five. My sister and I are both wearing cardboard headbands holding up single feathers in the back. Even though the Cherokee are an eastern tribe, the man in the photo, sandwiched between us, wore a full-length, Plains Indian–style feather headdress. I always wondered about that man, and how he must have suffered quietly with the indignity of pretending he was something that he wasn't while having his picture snapped by tourists a hundred times of day.

Today, over three-quarters of the population of Cherokee, North Carolina, is Native American. Most of them are descendants of those who managed to hide in the impenetrable mountains of western North Carolina and thus escape the Trail of Tears. I still remember the billboards from the 1960s (that were almost as prevalent as the "See Rock City" signs) advertising the Trail of Tears saga, *Unto These Hills*. The play, which is performed for several weeks every summer in a small amphitheater outside of Cherokee, celebrates the 1838 story of Tsali, who along with his wife, two sons and brother-in-law, were rounded up in the Smokies and force-marched by soldiers to one of the many stockades where Cherokees were being held before embarking on the tragic journey to Oklahoma.

At one point along the march, a soldier prodded Tsali's wife with a bayonet. An enraged Tsali attacked the soldier and after a struggle, killed him. The remaining soldiers fled, and Tsali and the rest of his family retreated into a cove on Clingman's Dome. The general in charge of enforcing the roundup of the Cherokees in the Smokies issued an ultimatum—if Tsali paid the price for the killing, the remaining Cherokees hiding out in the Smokies would not be deported and would be allowed to live in peace.

Tsali and the rest of his family surrendered. Tsali, his oldest son, and his brother-in-law were shot by a firing squad; the younger son was spared due to his age. Tsali's sacrifice is no longer commemorated every summer in the performances of *Unto These Hills*.[23] In a 2006 rewrite of the play, his story was removed.

Until the opening of Harrah's Casino about ten years ago, many of the Cherokee residents lived off the tourist trade in the spring and summer months and relied on public assistance in the off-peak season. Harrah's makes a distribution of about $12,000 each year to the roughly 15,000 members of the Eastern Band of the Cherokees. Additionally, each new member of the tribe begins accruing that annual $12,000 at birth, meaning that at age 18 he or she is eligible for a payout of $105,000 after tax distribution from the gambling fund.[24]

As we drove parallel to the Ocanaluftee River, I spotted the mid-century motel that we had stayed in in the early 1960s—it looked unchanged. The only thing that looked remarkably different was the fortress-like Harrah's Casino, which jutted up just past the main street still chock-full of tourist shops filled with plastic tomahawks, tom-tom drums and other trinkets made in China. We dropped Dave off at Harrah's—he wanted to have a few beers while he waited on his girlfriend. We watched as he walked past security into the entrance, wearing his poncho with his backpack still strapped on. I hoped he had remembered to take his Buck knife off his belt before entering.

SECTION HIKE 6
Newfound Gap, Tennessee, to Hot Springs, North Carolina
April 24–29, 2016 (67 Miles)

The last week in April looked to be beautiful in the southern Appalachians—the extended weather forecast called for nothing more than pop-up showers, and the temperatures were expected to be in a comfortable range—if anything, a bit too warm on some days, dipping into the 50s in the higher elevations during the night.

My wife dropped me off on a Saturday morning at Newfound Gap off of Highway 441—the only paved road that cuts through the Great Smoky Mountains National Park, and at 5,046 feet, the highest elevation for a gap that I had reached thus far on my section hikes.

The plan was to complete the remaining 30 miles of the trail in the Smokies, and then continue for almost 40 miles through the Pisgah National Forest, ending at Hot Springs on Friday. I had booked a hotel in Hot Springs for the Friday evening.

Although there was a slight chill in the air, I dressed in shorts, because I knew the exertion from starting a new hike wearing heavier clothing would soon make me hot and uncomfortable. This first day, I was forced, due to the shelter-only camping rules in the national park, to be ambitious with my mileage. The first shelter, Icewater Spring, was only three miles away, and the second, Peck's Corner, was a distance of ten miles from Newfound Gap. I was off to a late start, so I knew I had to move quickly in order to make it to Peck's Corner by evening.

Excited to be starting the latest phase of my trek, I covered the three miles and almost 1,000-foot ascent up to Icewater Spring Shelter in a little more than an hour. The shelter, at 5,920 feet, afforded great views of the valley below, which hikers can reach via the Sweet Heifer Creek Trail that I had passed earlier. Pressed for time, though, I lunched quickly and moved up the trail.

The next six miles, to Laurel Top, were easy to manage with their gentle ridgelines and staggering views of the mountains in the distance, still struggling, in late April, to produce the green sprouts of spring.

I met Summer Breeze and Ninja Roll along the way, and we talked as we hiked. They both were thru-hikers in their twenties who had started in Georgia a month earlier. Summer Breeze was a short, lithe hippy, with his chestnut mane of long, straight hair pulled off his face with a black and red scarf decorated with Jolly Roger pirate images. Without having to ask, I figured that Summer Breeze had earned his trail name from his laid-back, calm demeanor.

Ninja Roll was a slightly heavy-set, bald hiker from Louisiana. At one point, he had slipped while crossing some slick rocks over a creek and barrel-rolled himself out of potential calamity. An observer saw it, and thus a new trail name was born. He was now suffering from the after-effects of a binge in Gatlinburg the previous evening—he had taken a zero day in that town and found the local craft ale to his liking.

Like me, both were headed to Peck's Corner Shelter. We ascended Laurel Top and were approaching Charlie's Bunion when an attractive and petite young park ranger name Candace stopped and asked to see our permits. While it was cumbersome to remove my pack and dig through it for my permit, I was also glad to see that the rangers took their work seriously and were committed to keeping the park somewhat protected from the onslaught of thousands of hikers.

I took the small side trail off of the AT to catch the view from Charlie's Bunion, a rock outcropping which is part of the Sawteeth, a series of jutting, teeth-like stones that skirt the summits of a string of mountains in the central Smokies. The boulder that marks the top of Charlie's

Bunion leans precariously over the valley below, offering on this sunny day unobstructed views for miles to the west, including to Mount Le Conte, the third highest peak in the Smokies. Once again, I was in awe of the work of the CCC, which had constructed this spur of the AT that extended on to the Bunion.[25]

As beautiful as it is, Charlie's Bunion's bare rock face is not natural—a fire in the 1920s, a decade before the National Park was established, burned off the vegetation, and later flooding removed all the soil from the rock.[26]

The last major climb before reaching the shelter at Peck's Corner was Laurel Top, a 1,000-foot climb up to 5,907 feet. At the foot of the trail leading upward, I spotted Summer Breeze, sitting crisscross on top of a boulder, smoking a joint. I stopped and we talked for a while. I was curious about how thru-hikers managed to resupply their pot over the course of their extended hikes—none of the southern states, which comprise half the mileage of the AT, are within a generation of approving the use of recreational marijuana. In Atlanta, possession of a small amount of weed has been reduced to a misdemeanor subject to a small fine. But rural areas in the south were less forgiving, and local cops who might already have chips on their shoulders about outsiders exacerbated the risk.

I asked him if he had friends send it in the mail to him at various drop-off points, and he responded with a vigorous no. I did not want to probe any further, sensing he was getting defensive about it and continued up the balsam fir lined trail.

In the early evening I approached Peck's Corner Shelter, which follows an almost mile-long downward offshoot from the AT into a cove below. The stony path was hard to manage late on the first day of my hike.

At the end of the path, the shelter appears, a three-walled stone structure with a tin roof jutting outward, supported by three round wooden beams. Underneath the roof were a dozen or so hikers. I waved hello and continued past the shelter to a small spot a hundred feet away where I pitched my tent. The water source was down a small path that zigzagged down to a small spring bordered by mountain laurel.

After replenishing my water supply, I joined the hikers gathered under the shelter. I met Beth, who had recently completed her medical internship at Mt. Sinai Hospital in Manhattan and had just started a hundred-mile hike from Newfound Gap to Erwin, Tennessee. After finishing her hike, she was continuing her residency at a San Francisco hospital. Her Asian American friend, JoAnne, had flown from California to meet her in Knoxville, where they caught a shuttle to the trail. Beth was loud and full of enthusiasm, and I had a quiet respect for someone willing to hike the trail before starting a grueling new phase of her life. At that age, I, by contrast, would probably have headed to the beach with a cooler full of beer.

Ontario was also at the shelter. He had just been honorably discharged from the Army, having served in Iraq. He was planning his first big challenge on the trail for the next day—hiking 20 miles to Davenport Gap. He, along with Ninja Roll, were part of what I call a pod of thru hikers, who move at roughly the same pace, enjoy each other's company, and try to meet up in the evening to trade stories and make plans for the miles ahead.

I brought out my small plastic flask of Dawson County moonshine and passed it around. Ninja Roll shook his head no, still feeling the ill effects from the night before. Ontario took a swig and grimaced, as did Beth. A group of three men, about my age, walked into the shelter with a plastic pouch filled with red wine. They hung this from a peg, opened a spigot on the bottom, and decanted the wine carefully into their plastic cups. This was a group of old friends who got together once a year to hike different trails in the Smokies, and they were in the midst of a three-day backcountry trip.

There, under a late April pink moon, we laughed, traded stories and shared insights about what lay ahead on the trail. There was word of more bear sightings in the Smokies and a forest fire near Hot Springs, North Carolina, that was starting to spread. The thru-hikers talked about Trail Days in Damascus, Virginia; most of the thru hikers were planning on attending the three-day celebration and reunion of hikers held in that town each May. There was a long discussion about when cold-weather equipment such as heavy sleeping bags and thermal underwear should be shipped home to reduce weight. The consensus, notwithstanding the warm weather we were experiencing, was keep it until Memorial Day; cold snaps—known as "Blackberry Winters" in the mountains—were possible leading up to the beginning of June in the higher elevations of the southern Appalachians.

I envied the "trail legs" that the thru-hikers had developed that allowed them to cover so much mileage. Ontario mentioned how difficult Sassafras Mountain back in Georgia had been before he developed his trail legs. Looking back, it seems obvious there was nothing particularly onerous about Sassafras—it was just the first somewhat challenging mountain any of us had encountered on the AT. After 50 or so "Sassafras Mountains," the body adjusts.

I enjoyed talking with the millennials on my trips, largely because I have two children that were born in the 1990s and fall into the same age grouping. They are trying desperately to carve a path through life that is different; one that avoids the stressful lifestyle choices made by their parents. The AT affords them the opportunity, however briefly, to postpone these choices. The trail also provides, in a strange way, an order that does not exist in the havoc of everyday life. Despite the uncertainties related to weather, injuries, provisioning, etc., there is a linearity to the AT—there is a distance and a timeline, a beginning, a middle, and an end.

One member of the Brethren of the Wine Pouch came over and found out that I worked in banking and peppered me with questions about my employer. That was my cue to go to bed; the last thing I wanted to do was talk about work on the trail.

As the moon continued its slow ascent over the cove, I retreated to my tent and climbed inside my light, warm-weather bag, almost like a quilt, which kept me comfortable down to 40 degrees. Based on the weather forecasts of warm weather, I had left my heavier bag at home. Most of the crowd was still up talking, so I put in my earplugs and enjoyed a restful night of sleep.

I woke up early the next morning and went to retrieve my food bag, which I had hung on one of the shelter's bear cables. For some unknown reason, another hiker had hung his entire pack on the clip directly below my bag. When I lowered my bag, his pack came down as well, with a lot of momentum. I tried to dodge it, to avoid getting smacked on the head by 40 pounds of gear moving earthward at a high rate of speed, but the pack still hit my right shoulder, knocking me to the ground. I cursed loudly, hoping the culprit would hear me. But no one confessed, and I left the pack lying on the ground as I ate a quick breakfast and headed back up the trail.

There were two shelters left before I exited the National Park; one, at Cosby Knob, was 8 miles away, the other, just above Davenport Gap, was a distance of 15 miles. I decided to enjoy the more leisurely hike to Cosby.

At midday, I reached the summit of Old Black, which at 6,370 feet was the highest point of the remaining 15 miles I had left to hike in the Smokies.

Just off the trail after descending from the top was the wreckage of an F-4 Phantom Fighter that had crashed into the mountainside in 1984, instantly killing the pilot and his navigator. A cause for the crash was never determined. Parts of twisted metal fuselage and wings were strewn for hundreds of feet just off the trail. I walked off the trail to take pictures of what remained of the airplane, which was interspersed with new growth trees that had sprung up since the accident occurred more than 30 years ago.[27]

I passed the Brethren of the Wine Pouch upon climbing back up to the trail. They were headed to Maddron Bald Trail to complete another segment of their quest to hike all the trails in the Smoky Mountains National Park.

The trail was bordered by spruce and balsam fir as I continued my steep, 1,500-foot descent into Camel Gap. Insects, particularly gnats, were buzzing me, as they had the previous evening in the campsite, swirling around my face and biting me. I had not packed insect repellent for the trip because bugs had never been a problem on my previous spring hikes.

I do not know if there is some peculiarity about the Smokies that makes the appearance of insect pests at 5,000 feet and above a normal occurrence in mid-spring, or if the unusually warm weather created the perfect conditions for their early arrival in late April. But climate change is affecting the Appalachians—weather has become hotter and drier in the last 30 years, and five to 15 fewer freezing days occur each winter.[28]

For man, the southern Appalachians have long been a refuge from unpleasant temperatures—before the advent of air-conditioning, those who could afford it would leave humid and malarial conditions in low-lying areas and spend the hot months in places like Asheville, Lake Junaluska, Cashiers, and Boone. Similarly, animals retreated from the creeping glaciers during the last Ice Age and established new habitats in the southern Appalachians, which were spared the worst effects from the ice sheets.

Apocalyptic scenarios of soaring temperatures and massive flooding in coastal regions may drive waves of migration to higher elevations, which would obviously have a major impact on the rich and abundant natural resources of the mountains. I wonder, after years of watching millions of people evacuate the coasts during hurricane season, how much longer they will cling to their homes near the sea. The mountains would be at least a temporary refuge from the ravages of global warming.

As streams become warmer, native trout, which require colder water, will die off, and fraser and balsam firs, hemlocks, and red spruces, already under attack by invasive insects, would face extinction in the southern Appalachians. The northern flying squirrel, which moved south during the last Ice Age, would face extinction in Appalachia. One of the factors that contributes to the rich biodiversity of the Appalachians is the "resilient landscape." For instance, the Carolina wren and Carolina chickadee spend their entire lives on Mount Mitchell, the highest mountain in North Carolina. They never have to join seasonal migrations; they simply adjust their elevation on the mountain as the seasons change. But resiliency has its limits, and the question ultimately becomes, what happens to the chickadees when they run out of mountain?[29]

In terms of the AT, some climate models show eight inches less rainfall per year, sometimes more, which would greatly worsen drought conditions. Drought would also bring more frequent forest fires, and when combined with lack of water and more intense heat, might make a Georgia-to-Maine hike impossible to complete.

When I reached the approach trail to Cosby Knob in the mid-afternoon, there was a paper sign from the National Park Service warning "Danger! Bears Are Active in This Area!" This was a stock warning, so I did not find it worrisome. The more sinister notice was a sheet of notebook paper that also had a warning, scrawled in pencil, placed at the foot of the shelter sign and held down by a rock: "Last evening, a bear came into the shelter area and ran through it. We yelled and made noises, but he was not bothered. He finally left after a while." With that in mind, I trudged down the short path to find, hopefully, a spot in the camping area that would not attract the attention of a marauding bear.

Cosby Knob is a sprawling shelter area in a wide ravine bisected by a creek. North of the creek is the shelter, perched on one of the few flat spots. Adjacent camping spots seemed relatively flat, but they had already been claimed by a multitude of tents of different sizes and hues.

I took the flattest spot I could find, on the opposite side of the creek from the shelter, and pitched my tent. From head to toe, I would be sloping downward at about ten degrees, but that was simply the best I was going to be able to do that night.

I spent a great 30 minutes or so inside my tent, with my head propped up on my makeshift pillow, a tent bag stuffed with clothes. This had gradually become my favorite part of the day—the hard work of hiking was behind me, and I could just gaze at the shifting rays of the sun bouncing off the roof of my tent. I would use this time to check messages from home—the cell phone worked with maximum speed at higher elevations. Sometimes I would read a few pages of a slim paperback I brought along for the trip before dozing off into a nap. In and out of sleep, I would hear snippets of conversation and the sounds made by new arrivals as they dropped their packs and looked for places to put up tents or hammocks.

When I pulled myself out of the tent, Summer Breeze was hanging his hammock a short distance away between two poplars. We nodded our greetings, and I crossed over the creek and went into the shelter.

Everyone was discussing the bear and whether or not it would make another appearance. According to the scuttlebutt, the forest fire around Hot Springs was spreading, and there was some possibility that the AT in that area would be shut down. A music festival was also being held in Hot Springs that upcoming weekend, meaning that hotel and motel rooms would be scarce. Luckily, I had already booked a room for that Friday evening in town when my wife would drive up and meet me.

I took a spot next to Ninja Roll on the shelter's porch. He was hiking to the Standing Bear hostel just outside the Smokies. The hostel was famous for its small bar that served cheap Pabst Blue Ribbon beer. I asked Ninja if he planned on enjoying a few cold lagers after a day on the trail, and he shook his head sadly; "No, I just can't stop after a few."

As the sun set over the ridge to the west, I walked to my tent. I noticed that Beth, JoAnne, Summer Breeze, and a few others were start-ing a fire in the ring of stones adjacent to the shelter.

My tent was a good 75–100 feet away from the fire, so I was not too worried about their noise keeping me up. As I was beginning to drift off, I heard loud laughter. It was a woman, and it happened every 30–45 seconds: "huh, HA, HA, HA!!" I was determined not to let it bother me; after all, they had a right to stay up and enjoy themselves, and they probably had not heard of the unwritten code at shelters of quiet after sunset. But the noise continued, with loud outbursts bouncing off the cove for several hours. I inserted my earplugs, but still, the noise pen-etrated the plastic plugs, and I tossed and turned. There would be several minutes of silence, and I would relax, thinking they had gone to bed, only to have the stillness broken by another ear-splitting guffaw. At around 11, they finally went to bed, and I was able to drift off.

When I woke up the next morning, and I went over to the shelter, Beth and JoAnne were still in their tents. It turned out that everyone in that shelter had also been kept up by the noise, and Beth had been given a trail name: "Megaphone." As she walked over to the shelter to cook her breakfast, someone yelled out, "Hey, Megaphone!" She was taken aback and asked how she had earned that name. "Your voice is like a megaphone," said one hiker. "JoAnne is just as loud as I am," Megaphone responded in a huff.

I had about a seven-mile hike to Davenport Gap, the end of the Smokies on the AT. Beyond that, it was a decision on whether to stay at Standing Bear Farm, a hostel, just on the other side of the gap, or continue my hike over Snowbird Mountain, the first peak in the Pisgah National Forest.

After a mid-morning climb to the summit of Mt. Cammerer, it was an easy, five-mile descent down to Davenport Gap. As I reached the lower elevations, the heat started picking up. I stopped at Davenport Gap Shelter, the last shelter before leaving the Smokies, and the only one that still has a chain link bear fence in the shelter portico. I was eat-ing lunch with Ninja Roll when we heard the laughter, a half-mile up the trail. Megaphone, JoAnne and Summer Breeze passed by the shelter, and we asked where they were staying for the evening. When I found out they were stopping at Standing Bear, I made the decision to hike up Snowbird Mountain.

When the AT exits the Great Smoky Mountains National Park, it follows a road for a short distance over the Pigeon River, and then the AT insignia, painted on the road, points to the right, towards Interstate 40. It was confusing and poorly marked, and I had to retrace my steps several times before finally realizing that the AT continued under an interstate viaduct before continuing up a gravel road.

By the mid-afternoon, the sun was blazing down and temperatures approached 90 degrees. The occasional truck that passed by on the gravel kicked up clouds of dust, making the half-mile hike even more grueling.

A small wooden sign appeared on the right with a series of wooden steps, marking the start of the climb up Snowbird Mountain.

I was not prepared for Snowbird Mountain, mainly because I was filled with lazy, misplaced pride. The 70 miles of the Smokies were in my rearview mirror, and I felt like the most physical part of my trip, and maybe the most challenging part of the entire AT, was behind me. Snowbird was only a little over 4,000 feet in elevation, and I had climbed over more than a dozen peaks higher than that in the Smokies alone. I realized that I was starting at an elevation of only about 1,500 feet at Davenport Gap and the summit of Snowbird was a steady, upward hike of five miles, but I also knew I was ready for anything.

That afternoon, Snowbird Mountain kicked my ass. The heat was a contributing factor, but more than anything, overconfidence in my ability to manage a steady, uphill, five-mile hike in the mid-afternoon caused me to make a serious misjudgment.

About a mile up Snowbird, I started cursing my decision not to stay at Standing Bear, Megaphone's shrieks of laughter aside. I stopped every 100 feet or so to gather my breath and take another swig of water from my Camelbak, which was rapidly draining.

After baby-stepping over a series of steep switchbacks, I gave out at about 4 p.m., at Painter Branch, about halfway up Snowbird Mountain. I found a small, mossy overlook just off the trail that hung over the small creek below, which was hidden under a tangle of mountain laurel. I noticed that where the areas of the camping spot were bordered by bushes there were scraps of toilet paper, but I was too tired to care.

I threw off my backpack and leaned it against a small tree, which I used as a backrest while I took deep breaths, trying to slow down my heart rate. While I was resting, Sunshine and Moonshine, two young, athletic women, came by. They were looking for a place to camp, but there was no more room at my little overlook, which I soon learned was infested with flies.

Once I regained my energy, I fought my way to the creek below. There was no defined path, so I had to pull back rhododendron branches to get to the water source.

After I made my way back, a young couple I had passed earlier on the trail walked by and asked if there were any other places to camp in the vicinity. I told them I thought there was a place that might be suitable, just below me that I had passed on my way up the trail. They thanked me, and a short time later, the wife came back to my tent and gave me a small packet of powdered Gatorade, which I mixed with a liter of warm water. I thanked her profusely; all my energy reserves had been expended on the trek up Snowbird.

I had an early dinner of dehydrated corn enchiladas cooked in my Jetboil. I went inside my tent and stared at the rays of the dying sun dancing off my nylon roof, took a few tokes of weed, and drifted off into a deep, peaceful sleep.

I got off to an early start the next morning, knowing that I still had half of Snowbird Mountain yet to climb. Beyond that, I was hoping to get to the grassy bald of Max Patch to camp for the evening, a distance of 12 miles.

I was passed early in my hike by Moonshine and Sunshine; both with their hair pulled back in long ponytails, dressed like triathletes, their hiking poles flashing as they slalomed up the trail. As they went around me, they said they had found a great place to camp, a bit farther up the trail from me, with direct access to the creek.

I huffed and puffed my way up the mountain, with frequent stops to catch my breath. I had a number of false leads that I was close to the top, only to be disappointed as I rounded a turn to be faced with another series of switchbacks leading upward.

At midday, I finally reached the grassy top of Snowbird Mountain. To the left of the AT leading over the bald is an FAA aviation control building, a low-slung, white structure, topped by a beaker-shaped tower. After struggling with the climb up this ancient mountain, it was a jolt to see this futuristic-looking building placed at the summit. A fence surrounded it with warning signs against any form of trespass.

A man came out of the building to talk to me, and my first reaction was that I was somewhere where I was not supposed to be; I had somehow triggered a tripwire that alerted someone inside the building. But the man just wanted to talk about the AT and how he liked to hike on the weekends. His dream was to make it to Maine. I suppose it was pretty boring sitting inside the control building all day, and he probably needed a diversion every now and then.

The tall grass of the bald attracted flies, which made me quicken my pace over the half-mile portion of the trail at the top. As I descended into the forest headed to Deep Gap, the juxtaposition of modern science and ancient wilderness stuck with me.

The silence and serenity of the forest has attracted people for millennia. Ancient Celtic and Germanic tribes retreated into the woods, safe in the knowledge that Roman legions would never dare to pursue them in their sanctuaries deep in the forests. Religious orders have had hermitages in forests for centuries. The American trappist monk mystic, Thomas Merton, spoke for the need for our souls to search for paradise, the tree of life, in our place of origin, the woods. Doctors and therapists in North America are now recommending forest immersion, or "bathing," a practice long followed in Japan, as a way to reduce high blood pressure and stress.[30]

I have enjoyed the woods since I was a young boy. There was a large pine forest behind my grandparents' house, where we kids could go on long walks and build forts from fallen limbs. Later, forests were a place to escape adult supervision, to smoke and look at adult magazines and meet up with girls. The forests were alluring, mystical, and dangerous, all at once, and they beckon us to something we cannot identify but feel that is lost.

My favorite books as a child were stories that had forest settings, like *Little Red Riding Hood, The Town Musicians of Bremen,* and the tale of the Baba Yaga, the Russian witch who lived on the edge of a birch forest. As an adolescent, the Old Forest and Mirkwood and Lórien were always my favorite settings in the Tolkien trilogy. When I struggled in high school through the Shakespeare comedies *As You Like It* and *A Midsummer Night's Dream,* the forests were always welcome diversions, sanctuaries where fairies and changelings appeared.

Even when Shakespeare wrote *As You Like It* in the late 16th century, the Forest of Arden was a memory from his native Warwickshire. He wrote from nostalgia, because the actual forest had long ago been felled to make way for farmland. It was a Paradise Lost, an Eden, an imagined innocence that would never be regained but could be celebrated and yearned for in fiction.

It is not so much the actual physical noise of modern life that makes us seek peace in the forests—medieval London or late 19th century Manhattan were much louder from a sensory standpoint, in terms of sound, smell and sights. In my home inside the Atlanta city limits, the only ambient noises I ever really hear are the sounds of my neighbor's dog barking or a gas-powered leaf blower.

Almost every hiker carries a cell phone and a portable battery recharger, so it is not as if we cut ourselves completely off from the outside world. Handhelds are indispensable for communication, not only in emergency situations, but also for more mundane matters such as calling hostels or motels to check for room availability. Life goes on, and text messages with family members are needed to stay abreast of events on the home front and to let them know of my progress along the trail in order to schedule pickup points and times. Hikers have also largely stopped using foldout terrestrial maps of the trail (much to my chagrin—I love paper maps), and instead download apps that show them where they are and the satellite-beamed images of the features of the mountains that lie ahead.

Those who have hiked the AT have very firm beliefs on appropriate conduct on the trail, and there is a broad consensus when it comes to issues like removing trash and common courtesy at shelters. The use of social media, however, is an issue that divides many hikers. I fall into the camp of not using social media at all when I am on the trail. I do consider my time on the AT to be somewhat sacred, and a large reason why I go on hikes is to escape the constant background noise emanating from social media. I use my handheld to text home every other day to assure my family I haven't been eaten by a bear or fallen helplessly with a broken hip into a deep ravine. I will occasionally check emails, but I typically hike with my handheld in airplane mode so that I can snap pictures on a whim. I also will use the Guthook app to get a satellite read on the upcoming terrain.

One hiker told me, somewhat despairingly, that the first words of a new arrival into a shelter area used to be, "Where is the water?" Now it is more likely to be, "How is cell phone reception?"

Others will use their phones, particularly in the late winter and early spring when darkness arrives early in the evening, for downloading YouTube videos or movies from Netflix. I can understand that. If it is 6 p.m. and already dark, it is kind of pointless to try and go to sleep for the evening, and reading with a flashlight or headlamp gets tiresome in a hurry.

For whatever reason, I rarely see hikers using social media while on the trail. There are, of course, hiker groups on Facebook, but the posts tend to be more informational in nature—"be careful, this river in Pennsylvania has flooded," or "any recommendations for a good pair of hiking boots?" Maybe they are tweeting late at night or posting Snapchat videos when they cannot sleep in shelters, but I have never seen it.

There are also safety and practical reasons for limiting cell phone usage while on the trail—reception is typically very spotty, and overuse can quickly run down the battery. Many hikers, particularly women, are hesitant to upload their exact position on the trail and might delay Facebook updates for at least a few days so that any lurking creeps can't get a bead on exactly where they might be.

One hiker told me that he reports on social media only the bad things that occur to him on the trail so that his wife, who resents his hiking, doesn't think he is having too good of a time. I had to salute his innovative thinking to ensure a continued happy marriage while secretly enjoying his trips on the AT.

There are other hikers who resent the sanctimony of the "silence police" like me and continue to fully utilize social media while on the AT. At the end of the day, it is, like so many other things on the AT, simply a matter of "HYOH"—hike your own hike.

I approached Max Patch in the late afternoon. I had read a lot about this elongated mountain bald, which offers, for a northbound hiker, the first 360-degree view of the Blue Ridge Mountains. Max Patch was named many years ago by a local farmer whose horse, Max, liked to graze on the lush turf on top of the bald.

On the approach, there were more and more signs of civilization, including a cow pasture with a trail easement that passed through a cattle gate and wooden fence. Bored Hereford cattle watched me with no sign of alarm as I passed by.

At the foot of Max Patch, I filled my Camelbak and splashed my face with cold creek water. I felt the ionic charge and slight change in barometric pressure that subtly signals the imminent arrival of a mountain storm. I wasted no time in trying to reach the summit of Max Patch; I wanted to pitch my tent at the top, and I did not want to do it in a driving rainstorm.

By the time I reached the summit, black clouds were moving in quickly from the northwest. A crack of thunder was followed by the first heavy raindrops. I was on an open half-mile, exposed area on a mountain bald that made me feel vulnerable and frightened. I barely had time to soak in the panoramic, *Sound of Music* view of the Smokies, Black Mountains, Unakas and Great Balsams that provide one of the most scenic views on the AT.

I ran like hell.

The storm picked up momentum, with cold needles of rain stinging my face and neck as I raced to the sanctuary of the woods where the trail exited Max Patch to the east. Massive claps of thunder exploded over my head like artillery shells as I moved faster and faster towards the forest. I slid on a wet mud patch and barely caught myself with a hiking pole that I slammed into the ground just in the nick of time.

As I neared the forest, I noticed that most of the branches were still leafless, so there would not be shelter from the rain. But the trees still beckoned, a lighthouse on a stormy sea.

I collapsed under a massive water oak and caught my breath. Even in my state of panic, I knew that sitting under a huge tree was a terrible place to be if lightning struck anywhere nearby. But I did not care. I was no longer out in the open, no longer exposed, no longer a target for the fickle forces of nature.

After a while, the rain subsided, and I hiked at twice my normal pace to Roaring Fork Shelter, two miles away. It was a series of easy downhill switchbacks made treacherous by pools of water that had gathered in the numerous depressions along the trail.

By the time I reached the shelter, the sun was shining brightly. Thick drops of water hung lazily on the tree branches before gradually building up enough volume to plunk to the soaked ground below.

My impromptu sprint from Max Patch to Roaring Fork Shelter meant that I had hiked a total of 14 miles that day. The shelter, a three-sided log cabin fronted by a picnic table, was already full of hikers, their sleeping bags rolled out to mark their spots. I recognized Ontario and Ninja Roll; the rest of the occupants, except for a middle-aged retired Spanish military officer trail-named El Toro, were young men. I found a spot about 20 feet in front of the shelter at the bottom of a gentle downward slope. By this time, I had written off the rainstorm that left me shivering, frightened, and cold, as nothing more than a pop-up shower. The sun was back out in full force; all was good with the world.

I asked the assemblage who was up for a night hike to Hot Springs, almost 20 miles away. I got a chorus of derisive laughs in response. Most of them had made it off the trail just before the rain had arrived, but they were in no mood to tempt their luck.

Hot Springs, which is 270 miles north of Springer Mountain, is the first town the northbound AT actually goes directly through. Wesser, where NOC is located, had a couple of restaurants, a few motels and an outfitter, but it was not a true town.

So it was not surprising that all of the thru-hikers were planning on taking a zero day in Hot Springs. A couple of hot meals, resupplying at the local Dollar General store and outfitter, having a few cold beers, washing clothes and picking up packages at the local post office dominated the discussion.

Ontario was hoping for a CiCi's pizza restaurant, which is a hiker's nirvana—an unlimited buffet selection at an affordable price. Ninja was going to make a few calls back to Louisiana and try to round up some more money. El Toro, who spoke halting and uncertain English, nodded and smiled.

Two sandy-haired thru-hiking German men who were cooking noodles on their Jetboil had set up their tent next to mine.

I took a spot on the picnic table bench facing the inside of the shelter and prepared my freeze-dried lasagna. I felt invigorated by the events of the late afternoon and enjoyed recounting my wet adventure to the rest of the crowd. One had spotted me in my yellow slicker at the top of Max Patch just as he was making his exit into the woods.

This group of hikers abided by the hikers' code and, like my chickens back home, faithfully marched off to their sleeping positions at sunset.

I felt good when I climbed into my tent. As a precaution, I put in my earplugs, but there was no need—all the guys inside the shelter were quiet as they shifted their bags to the optimal position for dozing off. I settled in for a night of undisturbed sleep.

This time, rumbling thunder or bolts of lightning did not usher the rain in—the sound and light show happened later. This storm announced its arrival differently, with a brief but heavy surge in wind velocity. I sat up, turned on my headlamp, and peered outside. I could see the slow spiral of pine needles and twigs swirling downward. And then the rain came, in huge plops that thumped my tent.

The water did not seep into my tent; it flooded in. I knew that resistance was futile—there was no island inside my tent where I could try and escape the water. I just tried to position my torso-only air mattress in such a way that at least the upper half of my body remained dry.

I had only myself to blame. I knew I was in a precarious position if it rained that evening. And, as I later learned, there was a designated camping area on flat land adjacent to the shelter. I simply let misplaced optimism and impatience once again get the best of me, and I took a shortcut. My only solace was of the "misery loves company" variety; I knew that the two Germans were getting equally soaked. Schadenfreude, indeed.

In spite of constantly repositioning myself in a futile attempt to stay dry, I somehow managed about two hours of sleep that evening. The storm eventually passed in the early morning, but I was wet all night long.

I peeked outside my tent about 7 a.m. and saw brilliant rays of sunshine streaming in from the rising sun. I walked outside to survey the damage and saw deep puddles of rain in the 20 feet or so separating my tent space from the shelter. Although the occupants of the shelter had stayed dry, they were also kept up for a good part of the evening by the sounds of the storm.

I looked for any tree branch or large bush that was attracting sunlight and draped my wet sleeping bag, tent, and clothes over them. I could have started my hike as early as 8 a.m. that morning, but I waited until 10 to give my gear more time to dry out.

Some of the group were thinking about trying to cover the roughly 18 miles remaining to Hot Springs that day; most were planning on camping after 10–12 mile hikes, leaving a short walk in to the town the following day.

The Germans and I were the last to leave. "Was für ein beschissenes Wetter, ja?" (shitty weather, huh?), I offered. "Ja, aber heute ist doch wieder schön" (Yes, but it is beautiful again today), they responded. And of course, they were right. Yesterday's raw weather had passed through and been replaced by a mid-spring day blown in on the breath of angels.

The trail from the shelter went downward, running parallel to the rain-swollen Roaring Creek. I climbed Walnut Mountain and stopped at the shelter for lunch. El Toro was on top of the picnic table, sprawled out and snoring loudly. Apparently he did not get much sleep the previous night in the shelter, either. While it was funny that he was able to sack out like that in the middle of the day, I was also envious. I can never go to sleep that easily in uncomfortable surroundings, no matter how tired I am.

I climbed the summit of 4,686-foot Bluff Mountain in the mid-afternoon. I knew that the next 10 miles were an easy hike, with elevation gradually falling by 3,000 feet on the approach into Hot Springs.

I scouted various potential campsites along the trail as I made the slow climb down Bluff Mountain. There was one potential spot I briefly considered—a rocky area overlooking a small waterfall that spilled into a rhododendron-covered ravine below. I reconsidered, though, worried that I would wake up in the middle of the night to piss and walk off the ledge.

My patience was rewarded about a mile farther down the trail where I found the perfect spot—a flat apron of moss-covered ground about 15 feet off the trail; hidden enough to give privacy, but just open enough to let the remaining rays of the day's sunshine splash in.

After pitching my tent and hanging my bear pack, I cut two long sections of nylon rope and strung them between two trees. I hung my wet clothes on the clotheslines I had made and leaned back, with my knees pulled up, against the trunk of a tulip poplar. The bottom portion of the trunk jutted out slightly, fitting the contours of my lower back perfectly.

I took a deep breath and smiled. I was coming to terms with nature.

It had complete dominion over me, and I accepted that. It metes out punishment in the form of a powerful storm that chases us off of beautiful mountain summits; it rewards us with transcendent days such as this one that will forever be seared into our memories. It offers a rich bounty of biodiversity that nourishes our bellies and our souls; that same biodiversity presents us with perils that can harm us, whether we are wary or not.

It can reward an unsuspecting hunter with a seam of gold; it can be the backdrop to a tragic car accident that happened almost a century ago. It watches and observes but does not pass judgment. If the damage inflicted on it by humans is too severe, it will enact Newton's Third Law of Physics with an equal and opposite reaction. But this boomerang will not come from spite or anger. It will simply be an adjustment to the new realities, and humans may be swept up as part of the flotsam in the resulting backlash.

Nature just is, as it was and ever shall be.

I fingered the amulet that hung on a necklace underneath my shirt. On my different trips, I noticed that many hikers wore crosses or other amulets around their necks. I had chosen one, made of pewter, of the Norse rune *Fehu*.

To the ancients this symbolized wealth, cattle, or prosperity. The modern word in German for cattle, *Vieh*, is derived from *Fehu*. I was attracted to this particular rune because of a passage I had read a long time ago from an Anglo-Saxon epic poem:

Wealth [Fehu] is a comfort to all;
yet must everyone bestow it freely,
if they wish to gain honour in the sight of the Lord.

As we take, we must give back. That will be our ultimate legacy after we are long gone and forgotten by our descendants and pass into the mists of time. Nature is a reminder of that timelessness and grandeur; we are extras in an act that is a billion-fold more mysterious than our frantic, atomized lives.

The next morning heralded a day as perfect as the day before. I had an easy, seven-mile hike into Hot Springs. The hike was almost all downhill—Hot Springs has an elevation of 1,332 feet, only a little bit higher than Atlanta, and it would represent the lowest point yet for me on the AT.

I had a great pace, and I knew that I would arrive in town in plenty of time for lunch. There were several notices by the Park Service placed on signs that the AT had been shut down, until further notice, for an undetermined stretch of trail east of Hot Springs because of the forest fire.

As I descended the final mountain to the valley below, I heard the sound of children out in the local schoolyard playing during recess. It was a weird acoustic anomaly—I was still at least a mile above town, but I could hear the children shouting each other's names, laughter, even the teachers' admonitions. It was midday on Friday, and the air was electric with excitement. For the children and teachers, the weather was beautiful, the weekend was a few hours away, and summer break was just around the corner. For me, I was coming to the end of my longest extended hike—almost 70 miles. I had managed not to get lost, injured (other than both legs covered with bug bites) or even very tired or dirty—the rain on Max Patch had served effectively as a cold shower.

The AT spills out onto a street leading directly to the main road, U.S. Highway 25. It was disorienting for me to be hiking the trail through a town. This becomes more common farther north on the trail, but to actually be walking on asphalt with painted AT markings while dodging traffic was a new experience. At the trailhead, I walked by the century-old Laughing Heart Hostel, where many hikers were staying. Those who could not get a room (the hostel was fully booked during the peak hiking season in the spring) paid a small fee to pitch their tents on the sprawling grass lawn in the front. I spotted Summer Breeze's head, wrapped in his pirate bandana, poking out of a tent pitched on the lawn.

I ran into Moonshine, and she gave me directions to my hotel, the Iron Horse Station. After talking to her, I looked to the east and saw the damage of the fire—acres and acres of woodland had been burned out on the mountains to the east and north of Hot Springs. The smoke was gone, but the charred remains of the blaze stretched for miles.

I walked by a gas station and thought about buying some Gatorade, but there were at least 25 Harleys parked out front. Hot Springs was going to have an interesting mix of people that weekend—jam band music festival attendees, hikers, and leather-clad, Harley-riding orthodontists.

I stopped at a package store and bought my Gatorade, one liter of which I drained by the time I reached the Iron Horse Station, a brick, two-story structure that had a tavern, restaurant and shops on the bottom floor, with the inn rooms located on the top level. It was across the street from the original train station, and the trains, loaded with freight, periodically still rumbled through town.

After checking into my room and showering, I walked around my block. Hot Springs exuded an open, New Age, hippie vibe; with shops that sold healing candles, incense and tie-dye shirts. On the corner of my block was a Mayberry-style one room city jail. I had earlier noticed several century-old Victorian-style homes set back from the main street.

Down the block was an outfitter, and I walked in to buy some ointment for my insect bites. My eyes were drawn to a wooden sign hanging on the wall with a quote from John Muir: "The Mountains Are Calling, and I Must Go."

There was a small church where members were offering free pizza to hikers. I did not stop to find out if spreading the message was part of the package, but there were several people I recognized from the trail enjoying a slice.

I walked across the street to the Spring Creek Tavern, which featured a variety of North Carolina brews on tap and a welcoming staff with intriguing body ink art. I ordered a cheeseburger with all the toppings and a French Broad River Kölsch. Ninja and El Toro were at the bar, and I pulled up a chair next to them. Both of them were staying at the hostel and had already dropped off a load of laundry. I toasted both of them—they had arrived early enough that they were taking the rest of the day off in Hot Springs, but it was back on the trail the next day.

There was some speculation, probably unfounded, that a disgruntled hiker who had been arrested for marijuana possession in Hot Springs started the forest fire. The barmaid told us that earlier in the week helicopters had flown over the fire and doused it with water every few minutes. Their work was now done—the fire was extinguished, the smoke was gone, and all that remained were the blackened skeletons of scorched trees.

My wife arrived in the late afternoon, and I was so hungry, I ate again—this time splitting a veggie pizza with her. A few hours later, we went back to the hotel restaurant, where we ate local rainbow trout with green beans and new potatoes. In seven hours, I had eaten three full meals. I had turned into a ravenous Pac-Man, eating everything in front of me.

Across the street and railroad track from where we were staying, the music festival, featuring a number of jam bands, was taking place. We walked toward the sound of music, and met a young woman named Hunter who was doing the same. She was spending the summer in Hot Springs researching ancestral history—one branch of her family tree had been involved in a series of bank robberies in the area almost a century ago. We walked in together through the woods and entered the large covered tent where the band was playing. A thick cloud of weed haze hung over the stage, and several bongs were passed around the audience.

We bought some Green Man beers that were on tap and handed one to Hunter, and I paid a young hippy lady $20 for a shoulder and back massage and stretched out on a hospital gurney as she kneaded the sore spots.

I crashed hard at about 10 p.m.

We woke up early the next morning and went to the Smoky Mountain Diner, which was a favorite of hikers and was well known for its pancakes. I had a Southwestern Omelet with grits and coffee and spotted Megaphone and JoAnne. They were starting their hike to Erwin, Tennessee, later in the day.

After packing for the return back to Atlanta, I walked down the street past the hotel. Outside the outfitter, I saw Ninja Roll, Ontario, Moonshine and Sunshine loading up their gear in a van. Because of the fire, they were being forced to leapfrog the next fifteen miles of the AT; the outfitter was dropping them off at Allen Gap. I passed out my remaining fruit bars and gave them a few veggie jerky sticks to give to Megaphone, who was vegetarian. The engine started, we waved our goodbyes, and they were gone.

My wife and I enjoyed a nice drive back to Atlanta, stopping in Asheville for a nice leisurely lunch and pulling over to buy some antiques near Franklin and some ramps just across the Georgia border. We had come up with a mean recipe for ramps and linguine, sprinkled with pepperoncini.

The mountains gave way to the hills, which gave way to the congested approach to Atlanta, where we merged into the thick traffic and re-engaged with our busy lives.

PART III

Goodbye to the Bear

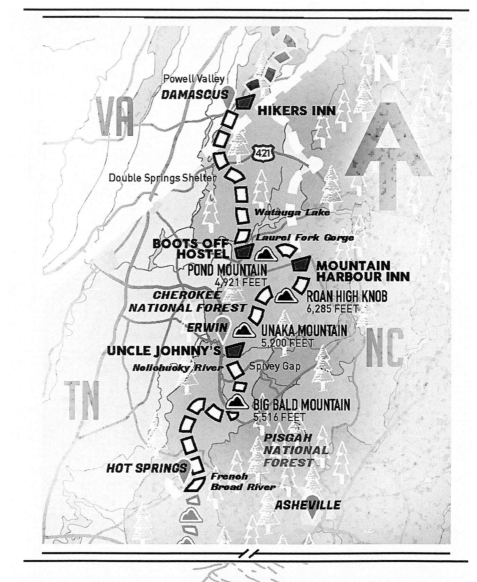

SECTION HIKE 9
October 7–14, 2018 | Roan Mountain, Tennessee to Damascus, Virginia

SECTION HIKE 8
April 29 – May 3, 2017 | Erwin, Tennessee to Roan Mountain, Tennessee

SECTION HIKE 7
October 9–14, 2016 | Hot Springs, North Carolina to Erwin, Tennessee

SECTION HIKE 7
Hot Springs, North Carolina, to Erwin, Tennessee
October 9–14, 2016 (70 Miles)

As was typical in the preparation of my other trips, work leading up to this hike was extremely heavy, which meant that my planning and ordering of supplies was piecemeal. An order of jerky would arrive one day; I would try to slip off to REI for Jetboil fuel another. I was starting my hike on a Sunday morning, and I did not shut my laptop down for work-related matters until early Saturday afternoon.

This hike was further complicated by two other issues—I was coming off a case of bronchitis, and Hurricane Matthew was still churning his way up the southeastern coast, with huge bands of rain moving hundreds of miles inland.

I went to a "Doc in the Box" on the Friday before my hike and got a prescription of antibiotics and a steroid shot. The doctor seemed to think it was all right if I went ahead, and that was all the encouragement I needed.

Matthew had hooked inland into the Carolinas, and indeed the storms had spread north in to the mountains of western North Carolina and eastern Tennessee. But weather forecasts by Saturday morning were showing that the high winds and rain would be gone by Sunday.

Because of my illness and work schedule, I really did not start getting in the proper spirit for the hike until my wife and I made the final approach to Hot Springs. The beautiful red barns of Madison County and changing leaves improved my mood; I was getting excited over the start of another hike.

I, like most southerners, enjoy autumn more than any other season, simply because summers are so brutal and long. As someone once said, people in the south don't look forward to Easter; that holiday means we are just getting that much closer to July.

Opposite: **Hot Springs, North Carolina to Damascus, Virginia—196 miles. Map by Kendall Young, WoodBatBrand.com.**

We all have our different rituals of preparing and looking forward to the fall. Shortly after the June solstice, I start tracking sunrises and sunsets and look for any subtle hints that the days are shortening. My chickens start gradually getting up later and retreating to their coop sooner, and this always reminds me of the sleeping patterns of hikers on the trail.

I have usually lived on heavily wooded lots, which have always produced generous amounts of firewood. I like to chop and split the deadwood that my trees so liberally supply; it is an activity that is physically demanding and relaxing at the same time, and I imagine the split wedges of hickory and oak bursting into flame in my fireplace after the first November frost.

The windows are opened in my house the first time temperatures dip below 70 degrees, usually on a late August evening. As the first poplar leaves turn bright yellow and acorns start falling from the oaks and prickly pods from the sweet gums make it painful to walk out on the deck barefooted, I start mentally preparing for the upcoming autumn hike.

We were spending the night at The Belle of Hot Springs, an historic, federalist-style, two-story, whitewashed bed and breakfast on the edge of town. It was owned by a mother and her daughter who had left Atlanta years ago to start new lives in the mountains of North Carolina.

Hot Springs was growing on me, and I had researched a bit of its history. More than a century ago, it was a tourist destination because of its elegant spa and soothing hot springs. Later, the small town of 650 hosted over 2,000 German civilians detained during World War I. On the large yard of the hotel that housed many of the detainees, the German prisoners built a faux Alpine village with buildings made to look like chalets with broad, gently sloping roofs supporting overhanging eaves and decorative wooden balconies underneath.[1]

I had planned a 70-mile, six-day hike to Erwin, Tennessee, with my wife coming back up to pick me up on Friday afternoon. We went to the Spring Creek Tavern that evening to watch some football and enjoy a pizza and a sampling of the local beers. When we headed back to the inn, the night had a bracing autumn chill as we crossed the bridge over the foggy Spring Creek.

I woke up early the next morning to a beautiful day. I was excited

The French Broad River, October 2016.

and ready to go. After breakfast in the dining area of the inn, I set off at about 8 a.m. The AT heads east from town for about a quarter mile, heading directly over the French Broad River Bridge.

The French Broad is a beautiful and ancient river—the world's third oldest, it stretches over two hundred miles to the north and west before merging in Knoxville with the Holston to form the Tennessee River.

The bridge stretches the length of several football fields, and there is a raised sidewalk on the shoulders for hikers and walkers to use. The wide river sparkled beneath me in a hundred small, churning eddies, while a thick mist rose over it to the east, which refracted rays from the rising sun, creating a mini-rainbow over the emerald-hued water below.

After crossing the river, the AT takes a sharp right turn downward and runs parallel to the French Broad for almost a mile before turning upward in a steady, 700-foot ascent to Lovers Leap Ridge. Along the way, I passed several homes where people had built houses a safe enough distance back from the river in the event that it overflowed in the springtime. I was now in the Cherokee National Forest; the Pisgah National Forest ended on the east side of Hot Springs.

As always, I started the hike with huge reserves of energy (fortified by the previous night's pizza), and the climb up Lovers Leap was not at all strenuous. There were a few strong wind gusts, but no rain—the last remnants of Matthew were moving beyond the southern Appalachians to points farther north. By late morning, I reached Lovers Leap ledge, a large bulging escarpment that looked south over the river and the valley below. The Sunday morning church bells from Hot Springs were pealing, and the chimes were reverberating off the mountainsides.

There were signs of the previous year's fire, but they were not as jarring as I had expected. Some charred trees were interspersed with green bushes and seedlings, but nothing like what I was anticipating, which was acre upon acre of burned-out woods, similar to the television footage from a western wildfire. In just six months, the forest had already started its slow cycle of recovery.

In the late morning, I passed a hiker headed south, and we stopped and talked. He was a thru-hiker who had reached Mount Katahdin less than a week ago. After reaching the summit and the end of his thru-hike, his girlfriend drove him from Maine back to Hot Springs; the previous spring's forest fire had forced him, like many others, to leapfrog 15 miles up the trail to Allen Gap. Now he had returned to finish the final portion of his thru-hike—his girlfriend had dropped him off at Allen Gap that morning, and he was hiking southward to Hot Springs to officially complete his thru-hike.

No one else would have ever known if he had hiked the entire trail except for this 15-mile portion. But his honesty and commitment would never have let him live with that small omission. He would finish his goal that afternoon and drive home with his girlfriend, freed from any future nagging doubt that he had not "done it right."

Notwithstanding the rains that had passed through the previous week from Matthew, the water sources as marked on the terrestrial map were dry—the last water I had seen was the French Broad River, now six miles behind me. I had fully stocked up with three liters before starting my hike, but the lack of water along the trail was becoming worrisome.

I passed a man-made pond created by an earthen dam with a wooden bench overlooking it. I stopped and had lunch and sipped my remaining water. The pond was not a good source for replenishment; the water had sections covered by a thin film of algae, and the last of the summer dragonflies buzzed over it.

As I climbed in elevation, the arrival of autumn was more apparent, especially with the maple trees turning red. I never tired of the splash of color, particularly since red leaves were fairly rare in Atlanta, and the leaves there did not reach their peak colors of amber and orange until early November.

I reached the summit of Rich Mountain in the mid-afternoon. I had climbed almost 3,500 feet and hiked eight miles since leaving Hot Springs, but I did not feel tired and decided to press on to Spring Mountain Shelter, another three miles, where there was the next identified water source. I had had no luck finding any drinking water during the day, and I had no Plan B if the spring at Spring Mountain turned out to be dry.

A state highway ran through Hurricane Gap, the last low point on the approach to Spring Mountain and the shelter. Two groups of college students were unloading from two vans and I knew the shelter would be overrun.

I was lucky when I arrived at the shelter in the late afternoon. There was a small trickle of water coming out of the spring in front of the log-cabin-style building. It took ten minutes, but I was able to fill three liters. Knowing that the college students were on my heels, I decided to hike on, hoping to find a place to sleep along the trail. A quarter mile later, I lucked out with a tucked-away spot just off the right side of the trail— home for the evening.

The weather had been cool during the day, but my face was lightly sunburned from facing the sun for a good part of my hike. I had covered 11 miles my first day out; so it was, after a quick meal, time for bed.

Morning has always been my favorite time in the mountains. The forest was resonating that morning with the sounds of wood thrushes, perhaps preparing for their migratory flights to Mexico, where they would winter before returning the next spring.

The sound of these early morning risers reminded me of the movie

Deliverance, in the scene where the character played by Jon Voight scaled Tallulah Gorge at dawn with his bow and arrow to hunt and kill the murderer of his friend. The silhouette of the killer, armed with his shotgun, can be seen on a cliff overlooking the river. As Voight silently positions his arrow and pulls back his bowstring for the fatal shot, the only sound that can be heard is that of the warblers and wood thrushes, performing their mating calls while the rest of the forest sleeps.

Pythagoras is famous for saying, "Unless you have something to say more pleasing than silence, don't break the silence." The creaking sound from the swaying firs, the trills and tweets of the songbirds, and the trickling of a gentle stream are more pleasing than silence. Most of us claim to crave stillness from time to time, but when confronted with absolute silence, we latch on to any sound, whether it is the rustling of leaves or the slight creak of a branch.

I packed my gear and got an early start. I was undecided on where I would be staying for the evening; I just planned to hike until I was tired and then search for a suitable place to pitch a tent for the night.

As I descended Spring Mountain, I spotted a poplar that was studded in a gorgeous wreath of scallop-shaped, mango-colored mushrooms called "chicken of the woods." The fungi of Appalachia represent a growing cottage industry for not only delicious foods like "chicken of the woods" and apricot-flavored chanterelles, but also for mushrooms valued for their medicinal properties. Paradoxically, trees in the region dying from invasive insects like the hemlock provide the perfect environment for mushrooms like the Asian reishi to flourish. Medicinally, this particular mushroom is said to reduce inflammation and balance the immune system.[2]

I have never foraged for food on the trail, but some hikers do. In addition to the easy to identify mushrooms and ramps, there are many edibles, including berries and fern fronds called "fiddleheads," dandelions, and even the ever-present pokeweed. All are seasonal and have to be properly cooked, and most of my energy was spent moving up the trail, leaving little time for adventurous side expeditions in search of exotic food.

The idea of foraging does bother some hikers, who worry that picking berries or mushrooms inflicts further damage on a trail already suffering from overuse. I personally see no harm in it, and if it enhances

Chicken of the woods mushrooms along the AT.

the experience for people to enjoy the exotic food fare of the AT, I feel that they will become even stronger guardians of its future. But the trail is living, and it has and will continue to undergo changes forced by the hand of man.

The southeastern portion of the AT has changed considerably since its formation, perhaps most dramatically with the elimination of 13 miles of trail below Springer Mountain. Most of the trail in the southeast is bordered by state and national parks, making alterations and slight changes in the route easier. Still, the AT is still not static; the route changes constantly, albeit not nearly as dramatically as it did in its early years (the first permanent route was not marked until 1971, 34 years after the AT was completed). Roan Mountain was originally not part of the trail, nor was the Grayson Highlands in Virginia; the original length of the trail was 2,054 miles, almost 150 miles shorter than it is today. Since its inception, an estimated 99 percent of the AT has been rerouted.[3]

A hiker named Rick walked up behind me, a quiet and painfully shy longhaired young man from Seattle who worked for Microsoft. He was hiking the section of the trail from Hot Springs to Damascus, Virginia. He had taken two weeks off work for this section hike. We stopped and ate lunch at the Little Laurel Shelter, where two malnourished bird dogs with GPS collars approached us, searching for food.

A late riser who had spent the night at the shelter told us they had arrived early in the morning and frightened some other campers—the dogs had sniffed and scratched on the outside of their tents, and in the darkness, they thought the shelter area had been invaded by a marauding bear. These pitiful and bone-thin dogs were surviving the best they could, following the trail where their best hope for food would be with hikers.

Rick let me use his portable cell phone battery recharger. Shamefully, I had run my battery down the previous day checking sports scores. Rick had decided to spend the evening at the shelter, and he was sweeping off his spot on the platform when I left.

As I "ridge ran" past Camp Creek Bald, the trail opened up, with several meadow hikes. I was enjoying the breaks from the "green tunnel" of a trail constantly bordered by tall trees. As beautiful as hiking in a dense forest is, it can also start to feel both monotonous and claustrophobic.

I set up my tent at a spot just below the meadow, in a large campsite that I had to myself—I had passed very few hikers over the course of the day. The camping area was in a small, dark and damp gap—not my first choice, but I knew difficult hiking lay ahead, and I wanted to call it a day after 12 miles on the trail.

I welcome solitude along the AT, but sometimes, on evenings like this one, it was unsettling to be alone. Gaps like this one exude an ominous aura. I start thinking of the serial killer who murdered the young woman who was hiking near Blood Mountain and who killed an elderly couple in the Pisgah National Forest.[4] Or maybe a ravenous bear would happen upon me and decide that his odds against a single camper were pretty good.

I went inside my tent as the sun settled over the ridge and checked for messages on my phone and read from my paperback to help calm my nerves. I briefly considered a couple of hits of pot to relax, but I was worried that this might magnify my paranoia.

Before I discovered the AT, I used to go to retreats at the Monastery of the Holy Spirit outside of Atlanta for solitude and escape from the confusion of everyday life. As the magical time of dusk approached, the Trappists, accompanied by an organ, would sing out beautiful prayers in antiphon at Compline, the hour before darkness:

> We praise you, Father, for your gifts
> Of dusk and nightfall over earth,
> Foreshadowing the mystery
> Of death that leads to endless day.

The Trappists believe that night prayer is a small dress rehearsal for death and eternal peace.[5] They acknowledge the proximity of death as part of their daily lives and never treat it as a vague or abstract future event. I had to laugh at the irony of my predicament—always searching for solitude, but then at moments like this, feeling uneasy with it. But I took comfort in the liturgy of the monks, who confront the notion of death each evening before retiring to their beds.

With the unsettling thoughts of rogue bears, serial killers, and fatalistic monks swimming in my head, I took a few swigs of moonshine and dozed off.

❦

I packed up early the next morning. I had managed a peaceful night of sleep, undisturbed by any observable threat. Eager to get out on the trail, I ate a granola bar, packed up, and headed out.

It was the start of my third day on the trail, and I had covered 22 miles. With almost 50 left to go, I wanted to make it at least to Flint Mountain Shelter, a distance of 11 miles. After covering that mileage, I would have four days to complete the remaining distance to Erwin, Tennessee.

The first two miles of the hike covered the boulder-strewn stretch of White Rocks, Blackstack Cliffs and Big Firescald Knob. The footing was treacherous, and the trail hugged the sides of cliffs in certain areas. As always, the AT is hard to follow when woods give way to boulders, and I had to really concentrate to pick up the white blaze markings. Climbing over rocks is also very hard on the knees, and I realized why so many people said the huge boulders in Pennsylvania made the AT in much of that state so difficult.

The boulders gradually gave way to forest, and I spotted my first mountain ash tree, its red berries in their full autumn glory, on the summit of Coldspring Mountain. This was my first encounter with this mystical tree, which was revered by the ancient druids in Britain, where it is called rowan. Also referred to as the "quickening tree," its branches were supposedly used by wizards as wands. The druid priests would burn rowan wood on funeral pyres, because it symbolized both death and rebirth. It was also one of the sacred trees burnt at the Beltane, the May Day celebration by pagans. It is a member of the rose family, and can live up to 200 years.[6]

I also passed the gravesites of the Sheltons, the "Overmountain Men," from Madison County, North Carolina, who fought for the Union during the Civil War. David Shelton, along with his nephew William and a 13-year-old boy named Millard Haire, were ambushed and killed by Confederate soldiers in 1864.[7]

The area had seen militia-style raids by both sides during the Civil War, including a raid on the nearby town of Marshall by unionists, in order to secure salt supplies. On a retaliatory raid, Confederate soldiers stationed in Hot Springs raided the Shelton Laurel community and engaged in indiscriminate killing of the old and young. Three boys, ranging from 13 to 17 years old, were rounded up and shot, execution style. The youngest, David Shelton (different from the David Shelton buried near Coldspring Mountain), begged for mercy, and said, "You have killed my old father and three brothers, you have shot me in both arms.... I forgive you all this—I can get well.... Let me go home to my mother and sisters." David Shelton was shot eight more times.[8]

My great-grandfather, Perry James "Jim" Grogan, also came from a mountainous region of divided loyalties during the Civil War. He was the descendant of Scots-Irish immigrants who had come to the Carolinas during the 1700s, eventually settling in the foothills of the Appalachian Mountains near modern-day Landrum, South Carolina. His earliest memory, at the age of the three, was attending his mother's funeral. Shortly thereafter, Jim's father and uncle left for Georgia. He remembered walking behind the wagon during the journey. His younger sister was left behind with his mother's family, and Jim never saw or heard from her again.

Raised in the shadow of what later became the Appalachian Trail in the small community of Juno in northern Dawson County, he had no personal stake in the fight. The rolling hills of his home did not allow for large, plantation-like farms, and his family had never owned any slaves. The planters of English descent in the flatter, lower Piedmont and coastal regions of the state were the main practitioners of slavery (although it did exist in the hills and mountains—the Cherokees, in fact, owned black slaves). Thousands of able-bodied men from the Appalachian areas of North Carolina, Tennessee and Georgia had pledged their loyalties to the United States—over 5,000 from Georgia alone fought for President Lincoln's Union.[9] At the start of the Civil War, Dawson County had a population of less than 4,000; the Confederate Army raised five companies (250 men) from the county, and the Union Army raised two companies (100 men).

I never learned if Jim Grogan faced a difficult decision on which side to choose when he enlisted at age 18 in the Confederate Army. It may have been as simple as the emotional tug of family loyalties from his small farm community or as complicated as a deeply felt support for the Southern cause.

By 1864, Private Grogan was no stranger to battle. In his two years of service, he fought in the Western Theater with the Georgia 52nd Regiment, Company I, known as the "Dawson County Tigers." The Georgia 52nd was made up of men from the northeastern Georgia hill and mountain counties of Dawson, Habersham, Towns, Union, Rabun, White, Franklin and Fannin.[10]

At the Battle of Kennesaw Mountain just outside Atlanta in June of 1864, a .54-caliber "minie" ball fired by a Union soldier hit Jim. The bullet entered the side of his right foot, one inch above his little toe, shattering bones and cartilage, before exiting on the left side.[11] When he was placed in a military ambulance, Private Grogan's mangled foot hung from a sling attached to the top of the covered wagon that was carrying him to the military hospital in Atlanta. The wagon had to travel a short distance to the east before swinging south on the road to Atlanta. At Marietta, the juncture between the eastern and southern roads, the driver of the wagon decided to stop and have a drink at a saloon. The drink turned into an all-night binge, and Jim Grogan spent a sleepless night in the wagon, wracked with pain. The next morning, a Confederate lieutenant passed by, and when he realized what had happened, had to be restrained from killing the driver.

After the wagon arrived at the hospital in Atlanta, Jim begged the surgeon not to amputate his foot below the ankle. The surgeon relented, and Jim was invalided out of the army and made his way back to his home in the mountains.

On October 16, 1864, with the war still raging, Perry James Grogan married Nancy Harben, and they had eight children together. When she was dying from fever in 1891, her last wish was for Jim to marry her sister, Minerva. Jim and Minerva honored her request, and had five children, the last of whom was my grandfather, born in 1902 when Jim was 58 years old.

Jim never recovered fully from his wound, and the damage from it eventually infected both legs. He suffered from varicose veins and running sores on both legs for the rest of his life and was unable to perform manual labor.[12] He died in 1923 and was buried at the cemetery next to New Hope Baptist Church, less than ten miles from Amicalola Falls, the start of the approach trail to Springer Mountain and the Appalachian Trail.

❧❦❧

I arrived at Flint Mountain Shelter in the late afternoon and pitched my tent just north of the structure, next to the creek. There were four other people staying there that evening, three young southbound thru-hikers who had recently graduated from college and another section hiker, Matt, from Macon, Georgia.

We ate on the picnic table fronting the shelter and exchanged information. One of the thru-hikers was trail-named "4.0." He had achieved somewhat legendary status in that year's class of Maine-to-Georgia hikers. He was known to leave off-beat messages in the shelter trail journals, and the other two thru-hikers, a young woman named Lisa and her boyfriend, Jeff, were pleased to have met up with him—"Wow, you are really 4.0?!?" Matt from Macon was like me—he was doing a section hike from Hot Springs to Erwin.

The trail name "4.0" was a jab at the hiker's grade point average, which apparently was considerably lower than that. He was funny and self-deprecating, so he embraced his trail name. Lisa and Jeff, the other two thru-hikers, had somehow managed to make it all the way to North Carolina without earning trail names. Lisa was small and petite and could almost have been mistaken for a male hiker until she took off her knit cap and shook out a beautiful mane of sandy-colored hair. I could not help but notice that she had a well-sculpted lower body, shaped and muscled by almost 2,000 miles of the trail.

We talked as they picked at their ramen in plastic cups. I asked them, as I usually did with all thru-hikers who are near the finish line, what the most difficult stretch of the trail is. Without hesitation, they responded, "Maine." Nothing, they said, can prepare a hiker for Maine, with its many rivers and creeks that the trail crosses directly over, and its long stretches of isolated wilderness.

Jokingly, 4.0 said that in Vermont if a river is too high at a trail crossing, trail volunteers will paint a yellow blaze signifying a detour to a fordable spot. In Maine, someone would simply hang up a sign with the blunt message, "Deal with it."

They were headed to Hot Springs the next day, a distance of 35 miles, so they were all getting up well before dawn to start their hikes. They were pleased to hear that there was a Dollar General in Hot Springs, where they could replenish their supplies of ramen and Snickers bars.

I pressed them for their knowledge of the trail that remained for me on this section hike. I love statistics as they relate to elevation, distance, and grade, and I tried to pry some useful information from them. They just shrugged, said it was moderately difficult. That comes with moving at such a rapid pace—the mountains, gaps, and ridges become a blur.

I was always looking for evidence that the most difficult stretch of the trail was behind me and asked if the Smokies were the last time the trail crossed a 6,000-foot peak until it reached New Hampshire. Matt from Macon reminded me that Roan Mountain, about 50 miles up the trail, surpassed that height.

We all turned in at dusk that night and said our goodbyes—they were heading south, and we were heading north. I had decided to get up early the next morning, too. Not as early as the thru-hikers, but I wanted to be on the trail by 6:30 a.m.—I still had almost 40 miles to cover in three days.

I was on the trail, as planned, an hour before dawn. The next hour or so would be hiking by headlamp, mainly downhill, alongside a dry creek bed. I made sure that the beams from the lamp caught the white blazes on the trees to ensure I did not stray from the trail. I had dressed for cool weather, but by daybreak at Devil Fork Gap, I shed my heavier clothing in favor of shorts and a T-shirt.

On a terrestrial map, Frozen Knob appears to be pretty unassuming, gently rising to a summit of around 4,500 feet. But, as always on the AT, looks can be deceiving, and once I reached what I thought was the summit, I saw that the mountain continued after a short saddleback.

When I was hiking on the quarter-mile saddleback, I was startled when someone spoke to me—I had not encountered a single hiker thus far that morning, and I was not expecting it. There was a man, wearing a kilt, munching an apple beneath the remnants of an old apple orchard. It was October, so these small green apples were ripe, and I picked a few and stowed them in my pack.

Brian was a 60-ish social worker from Asheville, doing a north-to-south section hike from Erwin to Hot Springs. He asked to use my cell phone, and I obliged him, even though I was concerned with a battery that was down in the red zone. "Meet me in the gap for a steak and a beer!" he yelled to a friend before handing me my phone back.

We talked and enjoyed the clear view for miles from the ridge. He knew the area well, pointing out Mount Mitchell, the highest mountain east of the Mississippi, which was at least 50 miles away but vaguely visible on this bright Indian summer day. It felt good to see some of the mountains that I had climbed, including Albert Mountain and Cheoah Bald.

Brian had friends he was staying with along his section hike, which meant he could "slack pack" with a lighter load. When I told him I was from Atlanta, he asked why I lived there. "Just trying to make a living," I responded. "Have you made it yet?" he said, as he wheeled and headed south towards Devil Fork Gap.

The day continued to warm, and I realized that this was my first section hike where there had been no hint of rain, nary a cloud in the sky for four days. I stopped at Hogback Ridge Shelter for lunch and had to walk a quarter mile to the creek to refill my Camelbak with water. Rick was already there. He had passed me at some point earlier, but I had not noticed. Maybe he had gotten an earlier start one morning and passed me when I was still in my tent.

The other occupant was a Native American Ojibwe from Canada named Pete. Pete was only about 5'4" and carried two carved, oak walking sticks, both of which were taller than he. At the top of each stick was an eagle feather tied with a leather strap through a drilled hole. Pete was garrulous, but difficult to follow. His thoughts were scattered, and he always expressed them with a broad smile. He had spent two consecutive nights at Hogback Ridge Shelter, which was odd because he was not injured and the weather had been perfect. He talked about Uncle Johnny's, the renowned hostel in Erwin, and how he looked forward to getting there. Prior to starting the AT, he claimed to have hiked the entire Florida Trail, from the Everglades to Pensacola. He asked Rick for some food and was handed a granola bar. I realized then that Pete had no money.

Matt from Macon walked in to the shelter area and joined us. He had caught up with me, despite the fact that he had not started his hike until 8 a.m. After a brief lunch, he headed back up the trail, joined by Pete. The three-mile hike from the shelter to Sam's Gap was hard—a lot of difficult roller-coaster ridges made worse by temperatures that had soared into the 80s.

When I finally reached Sam's Gap in the mid-afternoon, Matt from Macon was sitting with his gear under the overpass on Highway 26. I passed him and he asked how I felt on the hike from the shelter. "Definitely tired," I responded. "I don't feel good and am getting off the trail," Matt replied. I was stunned by this development. The previous night at the shelter, he seemed very knowledgeable and enthusiastic about the AT. He, like me, was progressing northward through a series of section hikes, and he had taken a week off work for this one. He had already called the outfitter in Hot Springs to pick him up and take him back to his car; the driver was en route. He told me Pete had made him feel uneasy. The two had hiked together down to the gap, and Pete spent much of the time trying to wheedle food and money. I could see Pete while we spoke, ascending the trail on the opposite side of the highway, stopping to talk to several hikers as they passed by.

I briefly considered joining Matt and leaving the trail. I was dead tired and still had 25 miles to go before I reached Erwin. I was also starting to feel uneasy about the situation with Pete, but decided to continue onward. I said goodbye to Matt, who said he would spend the rest of his vacation time visiting his grandmother.

I had no particular plan on where I was going to camp that night. All I could think about was getting myself a safe distance away from Pete. I stopped a day hiker whom I had noticed passed Pete on the trail. I asked him what he thought about Pete, and he gave me a quizzical look: "He seemed a little eccentric, but nothing too weird."

I passed Pete about a half-mile up the trail. He was moving very slowly. When I passed him, he asked me if was out for a day hike—he clearly did not recognize me even though I had spent a half hour at the shelter with him earlier that afternoon. I mumbled, "yeah," and sped around him.

I found new reserves of energy. Faster and faster I moved, over several small hillocks and over Street Gap and past a meadow that looked like a great place to camp. Given that Pete was moving so slowly, I was giving myself a huge margin of safety. In a little over two hours, I had hiked about five miles, and I continued to press on.

My fear was totally irrational. Pete was eccentric and penniless, but it is highly doubtful that he was a threat to anyone unless he was armed. I outweighed him by a hundred pounds, and there was nothing in his disposition that suggested any sort of hostility. But I was determined to make it to Low Gap, the last gap at the foot of 5,516-foot Big Bald Mountain.

I miscalculated. I had hiked past Low Gap, thinking it was the second gap before the ascent up to Big Bald Mountain. So I was unknowingly starting to hike the tenth highest mountain on the AT in the early evening, exhausted. Climbing Big Bald would be difficult under ideal circumstances, but it was murderous for me at that stage of the day. I stopped every hundred feet or so to catch my breath on the slow climb up. I was also out of water.

I was beginning to panic, because I needed to stop for the evening, but there was no place to pitch a tent. The trail hugged the mountain edge, with a drop-off to the left and steep tree and bush-covered banks to the right.

As I was sitting down alongside the trail on one of my mini-breaks, a young man and his golden retriever came running up the trail. He stopped and asked where I was headed. I told him the next available spot where I could pitch my tent. He was drinking a can of Wicked Weed ale during his run, which even in my wearied state I found interesting. He told me to follow him, he knew of just such a spot about "fifteen minutes" up the trail.

He continued his jog. Fifteen minutes for him was about 45 minutes for me. I continued to have to stop every hundred feet or so to rest, while he and his dog would stop and wait patiently for me to catch my breath. "Just up ahead!" he would yell down the trail at me. Slowly I would rise up, shift my pack, and lumber after him.

At dusk, we finally arrived at the finish line, a mossy patch of cleared space about 20 feet off the trail. Although it sloped downward at about ten degrees towards the ridge, I did not care. I slung my pack to the ground and thanked my Good Samaritan profusely.

He was staying with his father in an upscale development, Wolf Laurel, that abutted the AT along Big Bald. I could actually see the backyards and lights from the homes just off the trail. My benefactor offered to get me water, but I was not going to inconvenience him further. We shook hands and he continued his run up the trail, the tail of his golden retriever wagging as she ran beside him.

I managed to pitch my tent and eat a granola bar. It was already dark and hanging a bear pack was out of the question. Due to a misguided panic and one miscalculation, I had hiked 18 miles that day. As the darkness closed in and the October chill slowly penetrated my tent, I sank into a deep sleep.

❧❧❧

The next morning I woke up to temperatures near freezing. This was not a huge surprise, because I had camped at over 5,000 feet in elevation. I could have used something hot to drink, but I had long ago dispensed with the idea of brewing coffee in the morning while camping.

Instant, freeze-dried coffee tasted extremely bitter, and I usually ended up throwing most of my cup away. I ate a granola bar, packed my gear and set out.

I still had about 500 feet of elevation to contend with before I reached the summit of Big Bald, and the remaining portion of the trail leading up to the top was anything but easy—tight, rocky, switchback trails. It took me almost an hour to reach the peak.

My inadvertent 18-mile hike from the previous day had set me up nicely—I had two days to cover the remaining distance to Erwin, which also happened to be 18 miles. I was also getting an early start, so my goal for the day was to make it to No Business Knob Shelter, leaving an easy six-mile walk the following day to Uncle Johnny's Hostel, where my wife would be picking me up.

The gorgeous weather continued to hold up. The mountain opened up to a mile-long stretch of broad, grassy bald. I had an unobstructed, 180-degree view to the north, with one rippling ridge after another, stretching for as far as I could see on the horizon.

Balds and the reasons for their formation in the southern Appalachians remain a mystery. The highest mountain in Georgia is Bald Mountain (not to be confused with Big Bald), and I was always told that its summit was bare either due to lightning strikes or early settlers who grazed their cattle on the summit. Similar to the legend of Standing Indian Mountain, the Cherokee believed that a heinous flying beast terrorized the local tribes, and after praying to the Great Spirit, he sent lightning strikes against mountain after mountain until the lair of the monster was destroyed, along with all the trees on the summit.[13] The early mountaineer settlers referred to the balds as "hells," "wooly-heads" and "slicks."[14]

The fact is, though, that no one is sure why some mountains have balds, while others, in close proximity and sharing the same soil acidity and elevation characteristics of the bald mountains, do not. Roan Mountain, at 6,285 feet, has fir trees right to the summit, but the mountains just to the east of it in the Roan Highlands—Round, Jane, Hump, and Little Hump, do not. In short, balds represent "an ecological enigma and a conservation dilemma."[15]

Big Bald Mountain connects to Little Bald via a two-mile saddleback that featured clear views on that crisp autumn morning of the

Newfound Mountains and Roan Highlands. Right before I passed the Bald Mountain Shelter, I passed a group of field biologists who had set up netting in a brushy area just off the trail. They were tagging and releasing birds to get better information on their migratory patterns.

I stopped and chatted with them for a while. They said that the wood thrushes, due to loss of breeding ground habitat, had seen their numbers decline by half over the last 50 years. The thought of losing their trilling calls was shocking, but not altogether surprising. The bobwhite quail has seen precipitous declines in its numbers—I cannot recall the last time I heard the call of a bobwhite in the forests of north Georgia or western North Carolina. In my boyhood, I could hear them regularly in my grandparents' back yard, where I would try to imitate their call.

As I rounded the summit of Little Bald and started the slow descent down to Spivey Gap, I reflected on the previous day's events. I had no rational explanation for my behavior and why I was overcome with the need to put a safe distance between Pete and me. There was definitely a weird vibe around Pete, but he also seemed incapable of inflicting violence. The best explanation I could come up with was my almost complete lack of interaction with Native Americans, which is not that unusual given where I have lived my entire life. This thought depressed me, because I have read about and on an abstract level admired the cultures of the native tribes for years.

The hike down from the balds was a winding four-mile descent downward, with the exception of a steep, 1,000-foot confusing climb at High Rocks, a huge rock outcropping just above Spivey Gap.

I was feeling great by the time I reached the gap. I crossed Highway 19 and filled up my water at Devil's Creek. I reached the No Business Knob Shelter in the late afternoon. I was alone at the shelter, and I pitched my tent on a floor of pine needles about one hundred feet away from the front of the structure.

A young couple approached just before dusk, and they took off their packs and we talked. They were thru-hikers, and the young woman had just spent a week in an Erwin motel recovering from the giardia she contracted from drinking contaminated water. They had planned on spending the night at the shelter, but the water source nearby was dry. After discussing their options, they put their packs back on and headed to Devil's Creek, the nearest water source. I was sad to see them leave; I would have enjoyed their company.

As always on the last evening on the trail, I propped up my backpack against a tree and reflected on the trip. By tomorrow midday, I would have hiked 70 miles, a personal section hike record. I would also not have encountered one drop of rain, which was also a first-time occurrence.

As the daylight waned, I took a swig of moonshine and stared at the red and yellow leaves starting to slowly pinwheel downward. I loved the word for this time of year—fall, derived from the "fall of the leaves" or "fallowing," from the Old English verb meaning "to turn yellow-gold." It is a holdover from the original Elizabethan English spoken by the first British settlers in America that is no longer in use in Great Britain. I felt calm and at peace.

The next morning I was up early; I wanted to make it to Erwin by lunchtime to satisfy my cheeseburger and beer cravings. The six-mile hike was almost all downhill, featuring gorgeous overlooks on Cliff Ridge of the Nolichucky River (a tributary of the French Broad) and the gorge below. The colors along this portion of the Cherokee National Park were especially vivid—the scarlet leaves from dogwoods and red oaks interspersed with the golden yellow from tulip poplars and the occasional orange from a sweetgum. The view from Temple Ridge overlooking the gorge was particularly stunning, with the old train trestle built in 1907 still spanning the Nolichucky.

At noon, I walked out of the woods onto Highway 19. The AT continues for a short distance before it swings across a road bridge that extends over the gorge. Just on the west side of Highway 19 and a short walk to the bridge sits Uncle Johnny's, a splash of folk art and tie-dye connected to a sprawling stone and wood complex that houses a hostel, cabins, outfitter's store and shuttle service.

I walked up to the deck area that fronted the store. A large sign was hung from the bannister rail—"40¢ Snickers." I was spotted by a 70-ish, medium-sized man wearing a long-sleeved tie-dyed T-shirt and a broad-brimmed, cream-colored hat. He had long silver hair and a full-blown, white Santa Claus beard. He resembled a hippy Burl Ives.

"Welcome to Uncle Johnny's!" he shouted. "Need a room?" I walked up to the deck and shook the hand of John Shores, the proud owner. Years earlier, fed up with his corporate job in Birmingham, John happened across a house while section hiking on the AT and had a vision: there was no other place for miles along the AT that provided such ready access to hiking, fishing, sight-seeing and whitewater canoeing and kayaking. He talked to the owner and a plan was hatched. He bought the house, added showers, bathrooms and a nine-room hostel, and the dream became reality.[16] Today, Uncle Johnny's is regarded as an oasis on the AT, the best known hot shower and warm bed rest stop on the slog between Hot Springs and Damascus, Virginia.

"I don't need a room, but I could use a cheeseburger and beer," I responded.

"Well, we can arrange that. You like Lagunitas IPA?"

"Sure," I replied.

I handed him a twenty, and Johnny dispatched a driver down into town to pick up a cheeseburger with fries along with a six-pack. We sat out on the picnic table underneath the roof of the covered deck, and Uncle Johnny and I began to talk. His grizzled old mutt, Jerry Garcia, and his huge cat named Peeping Tom Cat accompanied us. Peeping Tom Cat liked to get on the beams overlooking people using the showers, much to the amusement of the guests.

Other than hiker snacks such as candy bars, Johnny's does not serve food, but does offer regular shuttles into the city of Erwin for guests in need of pizza and beer. "The average guest drinks nine beers," claimed Johnny, who would know after years of cleaning out bunkrooms and cabins. "Gotta be careful on where you buy it though," he continued. "Unicoi County has 18,000 residents and 180 churches."

The driver returned with my food, which I tried to eat while Peeping Tom Cat kept nuzzling my arm, hoping to get a bite. "You need to get yourself a Tilley hat," he said, referring to the hat perched on his head. "Best hat for hiking out there."

We each drank beer while Johnny filled me with stories about the Erwin area, including the macabre incident where Mary the Elephant was hung by local townspeople after killing her handler prior to a circus performance in 1916.

Johnny knew the tragic Civil War history of the area, where families were split between Union and Confederate loyalties. Friends and even members of the same families massacred men and boys in the mountains for supporting the other side.

We also discussed the history of "The Republic of Franklin." The modern-day counties of eastern Tennessee that are contiguous with the border of North Carolina were originally part of that state. In the 1780s, as payment for its Revolutionary War debt, North Carolina offered the area to Congress. However, the area that would become a new state to be named Franklin, did not receive the necessary two-thirds votes required under the Articles of Confederation. By then, the idea of a new state in a region that had long felt ignored by the leaders in the distant state capital of Raleigh had taken hold. When it became apparent that statehood would not be granted, Franklin declared itself a de facto republic in 1785. The state of North Carolina sent troops into the region, and a pitched battle ensued in early 1788, resulting in the death of three men. Soon thereafter, the leader of the Franklinites, John Sevier, was arrested and the rebellion was extinguished.[17]

It was clear then Johnny had a genuine affection for the area, and he had just completed a book on his hostel and Erwin. I bought a copy and had him sign it.

On our second beer, Rick came down from the trail and paid for a bunk for the evening. He said Pete would probably make it down later that day, and I mentioned Pete's plight to Johnny. "Don't know why people think they can hike the trail with no money," Johnny said, as he shook his head sadly.

My wife arrived as we were just finishing our third beers. Down below, a train roared through the gorge below, its whistle sounding. As I rose to leave, I asked him, "Is that train carrying coal?"

"Yep," said Johnny. "Clinchfield Railroad. There used to be fourteen trains a day carrying coal through town, now there is only one."

On that brilliant, Indian summer day in October 2016 as the sun began its long descent over Temple Ridge, I let that thought sink in.

SECTION HIKE 8
Erwin to Roan Mountain, Tennessee
April 29–May 3, 2017 (50 Miles)

It was clear by April 2017 that my job was not going to work out and that after almost four years, it was time to start looking for a new one. Time once again to freshen up the resume, get my "elevator speech" down pat and buy a new suit for interviews. Maybe even time to get the long-delayed teeth whitening done and add a little bit more dark color to the little pepper that remained among the salt of my hair. Closing in on age 60, I knew that corporate America valued above all else the perceived energy that accompanied the appearance of youth.

My daughter had been out of college and working for a year, and my son was about to graduate from high school and leave for college in August. My wife and I were on the verge of becoming empty nesters, and I was trying to wrap my head around both the good and the bad of that development.

I had now hiked too far north to ask my wife or father to drop me off at the starting point, which was more than an four-hour drive from Atlanta. I called Uncle Johnny's and was told I could park my car there; they would send a shuttle to pick me up when I finished my hike and bring me back to Erwin.

I was planning on hiking from Erwin to Damascus, a distance of about 125 miles; easily my longest trip to date. There were several places along the way, such as Mountain Harbour near Roan Mountain and several other hostels in the Hampton, Tennessee, area, where I could get off the trail for a night and resupply my pack.

The weather looked favorable; if anything, it might be a little on the too-warm side. I decided to take my warm weather sleeping bag, which would keep me comfortable down to 40 degrees.

I arose early on a Saturday morning and drove to Erwin. The good weather was holding up, but the temperature gauge in my car climbed steadily in to the high 80's. I pulled in to Uncle Johnny's at lunchtime and parked my car. The hostel and the grass-covered courtyard were full of hikers—those who could not get a room paid a small fee to pitch tents in the grass. The air was saturated with marijuana smoke, as several hikers sat at the picnic tables in the courtyard and passed around small bongs.

The contrast from my visit the previous autumn could not have been more stark—the entire complex was overrun with people, including hiking equipment vendors, who set up tents to ply their wares, and food hawkers, who set up just off the premises to sell hot dogs and sandwiches. Shuttles periodically arrived from town to pick up and drop off hikers.

Johnny was nowhere to be seen, so after dropping off my keys at the front desk of the store, I set off. The day was extraordinarily warm, close to 90 degrees, as I crossed over the bridge that led over the Nolichucky River. After crossing the river, the trail swung right and to the south, running parallel to the river and adjacent to the road for about a mile. Across the road was a church giving free meals to hikers; there were several who had walked over from Uncle Johnny's to take advantage of the offer.

After crossing a railroad track, the trail took a sharp left to the east and into the wilderness, following Jones Branch Creek, which fed into the Nolichucky. The extremely warm weather was more pronounced at this low elevation—I was starting at less than 1,500 feet. There were many tents just off the trail in this area, presumably hikers who wanted proximity to Erwin but did not want to pay for lodging.

I ascended the Nolichucky Gorge in a thick pine forest as the sun beat down. Felled trees interrupted a series of switchbacks—it was early spring, and the volunteer crews were still clearing out the trees and branches that had fallen the previous winter. I missed a detour and hiked in the wrong direction for a quarter of a mile until the trail disappeared, and I had no other option other than to return to my starting point.

Jan D. Curran wrote two books many years ago about his two thru hikes. The first one, *A Journey of Discovery,* detailed his experiences in the Erwin area, the only trail town he did not like. He found the locals to be rude and threatening, and at one point even had to hide in the woods from shadowy men.[18] I had never actually ventured into the town of Erwin itself, but I kept those stories in mind as I made my way to Curly Maple Gap.

My original plan for the day was to hike to Indian Grave Gap, a distance of eight miles from Uncle Johnny's. However, the heat was taking its toll on me, and I decided not to push it. After reaching Curly Maple Gap Shelter in the mid-afternoon, I called it a day after hiking a total of five miles. It had felt like August, not April, on my first day of hiking, and the meager amount of mileage I had covered left me both tired and dispirited.

The best spots for tents had already been taken and the shelter was full; apparently a lot of other hikers had reached the same conclusion that I had after leaving Erwin—the hot weather was zapping energy levels, and there was no point in pushing onward.

I found a spot next to the shelter's water source, a small, almost stagnant creek. I pitched my tent and climbed inside; I could hear new arrivals coming in, inquiring about spaces in the shelter, distances to the next shelter, etc. I stared at the sun-dappled ceiling of my tent and tried to doze off. As I was scratching my head, I felt a slight bump on the nape of my neck, a tick. This was not completely surprising—the trail leading to the shelter was thick and overgrown, and there were many occasions where I had brushed against bushes and trees.

I walked towards the double-decked shelter, which had a cinderblock foundation and tin roof. One of the occupants mentioned to me that she had spotted a snake in the water near my tent. I went back down to investigate, but I could not find it. I did notice, however, wasps buzzing around the area. Heat, wasps, snakes, and ticks—Curley Maple Shelter was not growing on me.

I met Doc and the Girl, a father and daughter duo that was thru-hiking. He was 64 and a retired lawyer from Iowa—he had also served as a medic in the Vietnam War and late in life obtained his law degree. She was in her late 20s and had just quit her advertising job in Manhattan. He was, like me, a slow mover, and had already decided that he would not reach the end of the trail in Maine until mid–October. "Last one to Katahdin wins," he said with a wry smile.

Three young men who were section hiking southward to Spivey Gap walked into the shelter area. One removed his boot and displayed a hideously stubbed and bloody big toe, with the toenail half off. After stubbing my toes on roots, I had lost several big toenails that gradually blackened and fell off weeks after a hike, but I had never suffered an injury as gruesome as this one. Doc was called to help apply the bandage, but nothing was going to save that nail. After performing that bit of first aid, Doc retired to his tent, where he remained for the rest of the evening.

I had been very lucky with injuries on my trips. Except for my first section hike, I had avoided one of the most common and debilitating of hiking injuries, foot blisters. I am by no means a gear geek, but my Vasque boots had served me very well in that department. Other common hiker injuries are sprains, ligament damage and tendonitis, and I had managed to dodge all those ailments, despite the fact that I am a notorious non-stretcher—I throw on my pack in the morning and set off on the trail without limbering up at all. Soreness in the back and shoulders from the pack load is the only pain I experience while hiking.

I was surprised by the food many of the thru-hikers had brought in—hummus, soft tortillas, and even some diced kale with salad dressing. They ate all the heavier food early in the hike to lessen their loads—most were not planning on getting off the trail until either Hampton or Damascus, a week to ten days away.

I went to bed at dusk under a crescent moon that cast little light over the open shelter area. The heat had not really receded by nightfall, and I tossed and turned before finally getting out of my sleeping bag and lying on top of it. It was the only time I had ever been on the trail where the heat had driven me out of my sleeping bag. I broke into a light sweat and did not finally nod off until early morning.

The next morning, I had no specific goal in mind other than to try and make up some of the ground I had lost due to my short hike the previous day. The trail stretched almost straight eastward, through Indian Grave Gap before rising steadily upward to 5,000 feet in elevation. I was back in the Pisgah National Forest, and the mountains I would be hiking over were known as the Unaka Range, a sub-range of the Blue Ridge that consists of a group of mountains that extend from the Nolichucky Gorge (which I had crossed the previous day) to the Watauga River farther north.

Unaka gets its name from the word "white" in Cherokee, probably because of the light-colored cliffs that are found throughout the range. The beautiful gemstone named Unakite, a pink and green speckled granite rock, is found in this range.[19]

The day was warm, but there was a slight breeze in the air. Some of the hikers said they had heard reports of rain moving through the area.

I covered the remaining three miles to Indian Grave Gap by mid-morning. There was a man handing out lemonade and bananas from the back of his pickup truck; I gratefully gulped down a cup of lemonade and crossed Highway 395 to start the ascent towards Unaka Mountain.

The wildflowers were starting to emerge—I passed purple wild irises, the small white petals from garlic mustard, and my favorite wildflower name, fleabane. This daisy gets its name from early settlers who would add the plant to their bedding as flea repellant.

At midday, I passed Beauty Spot, a circular parking area just below the ridgeline. This was the location where Jan Curran had felt threatened by locals who had followed him from Erwin, slowly circling in their pickup truck.[20]

At Beauty Spot Gap, I stopped for lunch and saw Doc and the Girl. They had finished their lunch earlier and were resting and telling passing hikers about a water source that was not marked on trail maps. I followed their instruction and walked one hundred feet down a path and refilled my Camelbak. It was yet another example of selfless behavior by members of the AT community, who were aware that other hikers were probably looking to replenish their water before hiking up Unaka Mountain.

Unaka Mountain does not garner much discussion among hikers, but it is a difficult climb back up over 5,000 feet, with a 1,000-foot elevation gain in one mile.

The author hiking up Unaka Mountain, April 2017.

I was about one-third of the way up the mountain when I realized that I had lost my map. I had forgotten to zip up the side pocket to my shorts, and the map had fallen out. This was disappointing, but not devastating—I was relying more and more on the Guthook app on my iPhone. But still, I liked to have my old-fashioned paper map to visualize the trail ahead.

As I made my slow climb up the mountain, I passed a small spruce tree decorated with Christmas ornaments, lace snowflakes and wind chimes. Nearby, there were solar lights placed in a heart shape. There was a plastic sign attached to an adjacent tree indicating that it was a memorial to Max Norrell, and the family would appreciate Facebook recognition from hikers who passed by. He was a young man who died at the age of 22. I do not know the circumstances of his death, but the memorial made me shiver—I have a son fast approaching that age, and newspaper obituaries seem filled with young men who die unexpectedly at early ages, so often from suicides.

Near the summit of Unaka Mountain I came upon a towering cathedral of red spruce trees. It was totally unexpected—these beautiful trees, each coated with several feet of lime green lichens at the base, were evenly spaced, in almost linear rows, like what is found in a German forest, and they rose 50, 60, 70 feet high. Their height blocked almost all sunlight from reaching the forest floor, which kept the thick underbrush that is so typical of Appalachian forests from growing. The level forest floor was a thick, plush carpet of rust-colored spruce needles. I had planned on continuing my hike for a few more miles to the shelter on the far side of Unaka Mountain, but I knew instantly that I had to camp in that spot.

Other than two other hikers from Tampa, I had the entire forest to myself. After setting up my tent, I walked around and explored the area. I talked to the other two hikers; they, like me, were planning on trying to make it to Damascus. They had been taking two consecutive weeks off each spring to eventually section hike the entire AT. They warned me of approaching bad weather, which surprised me. I had experienced nothing but brilliant sunshine and uncomfortably warm weather, but a cold front was about to move through, bringing heavy rain with it.

After a dinner of dehydrated lasagna cooked in my Jetboil, I went inside my tent and read for a while before dozing off. I slept for maybe two or three hours before I woke up. The wind had picked up considerably, and this was causing the giant spruces to sway and creak. The trees provided a canopy that protected my tent from the pelting of raindrops, but as the branches above me slowly collected water, they began to drip huge drops that plopped against the thin nylon of my tent cover.

I was staying dry, and the rain was not accompanied by thunder or lightning. More than anything, I was worried about an insect-weakened spruce toppling over and landing on or near me. The loud creaking noise from the strong winds made it worse—I stuck my head out of the tent, turned on my headlamp and took a quick inventory of the trees in the surrounding area. As far as I could tell, there were no trees that had fallen in the vicinity. They also seemed to have strong root systems, like the oaks and hickories that I was more familiar with. I managed to sleep in small 15- and 20-minute increments for the remainder of the night, always wary of the rocking-chair groans of the towering spruces.

⚜

I peeked out of the tent about 8 a.m., and the rain was pouring down. My two Floridian neighbors were already packed up and preparing to leave. They had both slept in hammocks the previous evening, and they said they found the weather peaceful; the winds provided a gentle swaying movement that rocked them to sleep.

I had never set out on a hike in the middle of a driving rainstorm before, but I felt I had to make up some of my lost ground. The first two days, I had only managed to cover a total distance of fifteen miles, and that left over one hundred miles to go before I reached Damascus. So I quickly packed up, gobbled down a granola bar, and set out.

I still had another 400 feet or so to climb before I reached the summit of Unaka Mountain, and the rain showed no sign of relenting as I started slogging down the cliff-lined and water-logged switchbacks on the far side of the mountain.

At one point, the rain was so heavy I climbed underneath a large boulder that overhung the trail and I found a low, dry place to perch and ride out the storm. I was soaking wet but still had enough of a sense of humor to snap a selfie of myself with my sopping hair plastered to the side of my face. I could only see the legs of the hikers who passed by, who were completely unaware that someone was huddled under a rock.

At midday, the rain showed signs of softening, and I continued my downward descent. I stopped briefly at Cherry Gap Shelter for lunch and learned that many of the hikers there were planning on staying at the Greasy Creek Friendly Hostel, about seven miles away. Despite its name, the hostel, which was an old 1940s-style converted farmhouse, enjoyed a reputation on the trail as a ramshackle but cheap and welcoming place to stay. It was about a mile off the trail, so that was a deterrent, but if the rains picked up again, a hostel was something I had to consider.

Any possibility of staying at the hostel was eliminated when I walked through Greasy Creek Gap without seeing the sign pointing in the direction of the hostel. I passed some southbound hikers, and I asked them how far it was to the hostel. They looked puzzled and told me I had passed the turnoff a mile back. The sun had broken out by this point, so I was not too disappointed and set my sights on Clyde Smith Shelter, just a couple of miles away.

I pulled off the trail and walked the short distance to the shelter in the early evening. The sun was still shining, but the weather had turned cold. All obvious camping spots were taken, so I had to take a small spot next to the trail that led from the AT to the shelter structure.

I set my gear down and headed down the hill to fill up with water. There I met Rafael, who was contemplating an end to his thru-hike. His knee was inflamed and it showed no signs of getting better. The condition had first appeared when he had crossed into North Carolina, and he had been dealing with it for almost three hundred miles. He said the only thing keeping him on the trail was the fear of embarrassment if he went back home. It would leave a void in his life—like all thru-hikers, he had set aside months of his life that were to be completely devoted to the trail. So the first few weeks would be uncomfortable, explaining to one person after another why he had ended his hike early. It was clear to me that he had had enough and would be leaving soon.

Rafael did have enough energy to get in a rather heated argument with Jules, a young blonde thru-hiker pulling on a joint. The two were vigorously debating whether a nearby vine crawling up a tree was poison oak. I filled up my Camelbak with water and headed back to the shelter while the two still argued.

I ran into Doc at the shelter, where he was eating at the picnic table. I pulled up next to him and talked. He admitted that he was really struggling with the physical toll the trail was taking on him. He spent almost all his time at shelters inside his tent, lying down and recuperating from the day's hike. At age 64, he had received the blessing of his doctor to thru-hike. He was slightly heavy-set and had high blood pressure, and his doctor had warned him to use "common sense." He said somewhat regretfully that he was holding his daughter up. "She'd be in Damascus by now if she didn't have to slow down because of me," he said with a shrug. There was no chance of the two separating—she clearly adored her father.

I climbed into my tent at dusk as the temperatures continued to drop. It was the last night of April, but it felt like it was near freezing, especially when the wind blew. I slept in three layers of clothing, including my gloves and skullcap. I had misjudged and brought my warm weather sleeping bag, so even in my swaddled condition, the chill of the night woke me up on several occasions.

⁂

I woke up early on the first day of May and crawled out of my tent to a 31-degree temperature. Other campers were slowly getting ready for the day, and the cold was fogging their breath.

Today was a big day—the trail led over Roan Mountain, which at 6,285 feet is the fifth highest peak on the Appalachian Trail. Roan had derived its name from the prevalence of red-berried Mountain Ash trees, which were called rowans in the homeland of the early English and Scottish settlers. At its lower elevations, such vegetation as southern as subtropical orchids can be found. But at the mountain's height, remnants from the ice age remain, including wood sorrel, witch hobble, and green alder, a shrub tree usually found in New England.[21]

I had managed only 27 miles in three days of hiking; normally, I would have covered another five or ten miles over this same time span. The weather was a big part of it, and after a brief respite for the next few days, the rain was forecasted to return in force by the end of the week.

I reached Hughes Gap in mid-morning and it represented the low point, at just over 4,000 feet, of the Roan Highlands, an almost 20-mile-long massif. Roan Mountain makes up most of the Roan Highlands, and it actually consists of five different peaks, one of which, Roan High Knob, at 6,285 feet, is renowned for having the highest elevation shelter on the AT. The other three sections of Roan Mountain that the trail would cross are known collectively as Grassy Ridge and are on the opposite side of Carver's Gap.

The initial approach to Roan Mountain was a comfortable grade, covering 1,000 feet over two miles. A hiker I passed along the way told me that switchbacks were introduced to Roan in the last decade; the challenge of a vertical path leading to the top was unimaginable to me.

I reached Ash Gap and enjoyed a leisurely lunch in a sun-splashed meadow. The day was warming up, and I had long since shed my fleece jacket and the lower, detachable portion of my synthetic waterproof pants.

The second part of the approach, climbing upward from Ash Gap, was steeper, but the dense coniferous forest provided a comfortable shade as I made my way up to the top. I reached the top of Roan Mountain in the early afternoon and traversed the camel hump of Tollhouse Gap that connected it with Roan High Knob. Along the way, I passed the sign marking the old Cloudland Hotel, which was built in 1885 and was touted as a summer getaway and health resort for well-heeled guests looking to escape the unrelenting heat of the eastern seaboard's summers. Guests took a 12-mile journey via stagecoaches from Johnson City, Tennessee, to reach the hotel. Fires burned constantly in the interior, as temperatures would drop into the low forties in the summer. The hotel, however, was too expensive to maintain due to its constant exposure to high winds, rain and snow. By 1910, it had been abandoned and now the only reminder of the former 166-room structure is the Rhododendron Gardens (the largest of its type in the world) that used to front the hotel.[22] I briefly imagined the ghosts of hotel visitors, resplendent in their Victorian finery, before heading back down the trail.

I passed the shelter and briefly considered staying there for the evening—in addition to being the highest shelter on the AT, it is also the only four-sided structure along the trail. I had checked my map, and there were spots marked for both camping and water at Carver's

Gap, where Highway 143 crossed. I was feeling pretty good, so I decided to continue on to Carver's Gap.

The descent was over a stony path that was an invitation to a sprained or broken ankle—this was probably the old route for the stage-coaches headed to the Cloudland Hotel. I reached Carver's Gap in the late afternoon, but I did not find the promised camping spot. I found a small, cleared out area in the woods, just to the west of the highway. I ignored the tattered remains of toilet paper that were on the other side of a large log that flanked one side of my spot.

There was a rest area at the top of the gap above my camping site, and I could hear tourists pulling over and talking. They had no idea I was just on the other side of a wall of trees. Again I was surprised by how far voices travel when they are not in competition with other ambient noise—I could easily hear conversations from a hundred feet away.

I cooked a packet of ramen noodles in my Jetboil, and since the weather was so cold, I ate it all, including the broth. Settling in was difficult, because I could hear the rush of cars speeding over the gap. Once again, I put on every bit of warm clothing I could find and cocooned myself inside my sleeping bag. Temperatures fell below freezing that night, and I shivered and worried about hypothermia.

The black bear appeared again in one of my fitful dreams. He had grown old, well past middle age. There were patches of baldness on his thick fur, and he reeked of the shit that he had rolled in. He sat on his bottom, like a human, with his arms stretched over his splayed legs and his paws draped over the insides of his knees.

The restaurant parking lot was nearly empty, and only a few lights were on inside. A breeze caused a tattered curtain hanging from an open window to flutter. I could hear the sound of a car passing by, its tires spraying water from the puddles that had collected on the highway. The mountains in the distance were dark and shrouded in mist and a sharp, cold wind blew through the trees, a premonition of an approaching storm.

I pulled up my collar as I approached his cage. He slowly raised his eyes to meet mine. There was no shine to his brown eyes, only a dull sadness. His head rolled forward, his head hitting his chest as he fell into a deep sleep.

A thin sheet of ice coated the surface of the water in my plastic bottle the next morning. The temperature gauge on my pack read 29 degrees. I brewed up the same meal from the previous evening, ramen noodles swimming in a steaming broth.

I walked the short distance to the rest area to dump off my trash. The trashcans were overflowing, so I went inside the bathroom to drop off my bag filled with food packaging. Gagging from the fetid smell, I forced myself not to look at the toilet, which had probably not been serviced in months.

Across the paved highway were a series of small balds that were, geologically, outcroppings of Roan Mountain. After crossing the highway, the trail enters a thicket of rhododendron before turning into a dense, balsam fir forest. After exiting the forest on Round Bald, the 360-degree views of the Appalachians that I had not seen since Max Patch suddenly came into view. With no tree cover, the winds cut through me as I wound my way over the exposed bald. My face was almost completely covered by a scarf, and my fingers were close to numb from the cold—I had only brought a pair of thin cotton gloves for my mid-spring hike.

I had just started my descent into Low Gap when three young male hikers passed me. I spoke to the sandy-haired heavyset one bringing up the rear who resembled Samwell Tarly from *Game of Thrones.* Rain, he said, was coming in, with snow in the higher elevations. Pretty much everyone was getting off the trail at the end of the day and riding out the storms at Mountain Harbour Bed and Breakfast at the next gap, which was crossed by Highway 19E.

I pondered my options as I ate lunch at Stan Murray Shelter. This trip was presenting just about every weather challenge possible, and I was ill-equipped for freezing, snowy weather. As I ascended Little Hump Mountain, I looked downward and to the west and spotted the iconic Overmountain Shelter, an old red barn converted to a shelter. The day had warmed, but it was not difficult to imagine a sudden change for the worse; I had seen it happen many times before along the trail.

Near the summit of Little Hump, I called the Mountain Harbour and was told that they were fully booked for the night. There was the possibility of paying a fee for a spot to pitch a tent in the camping area, but I was still eight miles away from the hostel and it was mid-afternoon.

I was not going to push myself to get to a camping spot that far away that would cost me money when there would be plenty of spots to pitch my tent along the way.

I also made the decision to call Uncle Johnny's and arrange for pick-up the next day at 11 a.m. I made the decision without any remorse—it was time to get off the trail; I had come on this section hike ill-prepared for a Blackberry Winter. Johnny took my call and wrote down the details for when I would be picked up the next morning off of Highway 19. After we hung up, he called me back an hour later and we went over the same details related to my pick-up that we had discussed earlier. I thought that was a little strange but did not think that much of it and continued up the trail.

I filled up with water at the creek in Bradley Gap and was halfway up the summit of Hump Mountain (the next peak after Little Hump), when I slumped down on to a thatch of thick heath grass that bordered the trail. I was exhausted—Hump Mountain was the last bald in the Roan Highlands, and it was a 600-foot goat trail straight to the summit. As I was staring at the clear azure skies trying to catch my breath, a woman and her dog walked up to me.

"Yankee" was a labradoodle, and her owner, Jeannie, was a thru-hiker who was "slack-packing" to Mountain Harbour Bed and Break-fast—she had dropped her pack off with a friend that morning at Carver's Gap, who in turn dropped it off at Mountain Harbour.

Yankee instantly recognized my state of exhaustion and flopped on the ground next to me while also taking deep breaths. Jeannie poured some water into a small plastic tray, and Yankee lapped it up.

Jeannie was from Massachusetts and hiking the trail alone, except for her faithful companion. She was very direct in that unique New England way that I liked and freely shared her opinions about the difficulty of the Roan Highlands. She and Yankee moved on, and I picked myself up and continued up the trail.

The Roan Highlands have massive boulders that are un-obscured by trees—they appear to have been tossed around by bored giants and then left there millennia ago. The stark landscape reminded me of the "tors" of Devon in southwest England as described in the Sherlock Holmes novel *The Hound of the Baskervilles*.

As I approached the summit of Hump Mountain, I saw Yankee

Hiking the Roan Highlands.

perched on a boulder, looking down the trail and barking. I called to her, and she gave me a quizzical look and then bounded up the trail back to her owner.

The stark bareness of the balds returned to forest lushness on the east side of Hump Mountain as I started my long descent down the Roan Highlands to Carver's Gap. I crossed a broad meadow bordered by a farm on its southern end. On the eastern edge of the meadow was a wooded rise called Doll Flats. As I began walking across the meadow, I could see that the small ridge was dotted with tents. I quickly decided that this is where I would spend the evening; it was still another three miles to the highway, and night was fast approaching.

As the trail skirts Doll Flats, there is a small, carved wooden sign that announces, "Leaving N.C." This marked the last spot of the 96 miles that the AT traversed in North Carolina—this does not count the more than 200 miles where the trail zigzags between the border with Tennessee—most days I crossed back and forth between the borders of the two states at multiple points without realizing it. I silently congratulated myself for finishing two of the 14 states on the AT.

I pitched a tent on the far western end of the ridge and hung my pack. Most of the hikers were already inside for the night. As the sun set over the summit of Hump Mountain, the temperature dropped dramatically, and I ate a hurried meal of dehydrated beef stroganoff before tucking in.

At nightfall, the sound of a freight train, in the form of a wind whipping across the meadow, roared through Doll Flats. I had never heard wind this loud, and I thought it might be what a tornado sounded like. My tent was situated in an east-west direction, and the force of the wind curled the top of my tent downward, almost touching the ground. The only thing keeping my tent from rolling down the trail like tumbleweed was my 230 pounds of dead weight anchoring the floor to the ground.

I got up in the darkness with my headlamp turned on and rearranged my tent in a north-south direction, thinking that the wind blasts would not be as bad but it made no difference—the gusts seemed to be attacking from every direction. I took a few swigs of moonshine and hunkered down for the night.

The next morning at daybreak, I walked outside and saw that my food pack, which I had hung on a nearby branch, had been pummeled like a piñata; the force of the wind had knocked it around until the string holding the bottom of the pack shut had opened, and its contents had been scattered over a distance of 40 feet. I guess the powerful winds had kept the bears and raccoons away—they could have walked into the campsite and had easy pickings for their treats. I talked with another camper who said wind speed had reached 80 miles per hour the previous night. I have no way of knowing how he could have recorded the wind velocity, but that sounded about right.

The wind had died down in the early morning, and the day started sunny and cold. I had an easy hike of four miles down the eastern slope of Hump Mountain, the final segment of the Roan Highlands.

I moved quickly down a series of easy switchbacks through woods that were brimming with life and the possibilities of a new day. I spotted a black-bellied salamander on a fern-covered rotted log before he saw me and slithered under a wet, mossy rock. A red-tailed hawk swirled above me, looking for prey before the bad weather once again moved in. A wood thrush provided a steady accompaniment of flute-like "eee-oh-lays!"

I arrived at my appointed pick-up spot on Highway 19-E fifteen minutes early. I called Uncle Johnny's and learned that there was a mix-up; apparently Johnny had not passed on my request from the previous day for a pick-up, so my driver would not be arriving for more than an hour after the scheduled pick-up time.

A steady stream of hikers followed me down the trail and stopped briefly at the highway. Many were staying at the Mountain Harbour Hostel, just a quarter-mile walk away. Others were looking for rides into the town of Roan Mountain, Tennessee, where they would look for lodging and the local Dollar General store to restock on supplies. One hiker donned his bamboo Chinese "coolie" hat—he claimed it intrigued passing drivers and made it more likely that he would be picked up while hitchhiking.

Everyone commented about the weather, and almost ever hiker I spoke with was going to ride out the approaching storm in local motels or hostels. The forecasts were still showing no break in the weather for the next two days, and the National Weather Service was not backing off its predictions of snow in the higher elevations.

Dave, the amiable owner of the Doe Rest Hostel in the town of Roan Mountain, passed by and stopped his van several times during my wait. He handed out free sodas to all hikers, and offered them rides into town. He and his wife had retired several years earlier, having lived in both San Diego and South Florida. When making the decision on where to retire, they studied weather and climate across the United States. They ultimately decided on the southern Appalachians because of its four distinct seasons and moderate temperatures.

I was at Mile Marker 388.2 on the AT and a little depressed. I kept expecting, at some point, that the trail would get easier. But that never happened, not when finishing the climb out of NOC or leaving the Smoky Mountains or completing my hike up Roan Mountain. There was always another mountain down the trail, equally if not more difficult. I was talking about this with a young woman hiker waiting for a ride in to town. She agreed, and offered, "I hear it gets easier after Mount Rogers in Virginia." There is always hope, I suppose.

My driver finally pulled into the parking area in an old, rusted 1970s Buick GS that reeked of cigarette smoke. He was a transplant from Pennsylvania who had moved into the area years ago, attracted by its beauty and low cost of living. We passed by one forlorn house after another with unkempt yards, rotting porches, and ancient vehicles left out to slowly rust in the weeds and high grass. Life in Appalachia has always been difficult—it is obviously isolated, and the soil is thin and rocky, which does not lend itself well to farming. And globalism has hollowed out the manufacturing base of textiles and furniture that was once so prevalent in these parts. But the despair now seems different, as if there is no hope.

I have a strong strain of "hillbilly" blood running through my veins, and my ancestors dealt with economic hardship differently. My great-grandfather made and lost a fortune selling moonshine—certainly nothing to be proud of, but it did require entrepreneurship and drive. During the Great Depression, my maternal grandfather would load up the vegetables he had grown on his small farm in the north Georgia hills and drive to Atlanta and sell produce from the bed of his truck.

His wife, my grandmother, bought a women's clothing store in nearby Gainesville and she, my grandfather and my mother moved there in the 1940s. That may not seem like an unsettling life event now, but back then, uprooting a family and moving from a small rural community to a medium-sized city to run a business would have carried a lot of risk. Although she never went to college (that simply did not happen in the early 20th century in her part of the world for a woman, even one as capable as she), my grandmother was an avid reader and learner even into old age (she lived until the age of 99). After a long day at her store, she would come home and complete a crossword puzzle and read textbooks on English grammar or Renaissance art, always striving for self-improvement. And when I was a small boy, she taught me how to read before I started school, giving me an immediate leg up when I started my formal education.

I had two great-uncles who took the "Hillbilly Highway" to Detroit in the 1930s to work in the Ford plant. They were joined by thousands of others from Appalachia who were able to get decent paying work on the assembly lines. The jobs they performed were largely unskilled, before full-scale automation, but they were also well paying. One uncle held a paintbrush coated in paint to place a white stripe dead center on model T's as they moved down the assembly line. While they took jobs in the industrial cities of the north, they never left their Appalachian roots behind. Their plight was captured in the famous Steve Earle song "Hillbilly Highway."

The high-paying jobs for unskilled labor are gone; there is no longer a Hillbilly Highway that will lead to economic salvation. The small cottage industries (hostels, outfitters, shuttles, etc.) that have sprung up as the AT continues to grow in popularity have eased the pain only slightly—most of the jobs tied to these businesses seem to be held by outsiders who moved into the region, attracted by its climate and beauty. By contrast, those who have multi-generational ties to Appalachia often feel trapped and left behind. Studies show that the white working class in America is the most pessimistic group in the country, much more than African Americans or Hispanics in the same economic strata. The inner spark that their ancestors possessed seems extinguished, and some blame their problems on outsiders, particularly the government and the "elites" and all too often, turn tragically to opiates to ease the pain.

The social ills that plague much of our inner cities ravage Appalachia to an even greater extent. Divorce and the decline of the extended family lead to fewer role models. Over the last century, my family has had its fair share of men who engaged in destructive, anti-social behavior that harmed and shamed their families. But they and others were shunned and even physically punished in their communities unless they "straightened up and flew right." And there were always success stories to point to, some cousin or uncle or aunt that had achieved success far from home.

As we drove closer to Erwin, where I had dropped off my car, I looked out the window as the bruise-colored clouds rolled in from the west. A short while later, we pulled in to Uncle Johnny's and I handed the driver $70 for the ride.

Johnny was behind the counter, and it was clear that he was not well. His head was drooped towards his chest, and when I asked him how he was doing, he looked up at me sadly and mumbled something I did not understand before letting his chin fall back down to his chest. I glanced at the young woman behind the counter, who gave me a knowing look, handed me a towel and offered me a free shower and a Gatorade for my troubles.

John M. Shores, Jr., died less than a year later at the age of 72. He will forever be remembered as a trail legend; a man who had a vision for his hostel on the Nolichucky, and he poured his soul into the place. My experience with him from the previous autumn was not unique— he treated everyone that entered his place like a long-lost friend and passed on his tips, encouragement, and entertaining anecdotes to anyone who had time to pull up a chair to listen. I am grateful that I had the opportunity to spend a couple of hours with him.

After a luxuriously long shower, I got in my car and headed south, eager to outpace the storm moving in. I stopped in Asheville at a combination bar and package store to restock my western North Carolina beer inventory, which had grown dangerously low back home. As I was nursing a beer and working on a crossword puzzle with some locals, a bolt of lightning knocked out the power in downtown Asheville. Rain soon came rushing in torrents down the street outside the bar, and I smiled inwardly, knowing I had made the right decision to leave the trail.

As I slowly drove home and stopped at roadside stands to pick up boiled peanuts, ramps, and mountain cider, I realized that I was at a crossroads with the AT. I was pushing farther and farther northward, and it was no longer an easy trip to get to my last jump-off point. I was also devoting one to two weeks each year of my vacation time to the AT, and my children were growing up fast, and I wanted to travel some more with them before it was too late.

The physical toll that the AT takes on someone like me, nearing 60, is also a factor that cannot be downplayed. There are lots of people in my age group and older who hike the trail, but each trip was getting more difficult. I was starting to feel like Doc—time on the trail not spent hiking was time I wanted to spend lying flat on my back inside my tent.

There is also the danger of hiking the trail, particularly alone. The odds of dying on the trail are phenomenally low—the mortality rate is much lower than the daily commute to work when taking into account the two to three million people that are on the AT annually. But they do occur, from trees falling on campers to heart attacks induced by strenuous uphill climbs, falls from steep precipices, and even drowning from fording flooded rivers in the northeast.

As I neared Atlanta, I started thinking that perhaps my most recently concluded hike might also be my last. At a minimum, I knew I would not be returning that fall—my family and I were finally taking that long-delayed trip to Europe over Christmas, and I needed to save money and allot vacation time for that.

Section Hike 9
Roan Mountain, Tennessee, to Damascus, Virginia
October 7–14, 2018 (77 Miles)

I started another job in finance in April 2018 and was spending most of my spare time with my wife building an antiques and collectibles business, which we had steadily grown over the previous five years. I had not given much thought to the AT in the year since I had last stepped off—my family and I had taken a trip over Christmas to Germany and Austria, and I was looking forward to planning and putting together similar trips in the near future, while my children were still young but unencumbered with their own families.

I was surprised in the spring of 2018 when a man I have known for years approached me at a charity event in Atlanta, and after several glasses of wine, expressed an interest in hiking the Appalachian Trail. I promised to keep that in mind, although I was uncertain if I would ever step foot on the AT again. This friend's (whose trail name, Wood Bat, was based on his lifelong involvement in youth baseball and his nostalgic yearning for the return of wooden bats, which were replaced years ago by the aluminum versions) enthusiasm about the trail, however, re-sparked my interest—his keenness was similar to mine five years ago when I first started to consider the possibility of hiking the AT.

I began making tentative arrangements over the summer for another trip in the autumn of 2018. It was an interesting and unique experience for me—thus far, I had hiked alone and did not have to consider the needs of a novice backpacker. With eight section hikes already under my belt, something important but obvious to me might be something that would be overlooked by Wood Bat. So I passed on random thoughts as they occurred to me on what type of gear he would need and how he should physically prepare himself for the upcoming ordeal. The back-and-forth was good for me—I am not a good organizer and planner—I tend to wing things and not prepare lists of what I might need on trips. This lack of organization had caused me some small amount of grief on previous section hikes when I left behind or did not order crucial supplies or needed gear.

Early October of 2018 was unseasonably warm, as was the entire month of September that preceded it. I was getting up early every morning and walking the steep hills of my neighborhood in warm and humid temperatures. I studied extended weather forecasts for northeastern Tennessee and the warmer than normal temperatures were expected to continue for at least the first half of our planned trip. There was also a chance of rain for at least two days, part of a cold front that would usher in cooler weather.

Wood Bat and I set off on our five-and-a-half-hour drive in the mid-afternoon of a Saturday. We were headed to the Mountain Harbour Bed and Breakfast off of Highway 19 East in Roan Mountain, Tennessee, and from there we planned on hiking to Damascus, Virginia. The terrain maps showed moderately difficult climbs—Shannon Hill, a member of the family that owns and runs Mountain Harbour, told me over the phone when I booked my reservation that the hike was "easy," and the most difficult part was the initial five miles climbing east from Highway 19. Of course, nothing on the AT is "easy" but I knew what she meant; it certainly looked less forbidding than the Roan Highlands, which lay on the opposite side of the highway that I had hiked a year and a half earlier.

Wood Bat and I weaved our way steadily north and east through the sightseeing and college football game day traffic. As we passed Cornelia, Clayton, Franklin and Sylva, I answered all of his questions and passed on any knowledge about hiking and camping that might be useful.

Wood Bat seemed to be mentally and physically prepared for the physical beating that the AT metes out. Lean and well over six feet tall, he had trained for months walking the hills of Atlanta with a weighted pack. His nature was both taciturn and thoughtful, and those attributes seemed to be well suited for the trail. He owned his own creative marketing business, and he and his wife had raised three sons, one of whom was on the cusp of receiving his final promotion from AAA to Major League Baseball.

We had hoped to arrive at Mountain Harbour around 7 p.m., but traffic and several stops along the way delayed our trip. As darkness set in, we called ahead to Mountain Harbour to let them know we would be arriving late. We were warned by Dave Hill that our dining options that time of night would be limited, so we ended up pulling into a diner in Unicoi, Tennessee, for a quick meal of country fried chicken, green beans and mashed potatoes. Several of the waiting staff were rail thin with scabs on their arms, and I could not help but wonder if they were meth addicts. Nevertheless, we now had food in our stomachs to tide us over until the next morning, when Mountain Harbour's legendary breakfast awaited us.

After we pulled in shortly before 9 p.m., we crossed a small bridge over a creek and walked up the steps to the main house; a rambling redwood-colored structure that was surrounded by a porch on three sides and was perched on a hill overlooking the creek. A large, inflatable fire-breathing dragon had been set up on the lawn for Halloween, and several goats foraged in the grass.

Located just three-tenths of a mile north of the AT, Mountain Harbour is perfectly located for NOBO hikers worn out by the Roan Highlands. SOBO hikers approaching from the less strenuous eastern approach are also drawn to Mountain Harbour for its legendary $12 breakfasts. Transplanted Californians Terry and Mary Hill purchased the property in 2003 and gradually added lodging space, a general store, and shuttle service. Terry passed away in 2016, and his widow Mary and their son Dave and daughter-in-law Shannon now run the facility.[23]

Dave directed us to our room in an old converted barn on the opposite side of the creek. It was a small, cedar-scented attic room with two twin beds on the floor. We turned on the fan, because it was still unusually warm at night in October, this deep in the mountains.

We slept soundly, aided by the fan that not only cooled off the warm room but also provided just enough sound to drown out any ambient noise.

⋘✕⋙

Breakfast started at 8 a.m., and we walked over to the main house to load up on calories before starting on the trail. The food was set up buffet-style in the kitchen, and we piled up our plates with egg casserole, sausage, fresh fruit, and homemade biscuits with sawmill gravy. We sat at the dining table with Rafiki and Scout, a couple from the north Georgia mountains that were going to section hike a different portion of the AT. A couple from Indiana was also there, in town for the nearby "tall tale" convention in Jonesborough, Tennessee.

Rafiki, a well-built middle-aged bald man who served as a probation officer in northeast Georgia, was recovering from surgery—he had had to have his ankle fused after a motorcycle accident several years earlier. Scout, a diminutive grandmother who worked as a court recorder, was excited to have him back on the trail—his injury had forced him to take a two-year hiatus from hiking.

We talked about the benefits of section hiking—I could never imagine myself as a thru-hiker, I enjoy the comforts of civilization too much. Scout agreed that the AT was better bitten off in small five- to seven-day chunks; she liked to stay abreast of news related to her extended family.

We collectively tried to come up with a story to help the couple from Indiana with a tall tale for the convention that they were attending. With Halloween approaching, the best we could come up with was a ghost that thru-hiked the AT, which I seriously doubted they would use.

Wood Bat and I finished our meal and headed back to our room to gather our gear, pay our bill and set out on the trail. Shortly before 9 a.m., we began the short walk south on Highway 19 East where we would join the trail. The humidity was thick, and even though it was still early in the morning, I broke into a heavy sweat before even setting foot on the trail.

Wood Bat walked right by the white blaze on a tree signifying the continuation of the trail. I had sent him an email earlier on trail signage and briefly coached him up again on the single white, double white (sharp change in direction) and blue blazes (side trails).

We set off into the Pisgah National Forest and up the trail towards Buck Mountain, a series of three distinct, moderately difficult climbs with a net elevation gain of about 1,000 feet. There had been rain the previous day, and it had brought out a small, yellow and black box turtle that was so well camouflaged I almost stepped on it.

I slipped on a slick rock and stuck my right hiking pole into the ground for support. The pole sank into mud, and as my body weight leaned into it, the metal pole snapped in two. Less than one mile into almost an 80-mile hike, and I was already down to one pole.

Wood Bat moved ahead, which was not unexpected. I had coached him on the need to "HYOH" (hike your own hike) and to not feel bad about separating and moving ahead. He rounded a turn well ahead of me and was gone from my line of sight.

The day continued to warm and the humidity thickened as I wound my way through a series of open meadows, my face and arms exposed to the bright sun. My boots and lower legs soon became wet from the high grass of the meadows, which was still soaked in early morning dew. Several ridge vistas opened up where I had great views of the Roan Highlands to the west.

I was able to practice a new breathing technique I had learned online from several section hikers. I was determined to reduce the discomfort of uphill climbs by breathing in through my nose and out through my mouth, slowly. "Breathe in roses, blow out candles," I kept reminding myself as I ascended ridges. I also practiced taking small, baby steps. It seemed to help; I was huffing and puffing less and taking fewer breaks.

As late morning approached, the trail passed by a family cemetery surrounded by a chain-link fence. As I rounded a corner, a near life-sized statue of a painted Jesus suddenly popped up, which gave me a start—my first thought was that it was a real person.

The trail passed over a gravel road next to a red brick and white chapel, Buck Mountain Baptist Church, which was holding Sunday morning services. I caught up with Wood Bat at midday at Jones Falls, a spectacular 100-foot waterfall that rose above our rocky perch just off the trail. Wood Bat had already eaten and was taking a series of photographs—he had come equipped with a professional-grade camera and a GoPro to record the trip.

We had covered roughly five miles and before Wood Bat set out again on the trail, we agreed to meet up again at Mountaineer Falls Shelter, a distance of four miles. The terrain looked manageable, mainly easy downhills and a mile-long stretch of trail that ran parallel to the Elk River.

I was encountering very few hikers, which was somewhat surprising. I had told Wood Bat we would meet up with a lot of SOBOs during our hike, but thus far, I had only met a few day hikers. The Elk River moved by slowly, covered with yellow poplar leaves that had fallen in the past few days. At some point early in the afternoon, I passed the "400" mark, signifying a total of 400 miles I had hiked on the AT.

On a gentle uphill, I ran into Wood Bat. He had stopped to rest, and it was clear from his raspy voice that he was tired and wanted to call it a day. We had hiked nine miles, and I understood. To keep us on pace to reach Damascus by Friday evening, I had hoped to hike a few more miles, but it was a completely new experience for Wood Bat—I had encouraged him to work out before our trip but at the same time warned him that no type of exercise routine can adequately prepare anyone for the unique rigors of the AT.

We replenished our water supply at Mountaineer Falls and hiked the short distance uphill to a campsite adjacent to the shelter. It was only 3 p.m., so we set up our tents in a leisurely manner before thunder rumbled in about a half hour later. I had picked up another tip online— put the tent tarp *inside* the tent; this prevented moisture from collecting between the bottom of the tent and the tarp. I had always been taught to put the tarp underneath the tent. As the rain shower moved in and pelted my tent with thick drops, I lay inside, snug and dry and unworried over the prospect of water seeping inside to soak my sleeping bag and air mattress.

The rain passed about 4 p.m., and we emerged from our tents to gather firewood. By nightfall, we had a decent blaze going, which I felt was somewhat wasted because the temperature had barely dipped below 70 degrees. I showed Wood Bat how to use a Jetboil, and we slowly ate our cooked dehydrated meals directly from the bags. We talked about the most important qualities a hiker needed to cope with the AT. I told Wood Bat there were no substitutes for grit and a positive attitude. I acknowledged that this was a pretty corny explanation, but a single-

Footbridge across the Elk River.

mindedness that constantly fends off negative thoughts was my best formula for success.

There are always things to complain about on the AT—the weather, the terrain, the lack of water, too much water, equipment malfunction, hunger, injuries, fatigue, etc. For the most part, I have no control over the things that cause discomfort on the trail, so I simply push them to the corners of my mind, to the extent possible. It simply does no good to focus on the negative. By my very unscientific calculation, I spend roughly 80 percent of my hiking time in some level of discomfort—I am winded from an uphill, putting stress on my lower body on a steep and rocky downhill, or feeling pangs of pain in my shoulders or lower back from carrying 32 pounds on my back. I simply accept the nagging aches and less than optimal hiking conditions. Dwelling on the negatives can quickly snowball into a miserable experience, and I constantly remind myself of how privileged I am to spend time walking along the spine of these ancient, beautiful, and unforgiving mountains.

The night was still warm when I crawled into my tent, and I used my sleeping bag as a pillow. I didn't unroll my bag until the early morning, when temperatures dropped into the low 60s.

❧

Monday morning dawned with every indication of the day being sunny, hot, and humid, with temperatures once again rising above 80 degrees. I dressed appropriately, in shorts, before setting out shortly before 9 a.m. I left the camp area a good 30 minutes before Wood Bat, secure in the knowledge that he would catch up and pass me in a few hours.

I wanted us to hike at least 12 or 13 miles that day, as we left the Pisgah and entered the Cherokee National Forest. The trail was pretty flat over this stretch, with a 500-foot uphill at the end of the day over White Rocks Mountain. This would put us in a good position to tackle Pond Mountain the next day—from the look of the map, Pond Mountain looked like our biggest challenge on the section hike; three miles of uphill with an elevation gain of 2,000 feet, followed by a three-mile descent.

I passed patches of purple and gold dwarf irises and red toadstool mushrooms. The aroma from resin-scented white pines, my favorite tree, was becoming more and more prevalent. The gray granite rocks that I always associate with the trail were giving way to pale limestone. There were numerous footbridges over the Laurel Fork, and they were covered with golden tulip poplar leaves. It was altogether a gentle section of trail, and I stopped frequently to soak in the beauty.

Wood Bat caught up with me just past one footbridge, when Space Ghost, a heavyset 50ish section hiker, passed us going southward. Space Ghost had started his hike in Damascus, and he was planning on going all the way to Standing Bear Farm Hostel, just north of the Smokies. In total, he was planning on a three-week section hike of over 250 miles.

Space Ghost told us of a nice spot to camp, a meadow about three miles beyond Moreland Gap Shelter. Before we parted ways, I asked him about Pond Mountain, which we would climb the next day. He shook his head, and grimly predicted, "You are not going to like it."

As I was ascending the White Rocks Mountain, a herd of white tail deer darted across the trail about 100 feet ahead of me. The number of deer in the United States is estimated at around 30 million, with North Carolina alone accounting for about 1 million of that total. After being hunted almost to extinction by 1900, the total number of deer had reached pre–Columbian levels by the year 2000—but after peaking in that year at 35 million, the total has been in steady decline since then, particularly in the western states. Hunters kill about 6 million deer a year, but this is more than a million less than were harvested in 2000.[24]

There are myriad reasons for the recent decline in population: wildfires, loss of habitat, drought, increases in chronic wasting disease, and the spread of coyotes are all factors cited for the fall in herd numbers. The Cherokee in western North Carolina lease some of their tribal land to exotic deer farmers, which is a controversial practice; deer confined in one area are more likely to transmit chronic wasting disease, a contagious brain disease that is always fatal.[25]

One deer predator from the west that is no longer a threat to the eastern population is the cougar, or mountain lion. The last cougar in the eastern states was spotted almost a century ago, and in early 2018, the U.S. Fish and Wildlife Service declared the eastern cougar subspecies extinct.[26] They were hunted to extinction for both taxidermy and agricultural reasons—farmers killed them because they were a threat to their livestock. There are many reports of cougars in the Appalachians, but if they do exist, there is no firm evidence to support their return to their native habitat. If they do exist, they are likely former pets that have been released.[27]

Other animals that formerly thrived in the Appalachians that are now extinct include the Carolina parakeet, a bright green and yellow bird that was the only parrot native to the eastern United States. The species was wiped out for its stunning feathers, which were used in ladies' hats. One reason for the ease in hunting them is that when wounded, an injured parakeet would scream distress calls. Other parakeets in the flock would hear it, and circle around the wounded bird until they were also shot.[28]

American passenger pigeons were once thought to number between two and three billion, which probably made them the most numerous bird species on Earth in the mid–19th century, and their winter roosting grounds were the riverbeds of the southern Appalachians. The Little Pigeon River, which I crossed over after exiting the northern end of the Great Smoky Mountain National Forest, and nearby Pigeon Forge, Tennessee, were both named for these creatures. Their meat became fashionable in large cities, and settlers cleared out much of their brush habitat, which caused many to starve (the birds lived off of beechnuts and acorns). Finally, with their numbers greatly diminished, the American passenger pigeon simply stopped breeding—ornithologists believe that their mating urges were triggered by the sound of their huge flocks, a noise that resembled sleigh bells.[29]

Perhaps the most tragic loss of flora was the demise of the American chestnut tree. This hardwood once comprised an estimated 20 percent of all the trees in the Appalachian Mountains. It is believed that one-third of the trees in the Smoky Mountains alone were once chestnuts. These trees thrived in elevations of between 1,000 and 4,500 feet, and they were heavily ingrained in southern Appalachian culture. Farmers in the mountains would let their hogs range free, much like farmers in Spain still do today when fattening their pigs to make jamón ibérico. American hogs would live off of chestnut mast on forest floors that were sometimes four inches deep. The largest trees could produce ten bushels of nuts a year. Wild game, such as deer, turkeys, squirrels and grouse depended on chestnuts as a main food source, and people also enjoyed their chestnuts, not cooked on an open fire, but usually in Dutch ovens.[30] Black bears were also heavily dependent upon chestnuts as part of their diets. Cherokees added the nuts from the chestnut to make their corn-meal dough. They also used its leaves to help with heart conditions and boiled the sprouts into an astringent tea to heal sores and wounds.[31]

The American chestnut grew to enormous sizes, sometimes measuring as large as 13 feet across, with crowns spreading more than 120 feet across the forest floor. In the spring, its buds would produce a white flower that looked like snow to those in the valleys below. Its wood was remarkably hardy and insect-resistant and provided settlers with the logs needed to build their cabins, barns, and fences, and even caskets. The beautifully grained wood was also used to make rustic furniture that is still highly treasured in antique stores across the country.

The American chestnut tree was destroyed by blight when an Asian chestnut tree was introduced to New York City in 1904. The Asian species was resistant to the fungus it carried, but the American chestnut was not. The fungus spread quickly, radiating outward in bands of 50 miles per year. By 1940, there were barely any trees left that were not dead or dying.[32] Lumber companies sped up their harvest of the remaining chestnuts before they were rendered useless dead hulks by the fungus. One farmer who lived in the Smokies used the huge hollowed-out stump from a felled chestnut as a corral for his animals for years.[33] Many of the original shelters built by the CCC on the AT used logs from felled chestnuts that had perished.[34]

The consequences were devastating to both people and animals in Appalachia. One resident recalled, "Turkeys disappeared, and the squirrels were not one tenth as many as before … bears got fat on chestnuts, coons got fat on chestnuts, and the woods was filled with wild turkeys, most all game ate chestnut." Another resident recalled, "Back when there were chestnuts, bear got so fat they couldn't run fast; now the poor bear run like a fox."[35]

Chestnuts had helped fuel the mountain economies; the nuts were gathered and hauled by wagon to urban centers for as much as $4 a bushel. In 1911 alone, one railroad in West Virginia carried 155,000 pounds of chestnuts to northern markets.[36]

The death of the American chestnut greatly accelerated the strong self-reliant subsistence culture of the southern Appalachians. Its effect is still felt today, with many mountain residents still struggling to make ends meet with few options other than serving in the tourist industry, working in the numerous retirement homes that dot Appalachia or moving to urban job centers.

I try to make sense of this ecological disaster, brought to the forests unwittingly by the hand of man. It certainly opened up space for other species to flourish, most notably oaks, poplars and hickories. But that seems to be a poor tradeoff, because the chestnut's economic utility and aesthetic beauty left a huge void in the eastern forests that will never be filled.

Arborists continue to experiment with blight-resistant hybrids, and have had some success, most notably a cross of the old American and the Chinese tree. But it is difficult to imagine any version of the old stately American classic ever returning to its former glory when it covered 30 million acres in the eastern forests.[37]

I walked down to the campsite into the meadow, which was former farmland, a little after 5 p.m. Wood Bat was already there, his tent pitched and his bear pack hung. The previous evening, he had taught me a new method of getting a pack over a branch—he tied a heavy branch to the end of the rope and slung it underhand, after several rotations, in a slingshot-type toss. By contrast, I had always thrown the rope in an overhand style grenade heave. His method seemed to work better, and my first toss was successful.

While we traded tight swigs of my Dawson County moonshine, I talked about my family history and its links to the Appalachian Mountains. Discovering gold, making moonshine, tragic deaths and dreams realized and dashed—when recounting the tales, I realized how unique, reckless and resilient my ancestors had been over the generations they had lived in the Appalachians. These attributes have been both points of pride and shame to my family in recent generations, and they were rarely discussed openly. It has only been in the past 20 years or so that these prickly subjects in my genealogy were researched and verified by one cousin and me.

As was the case during my previous section hike at Doll Flats, the winds came sweeping up the meadow during the night, although not with the same velocity as that night a year and a half earlier. My tent was bent over by the force of the winds, which were interspersed with moderate rainfall.

⚜

I awoke dry and no worse for wear the next morning and quickly packed and set off up the trail. Wood Bat was still getting ready when I put on my pack, and before I left, I reminded him that we were staying at Boots Off Hostel, on the far side of Pond Mountain.

The wind and rain had apparently been part of a cold front, because temperatures had dropped a bit from the previous two days.

The first four miles were mostly downhill, a steady descent into Dennis Cove, a cleared space just off the highway next to Big Branch Creek, where RVs and campers were parked in a perfect setting for "fat man camping,"

The next mile was flat or downhill, as I passed huge limestone rocks that were so linear in their shape that they appeared to be cut by the hand of man. The trail leading to the bottom of the deep ravine, into Laurel Fork Falls was rocky and treacherous, and I had to catch myself with my one remaining pole several times to avoid a fall.

The last couple of hundred feet leading to the bottom, I could hear the roar of the falls and see the fast-moving water gushing southward. The 55-foot falls were spectacular, and they were in fact so eye-catching that I inadvertently walked off the trail. After admiring the roaring falls for about ten minutes, I looked for the familiar white blaze that would indicate where I should resume my hike on the trail.

I looked across the creek and up the side of the falls and searched on the creek bank for any sign of the trail. Finally, after about 15 minutes, I retraced my steps up the trail and spotted a white blaze, indicating a sharp 90-degree turn 200 feet before the bottom of the falls. Later, I learned that Wood Bat made the same mistake and also became temporarily lost.

The trail soon dipped downward and hugged the creek bank, crisscrossing the creek on several wooden bridges before suddenly veering upward and southward towards Pond Mountain, a benign name originated by Thomas Jefferson's father, who surveyed this region on the border between Tennessee and North Carolina in the 1700s. He came up with

Wooden bridge in Pond Mountain Wilderness.

the name because of the many water sources found on the mountain's ridgeline.[38]

At just under 4,000 feet, Pond Mountain gained 2,000 feet in elevation over three miles, so I had plenty of opportunities to practice my new breathing technique—through the nose, *"breathe in roses,"* through the mouth, *"blow out candles."*

Pond, like Snowbird Mountain 250 miles away on the AT just outside the Smokies, was a tricky climb. It bobbed and weaved, shimmied and dipped before rising unexpectedly with bewildering turns where I never knew until I arrived at the bends whether the trail would head up or down. I would rather climb 5,000- or 6,000-foot mountains, which are almost always straightforward, rather than a much lower elevation but trickier Pond Mountain, which was always giving false hope that the summit was rapidly approaching. And I never actually reached the top of this mountain; the trail finally dipped downward for the long descent about 300 feet from the summit, which made the entire upward climb all the more maddening.

It was almost 4:30, and I had just over an hour and a half to make it to Boots Off Hostel before the shuttle departed at 6 p.m. to drop hikers off in Hampton, Tennessee, for food and supplies. As best I could, I raced down the mountain to try and make it before the shuttle departed.

I reached the bottom of the mountain with fifteen minutes to spare, but I still had a short uphill climb to the shelter. When I turned onto the driveway that snaked upward to the hostel complex, I embarrassingly had to flop onto the grass to catch my breath.

I walked to the check-in area and was met by Grumpy, a tall and well-built man with a braided beard, mullet haircut, and demon tattoos on his biceps. He laughed when I told him how Pond Mountain kicked my ass, and he tightened several straps on my backpack that had loosened over the course of the past three days.

Grumpy sold me a Powerade and directed me to my cabin. Wood Bat had arrived an hour earlier, and he had already had the opportunity to shower and decompress. I had just enough time to dump off my backpack and drain my grape Powerade before heading back out with Wood Bat to catch the shuttle.

It was a slow night—we were their only customers. Our shuttle driver, Bob, was a sheetrock installer who drove the van in his spare time. We climbed into the backseat—Bob's chihuahua, Molly, occupied the passenger side seat.

Hampton, like so many eastern Tennessee mountain towns, seemed faded and down on its luck. Old shotgun shacks lined the road into town, often with small front lawns piled full of disused toys and furniture.

Bob was quiet, and he dropped us off at a Subway in Hampton, where I ordered a 12-inch sub and a large cup of iced tea. We put our meals in a sack and continued on to a Dollar General store, where we hoped to replenish our depleted supply of food. I was somewhat surprised by the sparse offerings at the store; thru-hikers swear by them, but the only things I found were granola bars, Snickers bars and cheap ramen noodles. I had hoped that at least they would have some dehydrated food packets. I bought just enough food to tide me over for three more days.

Before we drove back to the hostel, Bob pulled into a convenience store to buy a 12-pack of Coors. Molly whimpered and her eyes darted around nervously as she stared outside while her owner was inside.

When we got back, I immediately piled my dirty clothes into a hamper (Boots Off washed them for $5) before heading to the shower to wash off three days of trail dirt and grime. The shower water poured through a large metal washtub with a perforated bottom that hung from the ceiling. The water flow was that of a strong, constant trickle, which was perfect for my sore and strained muscles and joints.

Refreshed, I went back to our cabin to eat my meal. By virtue of his earlier arrival, Wood Bat had rightfully claimed the lower king-sized bed, which was laid out perpendicular from the single bed situated in the top bunk frame. The beds took up most of the space in the eight-by-eight cabin, making it difficult for two large-sized men to move about at once. We took turns unpacking, throwing away trash and getting dressed for bed.

As I settled into my top bunk to read and relax before going to sleep, I reflected on having a companion hiker for the first time on a section hike. Wood Bat certainly had his quirks, as we all do, and I have more than most people. During the day, we were rarely together; he moved at a quicker pace, so our trail time together was limited to perhaps 15 minutes a day. There will always be differences between two people on extended hikes, but with me, these only became noticeable when we were "back in civilization"—when lights should be turned out, what optimal temperature settings should be in a room, what is the polite time to get up in the morning so as not to disturb the other occupant, etc.

Overall, Wood Bat seemed to be enjoying the experience; he asked a lot of questions (sometimes the same question three or four times—earlier that day, I threatened to tattoo "Boots Off Hostel" on his forehead if he asked me one more time where we would be staying that evening). But unusually for a novice hiker, he never complained about anything, and that quality made him a good person to have along on the trail. No one needs to be reminded of how tough the AT is when he or she is hiking it—that is self-evident, and whining only makes it worse.

I woke up early the next morning and silently climbed down the short ladder from my bunk to the floor. I went outside at daybreak and spotted Grumpy in front of the main building, holding a mug of coffee and smoking a cigarette as he looked over the hostel property and patiently waited for a new day to arrive.

I walked through a drizzle to the kitchen area on the bottom floor of the main building. Someone has painted a colorful "Christian Goth" mural on the concrete wall on one side of the kitchen. Grumpy had already set out our clean laundry in the hamper and had put out donuts, fruit and coffee. I ate alone, hoping to time it so that Wood Bat would arrive in the kitchen area at the time I was finished—I wanted to avoid the hassle of trying to load my backpack with two people in the small cabin bumping into each other.

When I left the kitchen, I ran into Grumpy. He somewhat lived up to his name—he was a man of few words, and he only seemed to open up when he felt like someone wasn't wasting his time with nonsense or meaningless pleasantries.

We talked about the trail that lay ahead. The next shelter, Watauga, had been shut for several years due to heavy bear activity in the area. Grumpy said that he expected that the shelter would be permanently closed and removed from trail maps in 2019. I asked him about bear activity and he responded with a hoarse laugh: "They won't be bothering you; they are on guard on account of it being bear hunting season." I had heard rifle fire, and even what sounded like automatic rifle fire, reverberate through the mountains in my previous three days of hiking, and now I knew the reason.

Grumpy recommended a place to stay in Damascus, Hikers Inn, which I promptly booked for Friday evening. I asked him about the trail between the hostel and Damascus, and he warned that the initial ten miles leading to Vandeventer Shelter were tough, but the trail leveled out after that, with only a few small steady uphills of 500 feet or less for the remaining 30 miles or so. "Forty-three miles to Damascus," he said, while blowing a stream of cigarette smoke through his nostrils.

The rain had picked up as I readied my pack for the hike that laid ahead. I knew that rain would last for most of the day; a cold front was moving in. On the porch of the cabin, I poured ramen noodles into a plastic water bottle. I had learned online from another hiker that noodles will soften up over the course of the day using cold water. After three or four hours, they soften enough to become edible. I showed Wood Bat the same trick before setting out.

The rain remained steady as I set out from the hostel. The trail blazes were confusing and seemingly led to nowhere until I spotted a double white blaze across Highway 321. The trail hugged the western shoreline of Watauga Lake, a Tennessee Valley Authority (TVA) reservoir established in 1948 when a dam was built on the Watauga River. As I made my way around the lake and towards the dam, I suddenly passed a steady stream of SOBOs—in rapid succession, I met Mocha, Slip and Slide, and a thru-hiker from Bristol, England, whose name I did not catch, but told me the summit to the ridge I was climbing was only "a few more switchbacks to the top." I learned long ago that thru-hikers tend to underestimate distance and degree of difficulty (while section hikers do the opposite), so I took his estimate with a grain of salt. Sure enough, there were at least ten more switchbacks before I reached the top.

Weather was the primary topic of conversation with the SOBOs— I received several confirmations that the rain would continue for the rest of the day, but more importantly, I learned of the storm that would be arriving the next day, on Thursday.

Before I set out on a section hike, I follow the news religiously when I am at home, and there was no indication when I left Atlanta the previous Saturday that a big storm was brewing in the Gulf of Mexico. I had studied extended weather forecasts for weeks for the section of the trail that I would be hiking, and rain, as part of a cold front, had long been predicted for both this day and the next. What I did not realize, until now, was that fast-moving Category 4 Hurricane Michael, which was only making landfall on the Gulf Coast of Florida that morning, would be moving rapidly inward before hitting my section of the trail early the next morning. A normal autumn rain ushered in by a cold front was going to be supplanted by inches of rain dumped by the third fiercest hurricane to strike the continental United States in its history.

Many of the SOBOs I spoke to were planning on staying at Boots Off Hostel that night to ride the storm out. One suggested that we stay at Vandeventer Shelter until the storm passed. But we had a timetable to meet—work schedules had forced Wood Bat and me to fit our almost 80-mile hike into an inflexible, six-day trip, and we had to soldier on, storm be damned.

To make matters worse, I had developed a pretty severe allergy, and I had to stop every ten minutes or so to clear phlegm from my lungs and blow out snot from my sinuses.

The rain lightened as I made my way around the lake and crossed the earthen Watauga Dam, which had a sheer, six- or seven-hundred-foot drop-off lined with slag on the side of the dam opposite the reservoir. I later learned that the reservoir covered the "first two Butlers," the small town now situated on a peninsula that juts out from the north-central part of the lake. The railroad company moved the first town of Butler, Tennessee, in the early part of the 20th century. The second Butler, which included 761 families along with the graves of their ancestors, was moved when the TVA lake was formed in 1948.[39] Scuba divers still dive into the old underwater ghost town to look at the old homes and buildings.

After crossing the dam, the trail takes a sharp turn to the left and follows the blacktop dam road before starting its gradual ascent up the 30-mile-long Iron Mountain Massif, which would be our springboard into Damascus. The steepest portion of Iron Mountain was the first five miles, which included a 2,000-foot elevation gain to over 4,000 feet.

Beyond Vandeventer Shelter, which marked the end of the five-mile upward hike, the trail flattened out for the remaining 30 miles or so to Damascus.

I was eating my lunch of cold ramen noodles in the early afternoon when Wood Bat caught up with me. He had gotten lost trying to find his way to the trail across Highway 321, and that had cost him 20 or 30 minutes. We talked about our options, and we agreed to try and hike to a campsite three and a half miles beyond Vandeventer Shelter where there was, according to the trail map, a water supply. We wanted to make as much progress as possible before the rains from Hurricane Michael arrived early the next morning.

When walking along the ridge of Iron Mountain, I could always see 16-mile-wide Lake Watauga on my right. I could spot distant marinas in one section, where the "New Butler" is located.

I reached Vandeventer Shelter around 3:30 as the rain picked up. There was no one inside, a somewhat worrisome sign that hikers were clearing off the trail in anticipation of the approaching storm. The trail was poorly marked at the shelter; I spent five or ten minutes playing detective until I finally found a white blaze.

The final three and a half miles to our campsite were navigated over winding, rain-slicked trails. I was getting pretty soaked—I had held off from wearing a rain jacket most of the day because the temperatures had warmed, and waterproof material, while somewhat impermeable to water, also does a very effective job of retaining heat. So it was a tradeoff—wet or hot. I finally opted for hot when the rains became too heavy.

I spotted our campsite, situated in a small cove just to the right of the trail, around 6 p.m. Wood Bat had set up his tent on one flattish side of the ridge. As I set up my tent farther down the cove on a grassy area, he came walking up with water. Our water source turned out to be nothing but a trickle into a small puddle. Someone had thoughtfully placed a tin can to help collect the small stream of water coming out of the ground.

The rain had stopped, but it was gloomy, and a mist rose from the forest floor—what the Germans called "the foxes making coffee." I moved quickly to set up my tent—I was wet, and after a 13-mile hike that day, I just wanted to crawl inside and decompress. I told Wood Bat when I was putting up my tent that he probably would not see me until the next morning. After removing a little bit of food for the evening, I somehow mustered up the energy to hang a bear pack.

I was comfortably set up inside my tent by 7 p.m. when the sun dipped over the cove. I ate a pack of potato chips I had picked up from the Subway the previous night in Hampton and also gobbled down a breakfast bar. I was pleased—we had covered the toughest part of the approach to Damascus, and my body heat was warming my wet clothes. I texted my wife and daughter a selfie, and my wife told me that Hurricane Michael was pounding Atlanta at that very moment. The volume of rain was so heavy that it had crushed the plastic tarp we used as a roof over our chicken coop. As I turned off my cell phone and prepared for sleep, I knew my dance with the storm would be coming real soon.

❧❧❧

Michael arrived at 4 a.m., with no shrieks from high winds or rumbling thunder—just buckets of rain appearing out of nowhere. Somehow, the heavy rain rocked me back to sleep until I woke again at 7. There was no letup—the rains continued to pound. Two trees crashed down in rapid succession; some distance away from me but still, too close for comfort.

I really was in a quandary about what to do—we needed to hike at least 12 miles or so to give us a reasonable distance for the hike in to Damascus the next day. But stepping outside meant getting instantly soaked—I knew my waterproof gear would prove ineffective in flash flood conditions. On cue, I received an emergency alarm notice on my cell phone from the National Weather Service that three inches of rain would be falling in my area, and that flood conditions would persist until 5 p.m.

The decision on what to do next was made for me when my tent started filling with water. Even the tarp that I placed inside was no shield against the water streaming in, and my choice became easy—I might as well hike if I was also going to be wet inside the tent. By the time I hoisted down my bear pack from the tree branch, I was dripping wet. Ironically, I was out of water and went back to the small stream that was identified as a source. The rain had poured in torrents down the hill into the small hole where the water collected. The force of the rain had turned the water brackish, and there was no way I was going to take a chance drinking it.

I yelled inside Wood Bat's tent, and he said he was prepared to hike as well. We agreed to meet up at the next identified water source, three miles up the trail at Iron Mountain Shelter.

Typically when hiking the trail, I will go out of my way to avoid standing water, but that sort of effort was pointless this morning. Water was gushing down the trail on the uphill climbs, and in the flat areas, a couple of inches had collected, which I just splashed through. Water was simply everywhere.

My demeanor was calm throughout the storm. I had learned several section hikes ago not to fight the weather, and I was determined to keep my mind from drifting into negative thoughts. Plus, I did not want Wood Bat to see me angry or discouraged. I just trudged forward, one muddy step at a time. Every half hour or so, I would get another emergency update alarm from the National Weather Service, with the outlook unchanged of flash flooding until the late afternoon. The internal jukebox returned to my brain: "Box of Rain," over and over again.

We arrived about 11 a.m. at Iron Mountain Shelter and collected water at the nearby spring. I had not had anything to drink since the evening before, so I was thirsty. Wood Bat asked me for a weather update, and I told him it should rain until the late afternoon. "Tomorrow is going to be pretty, though," I said with a smile.

We sat under the tin roof of the shelter while the downpour continued. Wood Bat left after a while, and I was left alone to contemplate our predicament. We had a little over a day and a half to finish the remaining 27 miles to Damascus, and the rest of the afternoon would continue to be a weather challenge. We had not passed any hikers that morning; it seemed that everyone had found a place to hole up and ride the storm out.

Then I heard a wood thrush: "eee-oh-LAY," and the rain stopped almost immediately thereafter. I smiled and stepped back on the trail. The next five miles of descending Iron Mountain towards Highway 91 were easy, gently winding trails. I was able to move quickly with the rain continuing to hold off until I reached the highway where Wood Bat was waiting, eating his cold ramen noodles. We were uncertain on where to camp for the evening, so we agreed to meet up once again at

Double Springs Shelter in another three miles. About that time, the rain started falling again.

The AT continued across the highway through a cow pasture. We walked through the wet turf while Holstein cattle mooed half-heartedly and gave us bored looks. The combination of rain and mist made following the white blazes difficult, and I had to stop several times to re-establish where the path led.

We continued through the pasture for a mile until the trail dipped back into the forest. At that point, Wood Bat passed me—I was worn out as the trail started its 500-foot ascent the remaining two miles to the shelter. I tried the "breathe in roses, blow out candles" breathing exercise, and it helped some, but I still had to stop every 100 feet or so to catch my breath. My allergy was giving me fits, and I was constantly clearing my sinuses and lungs.

The rain was coming down harder when I passed the only hiker I would see that day other than Wood Bat. He was a young SOBO named Big Al with a huge grin on his face and a flashing boombox attached to the top of his pack—he felt like the loud rock music and lights would "keep the bears away." Big Al was in his 30s and had recently received a disability discharge from the Army. He was a SOBO who had leap-frogged from New York to Harper's Ferry, West Virginia, because the weather was "too cold" in the northeast.

He had spent the previous night in a tent next to Double Springs Shelter, and like me, he got soaking wet in the early morning. He gathered his gear and went inside the shelter where he slept until 2 p.m. He had left the shelter just an hour or so earlier to cover as much of the trail as he could before darkness set in. He gave me an estimate of the remaining mileage to the shelter, and I turned and watched him hike down the trail, his boombox flashing red and blue lights. His enthusiasm gave me a temporary lift, and I picked up my pace to cover the remaining distance to the shelter.

Around 4 p.m., I walked into the shelter. Wood Bat was there, along with a small, lithe, bearded man in his 60s named Ned. Wood Bat and I discussed our options—we had 19 miles left until we reached Damascus, and that was a long way for me to hike in a day; in fact, it would represent the longest distance I had ever hiked. But we were both tired— 11 miles of hiking in the rain had taken its toll. I discussed the possibility of going another two or three miles to set us up for a shorter hike the next morning, but that rather easy downhill section could be covered in an hour the next morning when we were fresh. So we decided to spend the night at Double Springs, only the second time I had actually slept inside a shelter—I was in no mood to try and set up my wet tent, particularly while it was still raining.

We began setting up for the evening, hanging up our wet clothes and putting our bedding on the wood platform of the shelter. Ned's trail name was "Jiffy Pop," given to him by his daughter while hiking in Maine due to his insatiable craving for popcorn on one of their hikes. He had spent all day in the shelter staying dry while the storm raged. Like us, he was section hiking to Damascus; unlike us, he was planning on covering the remaining distance in two days.

It was soon apparent that Jiffy Pop was a storyteller. He had a calm, relaxed demeanor, and he could weave his experiences in language that was interesting and entertaining. He had graduated from the University of New Hampshire and started a career in forestry before moving on to arboriculture and later, surveying. The common theme of his career was spending time outdoors, and he spent a lot of his spare time hiking Baxter State Park in Maine.

Divorced and open for a new adventure, he studied the eastern seaboard looking for a suitable place to spend his retirement years. Connecticut, where he lived at the time, was out of the question because of its high cost of living. He briefly considered the coast of Maine, but he was similarly priced out there because of the lack of affordable housing. He settled on Hickory, North Carolina, which was roughly situated equidistant between the coast and the AT and also close to Charlotte, for when he felt the need to venture into a larger city.

In order to meet people and keep himself somewhat busy, he worked as a groundskeeper at the golf course of the local country club a couple days a week. He never played golf himself, but "liked to watch other people play."

Jiffy Pop had started this section hike in the Smokies and was ending his trip in Damascus, where he would be meeting his girlfriend at the same place Wood Bat and I were staying, Hikers Inn. He and his girlfriend planned to bicycle down the Virginia Creeper Trail during their stay in Damascus.

At about 5, the rain stopped and the sun briefly appeared before clouds moved back in. The weather forecast had been accurate; we knew the worst was now behind us.

Jiffy Pop was encouraging about our chances of covering the 19 miles to Damascus the next day. Earlier that morning, another hiker, Poncho, had left the shelter headed to Damascus. He was hiking without his boots, which had fallen off the back of his pack several days ago while he had been making his way up the trail with his earbuds in listening to music. Of course, he had been hiking while stoned, and he did not realize his boots were missing until the end of the day. I liked my chances of making it to Damascus the next day if Poncho could do it in the rain without his boots.

The previous night at the shelter, Poncho and Big Al had smoked weed and then decided to go into the woods and chop wood for a campfire with the machete Poncho had in his pack (along with a transistor radio). Jiffy Pop estimated that Poncho had a backpack that weighed at least 60 pounds, and he weighed only a little more than twice that amount. My confidence in my ability to cover the remaining mileage to Damascus the next day was growing by the minute.

Jiffy Pop had spotted three bears, a mother and her two cubs, in an acorn-rich area near the top of Pond Mountain. The mother spotted him and shimmied down a tree, closely followed by her two cubs. He could not believe how an animal that large could move so swiftly and at the same time make so little noise.

We discussed the rifle blasts we had all been hearing in the past week related to bear hunting season. Jiffy Pop explained how the specially trained dogs I have seen throughout my trips with GPS collars were used: hunters bait a station with food, a hungry bear finds the food, helps himself to a meal, and leaves the area. The hunter then takes the dogs to the station so they can pick up the scent of the bear. The pack of dogs tracks the now-frightened bear, which follows its instincts and climbs a tree. The dogs gather under the tree, barking, while the hunter, usually some distance away, sees the GPS signals emanating from one area. The hunter then goes to the area and shoots the bear down from the tree.

My first reaction was that this was a barbaric practice, but is it really worse for the bear than, say, bow-hunting? How many single shot arrows kill a bear instantly instead of wounding them, where the bear then has to be tracked and shot several more times before dying? There are no easy answers when it comes to culling the wildlife to try and maintain an optimal balance that is best for both humans and animals.

Wood Bat prepared a dehydrated meal of breakfast hash over the Jetboil. It was perhaps the most tasteless meal I had ever had while camping, but I was nonetheless grateful; my own supply of food was almost fully depleted.

Jiffy Pop was settling in for the evening, strictly adhering to the "down at sunset" rule. He had a bear canister, so he did not have to worry about hanging a pack. When I finally returned from hanging mine, it was near dark, and Jiffy Pop was already perfectly set up for bed, with an air mattress that rose three inches from the wood platform flooring of the shelter. He looked as comfortable as could be possible on the trail. He told us before turning in that he wanted to be up by 6:30 a.m. and on the trail by 8.

❧⊱⊰❧

Wood Bat and I climbed into our sleeping bags. I was skeptical about my ability to sleep in a shelter because of my past history of noise sensitivity. However, on this night, I fell asleep at nightfall, and did not arise until 6:45, when Wood Bat was giving Jiffy Pop the time. Except for a couple of fitful interludes, I had slept for almost 12 hours.

I announced to the shelter that I had "slept great" that night, and no one said anything. Instantly, I knew I was "that guy." I asked Wood Bat, "Did I snore?" "Like a pro," he responded. Luckily for Jiffy Pop, he was deaf in one ear and put his good ear down on the platform to muffle the sound of my snoring. I felt sheepish, because I have always been the one to complain about other people snoring, so I apologized profusely.

The temperature was 40 degrees at 7 a.m., and Jiffy Pop was not moving from his spot. I forced myself out of my bag at a little after 7 and spent a good fifteen minutes trying to locate my bear pack—it was still dark outside, and it was hard to see, even with a head lamp. I returned to the shelter after finding it, packed up, drank some coffee and ate a granola bar and finally set out about 8:30. Wood Bat was still getting ready, and Jiffy Pop showed no sign of movement inside his sleeping bag. I was completely wrapped up, including a heavy jacket, skullcap and gloves.

The hiking was steady, down sunlit slopes slowly warming with the rising sun. White pines became more prevalent—I caught whiffs of their resinous aroma as I quickly covered, one, two, three miles. The bronze trunks of the firs and spruces reflected the weak glare of the early autumnal light, which was my first stark reminder that yet another year would soon be fading away. The heavy rains from the previous two days had caused mushrooms to sprout on the rotting trunks of every dead tree along the trail. As I passed Low Gap, roughly the five-mile mark on the way to Damascus, I knew I was going to be able to make it. It would not be easy—nothing ever is on the Appalachian Trail—but the 19 miles would be finished by the end of the day.

I met "Gandalfin," a SOBO from Cincinnati who averaged 20 miles a day on the trail while listening to podcasts of NFL games. I did a quick calculation in my mind and mentioned that he had just under a month to go. "I can't fucking WAIT," he said. "It has been great, but I am ready to get off." This was a sentiment I often heard expressed by thru-hikers.

Gandalfin noticed my gloves, which were red and black and had the Atlanta Falcons football team insignia. He asked me my trail name, and I told him I did not have one. "You do now," he said. "You are Dirty Bird!" I laughed, and he continued up the trail. I heard him yell out one more time, "Dirty Bird!" I could live with that name—it was somewhat accurate—I owned six chickens (who are certainly filthy) and I probably resembled a grizzled old bird after almost a week on the trail.

The hiking was easy enough that I was able to reflect on my life— I was turning 60 years old in a few weeks, a milestone that I strangely was not dreading. I was beginning to look forward to the freedom of retirement, which was becoming more and more of a reality with each passing day. My career had been a roller-coaster, with some great years that allowed my family and me to live and travel abroad, punctuated by job losses that created emotional and monetary stresses. I had long been bored by my string of jobs in financial services and had, along with my wife, established a side business focused on antiques and collectibles that was becoming more successful with each passing year.

I was becoming more and more excited over the prospect of an active retirement, focused on work that I found compelling rather than grinding at a corporate job to shield my family from financial hardship. I was not naïve about age and its inevitable pains and infirmities, but I was also proud that I had made it this far and earned my stripes, so to speak, in this rough and tumble world.

As I inched closer and closer to Virginia, my family ties to the region were diminishing, with the lone exception of William Parks of Powell Valley in southwestern Virginia, near Damascus. William Parks was my great-great-great-great uncle and was also the uncle of Benjamin Parks, Jr., who discovered gold near modern day Dahlonega, Georgia. He was 38 years old in the spring of 1776, shortly after the start of the Revolutionary War between the fledgling states of the eastern seaboard and the British Empire.

The Cherokee Indians, fearful of further western expansion by American settlers into their homelands, had allied themselves with the British. "1776 dawned with a fury of Indian depredations hitherto unknown from the Cherokees whose proximity to the western settlements made them a more formidable foe than the Shawnee, although the Shawnee attacks did not cease. The Revolutionary War was raging and the western settlers were faced with an enemy to the east, one to the south and another to the north, with British agents abetting and arming the hostile Indians, and in the midst were Tory traitors waiting and ready to strike."[40]

The situation quickly grew desperate as Cherokee attacks increased along the valleys of the Clinch, Holston, and Powell rivers. The attacks typically occurred with little or no warning, and this added to the sense of panic among the settlers. Cherokee harassment in the region forced settlers to live in forts for most of 1776, which added to their suffering—the planting season was missed, and this made the settlers reliant on food that had to be shipped by pack train from the east (and these pack trains also had to be guarded—the narrow gaps of southwest Virginia made the supply wagons particularly susceptible to Cherokee attacks).

William Parks owned 400 acres of land on Indian Creek in Powell Valley, Virginia, by settlement right of 1773, and held an additional 1,000 acres via "pre-emption warrant."[41] In May of 1776, Parks, like many other settlers from the area, had taken refuge from the Cherokee attacks at Martin's Station, a fort located in what is now Lee County, Virginia. The men inside grew bored and frustrated by the lack of communication from the military forces protecting the region and held a council and decided to all head home if nothing was heard in the next three days.

William Parks insisted on leaving that day to go eight miles south of the fort to put up a few poles in the shape of a house, cut down some trees, dig some holes in the ground, and plant some corn so as to secure a "corn right." He would have enough time to take care of all of this and return within three days and join the others from the fort to return to their settlement. He left that evening with his nephew and a "negro man" slave to secure the corn right.

On the appointed return date, his nephew returned, but there were no signs of William Parks or the slave. The men in the fort found his tracks and went to where "Indians had been lying" among some limestone rocks on the Kentucky Trace. There they found Parks, lying facedown and dead. He had been shot through the heart and scalped, with "a war club left in his brain." The settlers made a makeshift sling from tree bark, placed Parks's body in it, and carried him back to his cabin where he was buried. No mention was made in the reports on the fate of the slave.[42]

The symmetry of my family history and the path of the first 500 miles of the Appalachian Trail struck me once again, particularly as it involved once again a tragic encounter with the Cherokees. It was hard to view Parks as a victim—his impatience and greed won out, notwithstanding the fact that he knew that there were Cherokees on a war footing in the area. He chose to disregard the risks and put his life and the life of others in peril, and he paid the ultimate price.

I could glimpse Damascus through the rustling leaves beginning to "fallow" into yellow and gold while still stubbornly clinging to the tree branches as I started my final descent towards town. My family was like these mountains—rugged and harsh and certainly rough around the edges, but also as fierce and unyielding as the weather-beaten peaks I had slowly climbed over the past five and a half years. The trajectory of their lives, like the southern Appalachians, was marked by precipitous climbs to the top, followed by dizzying falls. They are at rest now, eternally part of the valleys and towns of these timeless mountains, their bones protected by the leaves and soil from the icy winds, rain and snow.

At about 5 p.m., I reached a rough sign on the trail announcing the

Wooden sign marking the Virginia border with Tennessee.

border crossing into Virginia and Jefferson National Forest. I was three-and-a-half miles from Damascus, and I had hit the wall. I was willing myself forward with every step to get me to the end of the trail.

A small man appeared, climbing up the trail heading south. As he came closer, I noticed he was wearing an oversized fluorescent orange hunter's cap. He was barely over five feet tall, was missing a few teeth, and was carrying a neat stack of forest sticks bound together and tied on his back, like one would expect from a medieval forester. He also was carrying a medium-sized aerated plastic cage. I was curious, so looked through the top of the clear plastic and spotted two large rats, one brown, the other white.

"I am going to the Tennessee border," he announced. "Just a half mile ahead," I informed him. "I knowed that," he responded, while offering me a closer look at his pet rats. I learned that he liked to take his rats camping with him, and their favorite spot was a campsite adjacent to the border sign. He had named the brown rat Sable, and the white one Falkor, in honor of the dragon from the movie *The Neverending Story*. He let them out of their cages at the campsite, where they would roam, always returning before he left. "Someone down the trail told me their names were Dee and Con. I gave him a look that coulda keelt."

I later learned that I had met "Rat Man," a man well known locally. He lived in the woods around Damascus during the warmer months. Residents speculated that he must have some money, because he always left for the winter, returning in the spring. It sounded like he was harmless and never begged for food or money; he was much more likely to show up on a homeowner's front porch just to talk, usually for an extended time.

Twilight was falling on Damascus when the trail dumped me off on the edge of town just before 7 p.m. If my hike had lasted ten minutes longer, I would have needed my headlamp to navigate the last portion of the wooded trail. I was disoriented by being in a town again, especially with night falling, and took several wrong turns before arriving at the inn.

I knocked on the door of Hikers Inn along East Laurel Avenue in the historic district of town. Lee, the co-owner of the inn (she and her husband had bought it in 2010), opened the door and warmly greeted me, taking me upstairs over the creaky, carpeted steps to my room on the second floor.

Wood Bat was already there, sitting on one of the two twin beds. He had arrived an hour earlier and had showered and settled in. I took a long shower, as much as to ease my aching muscles as to cleanse the grime from three days of hiking. My hike that day was the longest I had ever completed, and my entire body was one throbbing mess.

We hobbled down the street (Wood Bat was feeling the pain as well) and got a booth at Damascus Pizza. Strangely, I was not ravenously hungry and did not attack my cheeseburger. I actually left some food on my plate as a I sipped a Trail Daze Lager IPA (which I thought was contradictory) made in Damascus and watched the karaoke performers.

The cold and fog was settling in on this small, friendly trail town as we made our way back to the inn. Damascus calls itself "Trail Town U.S.A.," and I had seen nothing to dispute that claim. There were inviting eateries, outfitters, warm and historic inns, a microbrewery, and yes, even a Dollar General.

⟨⟨⟨⟩⟩⟩

Early the next morning I went downstairs and talked to Lee, who fell in love with Damascus when resupplying her Belgian husband, Paul, in that town during his thru-hike in 2010. They bought the almost 100-year-old Victorian-style house with gingerbread trimmings and a wrap-around porch and converted it into a bed and breakfast with a hostel in the back courtyard.

In honor of Paul's Belgian heritage, the couple had hung Flemish prints of Bosch and Brueghel throughout the house, which had beautiful hardwood floors and American chestnut baseboards. We talked about the local characters, including Rat Man. I learned that the local grocery store stayed open past midnight once a month to accommodate those in town living on fixed incomes who would buy food and other necessities as soon as their disability or Social Security checks were deposited. It was a reminder that, despite the visual appeal of the town, there were many who lived desperate lives within Trail Town U.S.A.

We paid our bill and walked to the local outfitter, where we met John, a bald and heavyset middle-aged man with glasses, who would be driving us back to Mountain Harbour to pick up our car. John was a former Marine who had been living outdoors and sleeping in his hammock for over ten years. He was very matter-of-fact about his living arrangements and was clearly unbothered by being technically homeless. We had interrupted his breakfast at the local café when he got the call to drive us, but he was not upset and seemed eager to share his knowledge of the local area while making a little money.

We drove south towards Roan Mountain and crossed the border back into Tennessee as the fog was lifting and the sun was rising over the valleys bathed in an early autumn sheen of green and gold. We passed towns and hamlets with long abandoned stores and factories. The only businesses that seemed to be flourishing were the Dollar General stores—I lost count after five on the number of Dollar Generals we passed on the 70-mile drive back to Mountain Harbour. I asked John why these towns seemed so bereft of opportunity compared to Damascus, and he told me that Damascus had also had more than its share of business failures, they just were not so visible.

I was surprised by the number of houses and trailers we passed that flew the Confederate flag and could only surmise that the occupants knew little about the divided loyalties of that area during the Civil War. Or if they did know, they no longer cared. The first "Trump/Pence 2020" signs were already starting to sprout up in yards along the highway.

There was a sadness that pervaded this stunningly beautiful land, and the absence of hope was palpable. I could discern no displays of enterprise, no sense of purpose that was visible as we continued southward. I could understand it, in a certain sense—change had not treated the people of Appalachia well in recent years. Natural gas and oil from fracking and new alternative energies had supplanted coal and left that industry to die a slow death, while automation and globalization had ravaged the local labor-intensive manufacturers. If nothing else, generations of Appalachians had always prided themselves on their ability to survive unaided in difficult conditions. Now, even that satisfaction connected to self-reliance appears to be gone.

The ridges and mountains we had climbed were on my right—Iron Mountain, Pond Mountain, and Watauga Dam. John told us the story of the "three Butlers," two of which were now at the bottom of the reservoir.

John knew Grumpy at Boots Off Hostel and had worked for Uncle Johnny in Erwin a number of years earlier. He reminisced about how Uncle Johnny knew the cost of everything, down to a packet of coffee creamer. We laughed as we shared place and people names that were unknown to me a month ago but now easily rolled off my tongue. I felt at ease here in this area where the borders of Tennessee, North Carolina and Virginia meet.

I was going to miss this shared knowledge, this culture, this community that I, along with thousands of others, had been absorbed into simply by hiking the trail. It is a culture of instant acceptance and trust, one that silently recognizes the shared hardships, and it is built on a mutual respect for anyone who had toiled through the sweat, pain, and joy of the AT. It is also unique in today's America because it is devoid of tribalism—gender, race, religion, age and all the other issues that divide the country disappear as soon as one puts on a pack and steps foot on the trail.

John dropped us off in the parking lot of Mountain Harbour before noon, and Wood Bat and I started our slow journey back to Atlanta. Tourists were beginning to swarm into the area in search of newly picked apples and other mountain delicacies, gorgeous vistas and crisp autumn temperatures.

My gaze continued to drift upward to the windswept ridges, the rustling leaves, the verdant coves and the trickling streams of the Blue Ridge. I knew that in the years to come I would be pulling out old maps and looking at pictures to jog my memory of the names and places I had hiked over the last five and a half years.

The images of the people I had met along the trail flashed through my mind—all of their faces, their voices, the laughs, the conversations, the advice, and the worries that we all shared. Retina, Caveman, Matt, Bluto, Gentleman Jim, Megaphone, Ninja Roll, Uncle Johnny, Doc, Wood Bat, Grumpy, Jiffy Pop, and so many others.

My journey had come to an end, and I felt privileged that these mountains had taken me in; I had not conquered them, they had conquered me, and I was the better for it. As John Muir famously said, "In every walk with nature, one receives far more than he seeks."

The bear, like me, was old and flecked with silver when he reappeared in my dream. The restaurant was shuttered, with a yellowed notice of foreclosure taped to the door. He did nothing to acknowledge my presence as I approached the cage. The lock was fragile from years of rust and neglect, and it snapped easily when I pulled the door open.

The bear sensed something extraordinary had happened as the door creaked open. He slowly rose up and shook off years of accumulated filth as he lumbered to the exit. He paused at the open door and gently nudged his muzzle against my right hand. I stroked his ancient head like I would my dog, behind the ears and the back of the neck. He walked gingerly past me and through the doorway, still unsteady after years of confinement.

The landscape had changed. There was now a broad, emerald river in front of us, with sparkling white rapids. I recognized it instantly as the French Broad. The bear ambled to the edge of the river before stepping in. He had misjudged the depth and plunged below the surface before his head reappeared, and he pulled himself up on some shoals. He sprayed water as he vigorously shook his mane.

The mountains were purple silhouettes framing the uplands across the river, and the bear picked up his pace as he crossed the remaining distance and clambered up the opposite bank. I followed him with my eyes for as long as I could, and he grew smaller and smaller as he sprinted towards home.

Notes

Introduction

1. "The Geologic Origins of Kennesaw Mountain," The National Park Service, https://www.nps.gov/kemo/learn/historyculture/upload/Geology_SB.pdf, accessed August 25, 2018.

Part I

1. Appalachian Trail Thru Hike Statistics, August 13, 2017, https://www.outdoors.org/articles/amc-outdoors/equipped/the-latest-appalachian-trail-thru-hike-statistics.

2. David Clark, *Blue Ridge Facts and Legends* (1955), p. 50.

3. William L. Stuart, "The Gemstone Chronicles," October 27, 2014, https://www.williamlstuart.com/2014/10/27/calhoun-mine/, accessed May 21, 2018.

4. David Williams, *The Georgia Gold Rush: Twenty-Niners, Cherokees, and Gold Fever* (1993), pp. 24–25.

5. "A Visit to Uncle Bennie Parks—He Tells the Story of His Find," *The Atlanta Constitution*, July 15, 1894, p. 2.

6. David Williams, *The Georgia Gold Rush: Twenty-Niners, Cherokees, and Gold Fever* (1993), 79.

7. *Niles Register*, May 4, 1833.

8. John Ehle, *Trail of Tears: The Rise and Fall of the Cherokee Nation* (1988), p. 223.

9. *Ibid.*, pp. 222–223.

10. *Ibid.*, p. 225.

11. "A Visit to Uncle Bennie Parks—He Tells the Story of His Find," *The Atlanta Constitution*, July 15, 1894, p. 2.

12. *Ibid.*

13. Bill Osinski, "Gold Rush Descendants Hold Golden Gathering," *The Atlanta Journal-Constitution*, September 9, 2002.

14. Bo Emerson, "Mountain Crossing a Hikers Paradise," *The Atlanta Journal-Constitution*, April 17, 2010, https://www.ajc.com/travel/newsmedleystory1296876/6eDOFyNNypx6Qn9PSq8uHN/, accessed June 2, 2018.

15. Georgia Mysteries, February 28, 2009, http://georgiamysteries.blogspot.com/2009/02/blood-mountain-home-to-unknown.html, accessed May 2, 2018.

16. Reverend Michael Kane, "Quitting the AT," April 2, 2015, https://revkane.com/2015/04/02/at-happiness-quitting-the-appalachian-trail/, accessed May 31, 2018.

17. Bo Emerson, "Mountain Crossing a Hikers Paradise," *The Atlanta Journal-Constitution*, April 17, 2010, https://www.ajc.com/travel/newsmedleystory1296876/6eDOFyNNypx6Qn9PSq8uHN/, accessed June 2, 2018.

18. *Ibid.*

19. Jess Bidgwood and Richard Pérez-Peña, "Geraldine Largay's Wrong Turn: Death on the Appalachian Trail," *New York Times*, May 26, 2016, https://www.nytimes.com/2016/05/27/us/missing-hiker-geraldine-largay-appalachian-trail-maine.html, accessed August 29, 2018.

20. Raymond A. Cook, *Mountain Singer: The Life and Legacy of Byron Herbert Reece* (Atlanta: Cherokee Publishing, 1980), p. 187. Poem reprinted with permission from Ken Boyd.

21. "Interesting Facts," Appalachian Trail Conservancy, http://www.appalachiantrail.org/home/community/2000-milers, accessed July 14, 2018.

22. Christian Boone and Ron Cook, "Ten Years Later, Hiker Murder Still Haunts Those Closest to Case," *The Atlanta Journal-Constitution*, December 27, 2017, https://www.myajc.com/news/crime—law/ten-years-later-hiker-murder-still-haunts-those-closest-case/CSgydKXZNfG738F34UdWYN/

23. Joseph Earl Dabney, *Mountain Spirits: A Chronicle of Corn Whiskey and the Moonshine Life* (1974), p. 34.

24. *Ibid.*, p. 51.

25. *Dawson County; Georgia Heritage, 1857–1996*, Dawson County Historical and Genealogical Society, p. 51.

26. Esther Kellner, *Moonshine: Its History and Folklore* (1971), p. 222.

27. *The State of Georgia vs. H.E. Parks*, transcript of the trial, May 16, 1925.

28. *The Gainesville News*, July 9, 1924, p. 1.

29. Raymond A. Cook, *Mountain Singer: The Life and Legacy of Byron Herbert Reece* (Atlanta: Cherokee Publishing, 1980), p. 201. Poem reprinted with permission from Ken Boyd.

30. *Ibid.*, p. 127.

31. *Ibid.*, p. 133.

32. Kathryn Seelye, "As Hikers Celebrate on Appalachian Trail, Some Ask Where Will It End?" *New York Times,* August 19, 2015, https://www.nytimes.com/2015/08/30/us/as-hikers-celebrate-on-appalachian-trail-some-ask-where-will-it-end.html, accessed July 7, 2018.

33. "How One Man Removed 1,720 Pounds of Backcountry Trash" http://www.cleverhiker.com/blog/how-one-man-removed-1720-pounds-of-backcountry-trash, accessed July 8, 2018.

34. "Interesting Facts," Appalachian Trail Conservancy, http://www.appalachiantrail.org/home/community/2000-milers, accessed July 15, 2018.

35. Standing Indian Mountain, Wikipedia, https://en.wikipedia.org/wiki/Standing_Indian_Mountain.

Part II

1. Western North Carolina Vitality Index, Precipitation Variability, accessed June 5, 2018.

2. Biodiversity of the Southern Appalachians, Highlands Biological Station, accessed June 12, 2018.

3. Todd Walker, "How Cherokees Used Trees of Southern Appalachia for Food, Medicine, and Craft," Survival Sherpa, March 8, 2016, https://survivalsherpa.wordpress.com/2016/03/08/how-cherokees-used-trees-of-southern-appalachia-for-food-medicine-and-craft/, accessed June 12, 2018.

4. Tom Bennett, Hiwassee River Watershed Coalition, Inc., https://hrwc.net/towns-county-ga-preserves-the-top-of-bell-mountain/, accessed June 13, 2018.

5. Civilian Conservation Corps Legacy, http://www.ccclegacy.org/CCC_Brief_History.html, accessed June 14, 2018.

6. Nantahala National Forest, U.S. Forest Service, Accessed June 17, 2018.

7. Elizabeth Hoyle Rucker, *The Genealogy of Peiter Heyl and His Descendants, 1100 to 1936* (1938).

8. "Minister's Wife Is Killed in Auto Accident," *Forest City Courier*, October 5, 1922, p. 1.

9. *Ibid.*

10. "Mrs. M.B. Clegg Is Dead from Injuries," *Asheville Citizen-Times*, September 29, 1922.

11. *Ibid.*

12. "Death Claims Reverend M.B. Clegg at Home Here," *Asheville Citizen-Times*, April 6, 1947.

13. Zell Miller, *The Mountains Within Me* (1976), pp. 82–85.

14. "The Road to Nowhere," Western North Carolina Attractions, https://westernncattractions.com/the-road-to-nowhere/, accessed July 8, 2018.

15. Zach Davis, "21 Appalachian Trail Statistics That Will Surprise, Entertain and Inform You," REI.com, accessed August 10, 2018.

16. The Great Smoky Mountains, The National Park Service, https://www.nps.

gov/grsm/learn/nature/index.htm, accessed July 10, 2018.

17. Bruce Henderson, "Trails Closed After Bear Attack in Smokies Park," *Charlotte Observer*, June 8, 2015, https://www.charlotteobserver.com/news/local/article23487439.html, accessed July 12, 2018.

18. Andrew Weil, "Appalachian Trail Hiker Describes Agonizing Bear Attack," WBIR, Knoxville, May 26, 2016, https://www.wbir.com/article/news/local/appalachian-trail-hiker-describes-agonizing-bear-attack/51–216960737, accessed August 29, 2018.

19. Great Smoky Mountains Guide, Appalachian Bear Rescue, October 26, 2015. http://www.greatsmokymountainsguide.com/appalachian-bear-rescue/, accessed July 12, 2018.

20. Steve Ahillen, "Black Bears Stayed Put During Gatlinburg Wildfires," *Knox News*, November 22, 2017, https://www.knoxnews.com/story/news/local/tennessee/gatlinburg/2017/11/22/gatlinburg-wildfire-black-bears-stayed-put-study-university-tennessee-students-shows/747193001/, accessed July 13, 2108.

21. Jason Fishman, "3 Cherokee Legends from the Great Smoky Mountains," June 3, 2016, https://www.visitmysmokies.com/blog/smoky-mountains/cherokee-legends-from-the-great-smoky-mountains/, accessed July 14, 2018.

22. Leon Lutz, "Woman Sets New Unsupported Record on Appalachian Trail," *Gear Junkie*, September 25, 2015, https://gearjunkie.com/appalachian-trail-unsupported-record-2015. accessed July 15, 2018.

23. David Clark, *Blue Ridge Facts and Legends* (1955), p. 64.

24. Issie Lapowsky, "Free Money: The Surprising Effects of a Basic Income Supplied by Government," *Wired*, November 12, 2017, accessed July 28, 2018.

25. "Charlie's Bunion," Wikipedia, https://en.wikipedia.org/wiki/Charlies_Bunion, accessed July 17, 2018.

26. Charlie Bunion Hike, Great Smoky Mountains, https://www.romanticashe ville.com/charlies_bunion.htm, accessed July 17, 2018.

27. David J. Scott, GoSmokies.com, April 12, 2013, http://gosmokies.knoxnews.com/photo/albums/smokies-f-4, accessed July 19, 2018.

28. Jillian Randel, "Appalachia and Our Changing Planet," *The Appalachian Voice*, April 1, 2011, http://appvoices.org/2011/04/01/appalachia-and-our-changing-planet/, accessed July 20, 2018.

29. Kevin O'Donnell, "Climate Change in Appalachia: A Study Shows That Appalachia May Provide a 'Stronghold' of Natural Resilience—But Don't Get Complacent; Or, What Happens When the Chickadees Run Out of Mountain," Now and Then FUTURE, East Tennessee State University, p. 36.

30. Amitha Kalaichandran, M.D., "Take a Walk in the Woods. Doctor's Orders." *The New York Times,* July 12, 2018, https://www.nytimes.com/2018/07/12/well/take-a-walk-in-the-woods-doctors-orders.html?smid=tw-nytimes&smtyp=cur, accessed August 5, 2018.

Part III

1. Welcome to Madison County, North Carolina, Visitmadiosncounty.com, https://www.visitmadisoncounty.com/who-we-are/town-of-hot-springs/the-german-village-wwi-internment-camp/, accessed July 31, 2018.

2. Elizabeth Laubach, "A Magical Mycology Tapestry," *The Appalachian Voice*, June 14, 2016, http://appvoices.org/2016/06/14/magical-mycology-tapestry/, accessed August 27, 2018.

3. "75th Anniversary of the Completion of the Appalachian Trail," The Appalachian Trail Conservancy, June 9, 2012, http://www.appalachiantrail.org/promo/75th-anniversary, accessed September 10, 2018.

4. Clarke Morrison, "Serial Killer Gets Life Sentence in N.C. Slayings," *Asheville Citizen-Times*, April 25, 2013; accessed August 2, 2018.

5. Msgr. Charles Pope, "The Night

Prayer of the Church as a Dress Rehearsal for Death," March 5, 2015, http://blog.adw. org/2015/03/the-night-prayer-of-the-church-as-a-rehearsal-for-death/, accessed August 3, 2018.

6. Susa M. Black, "Tree Lore: Rowan," https://www.druidry.org/library/trees/tree-lore-rowan, accessed August 30, 2018.

7. Karen Chavez, "Asheville Woman Pens 'Civil War Sites on AT,'" *Citizen-Times*, January 21, 2016, https://www.citizen-times.com/story/life/2016/01/21/asheville-woman-pens-civil-war-sites/78795242/, accessed September 2, 2018.

8. Philip Gerard, "Atrocity at Shelton Laurel," *Our State*, April 29, 2012, https://www.ourstate.com/atrocity-at-shelton-laurel/, accessed September 2, 2018.

9. "Georgians in the Union Army," The Georgia Historical Society, August 6, 2015, https://georgiahistory.com/ghmi_marker_updated/georgians-in-the-union-army/, accessed May 22, 2018.

10. The Home of Barton-Stovall's Georgia Infantry Brigade, http://www.oocities.org/athens/agora/9743/, accessed May 19, 2018.

11. Application for military pension, State of Georgia, Perry James Grogan, February 4, 1890.

12. *Ibid.*

13. David Clark, *Blue Ridge Facts and Legends* (1955), p. 58.

14. *Ibid.*

15. Peter D. Weigl and Travis W. Knowles, "Megaherbivores and Southern Appalachian Grass Balds," *Growth and Change* 26, 3 (1995): pp. 365–382.

16. John Shores as told to Stephen Tyler, *A Hostel on the Nolichucky*, 2016.

17. "Battle of the State of Franklin," Tipton-Haynes Historical Website, http://www.tipton-haynes.org/research/history/colonel-john-tipton/battle-of-the-state-of-franklin-february-27-29-1788/, accessed September 3, 2018.

18. Jan D. Curran, *The Appalachian Trail: A Journey of Discovery,* 1991, p. xviii.

19. R.V. Dietrich, "Gemrocks: Ornamental and Curio Stones," http://stone plus.cst.cmich.edu/Default.htm, accessed August 16, 2018.

20. Jan D. Curran, *The Appalachian Trail: A Journey of Discovery,* p. xviii.

21. "Roan Mountain and Roan Mountain State Park," Sherpa Guides, http://www.sherpaguides.com/north_carolina/mountains/black_mountains/roan_mountain.html, accessed August 25, 2018.

22. "The Cloudland Hotel: A Mammoth Landmark of Its Day," Mitchell County Historical Society, April 2, 2017, accessed August 19, 2018.

23. Obituary for Terence "Terry" Wayne Hill, Tetrick Funeral Home, March 30, 2016, https://www.tetrickfuneralhome.com/obituaries/Terence-Hill/#!/Obituary.

24. "The Decline of Deer Populations," Deer Friendly, http://www.deerfriendly.com/decline-of-deer-populations, accessed August 4, 2018.

25. Craig Holt, "Commission Votes to Continue Restrictions on Farm Raised Elk and Whitetails," *Carolina Sportsman*, October 30, 2014, http://www.carolina sportsman.com/details.php?id=4601, accessed August 4, 2018.

26. Sarah Gibbens, "Eastern Cougars Declared Extinct, But That May Not Be Bad," *National Geographic,* January 25, 2018, https://news.nationalgeographic.com/2018/01/north-american-eastern-cougar-mountain-lion-extinct-spd/, accessed August 4, 2018.

27. Chris Bolgiano, "Living with Cougars in the Appalachian Mountains," by The Potomac Appalachian Trail Club, Flora and Fauna, http://www.patc.us/re sources/florafauna/cougar.html, accessed August 4, 2018.

28. John Nolt, "Lost Species of Southern Appalachia," The University of Tennessee, Knoxville, https://web.utk.edu/~nolt/radio/lostspecies.html, accessed August 4, 2018.

29. *Ibid.*

30. Donald E. Davis, "Historical Significance of American Chestnut to Appalachian Culture and Ecology," Dalton State College, Social Sciences Division, 2005, pp. 2 and 3, https://ecosystems.psu.edu/

research/chestnut/information/confer-ence-2004/conference/davis, accessed August 5, 2018.

31. *Ibid.*, p. 3.

32. *Ibid.*

33. David Clark, *Blue Ridge Facts and Legends* (1955), p. 129.

34. "Building the Shelters," Appalachian Trail Histories, http://appalach iantrailhistory.org/exhibits/show/shelters/ shelterbuilding, accessed August 10, 2018.

35. Donald E. Davis, "Historical Significance of American Chestnut to Appalachian Culture and Ecology," Dalton State College, Social Sciences Division, 2005, p. 3, https://ecosystems.psu.edu/research/ chestnut/information/conference-2004/ conference/davis, accessed August 5, 2018.

36. *Ibid.*

37. Chestnut Hill, Nursery and Orchards, http://www.chestnuthilltreefarm. com/store/c/31-Dunstan-Chestnut-Trees. aspx, accessed August 31, 2018.

38. "Pond Mountain Game Lands," The Blue Ridge Conservancy, https://blue ridgeconservancy.org/pond-mountain-gamc-lands-1/, accessed October 20, 2018.

39. Meghan O'Brien, "Most People Have No Idea There's an Underwater Ghost Town Hiding in the American South," *Only in Your State*, July 9, 2016, https:// www.onlyinyourstate.com/tennessee/tn-ghost-town-underwater/, accessed October 22, 2018.

40. Emory L. Hamilton, "The Killing of William Parks in Powell Valley," from the unpublished manuscript *Indian Atrocities Along the Clinch, Powell, and Holston Rivers*, pp. 21–22.

41. *Ibid.*, pp. 37–38.

42. *Ibid.*

Bibliography

Clark, David. *Blue Ridge Facts and Legends*. Charlotte, NC: Clark Publishing, 1955.

Cook, Raymond A. *Mountain Singer: The Life and Legacy of Byron Herbert Reece*. Atlanta, GA: Cherokee Publishing, 1980.

Curran, Jan D. *The Appalachian Trail-a Journey of Discovery*. Moore Haven, FL: Rainbow Books, 1991.

Dabney, Joseph Earl. *Mountain Spirits: A Chronicle of Corn Whiskey from King James' Ulster Plantation to America's Appalachians and the Moonshine Life*. New York: Charles Scribner's Sons, 1974.

Davis, Donald E. *Historical Significance of American Chestnut to Appalachian Culture and Ecology* 2004, https://ecosystems.psu.edu/research/chestnut/information/conference-2004/conference/davis.

Dawson County; Georgia Heritage, 1857–1996. Dawson County Historical and Genealogical Society, 1999.

Ehle, John. *Trail of Tears: The Rise and Fall of the Cherokee Nation*. New York: Anchor Books, published by Doubleday, 1988.

Emerson, Bo. "Mountain Crossing a Hikers Paradise." *The Atlanta Journal-Constitution*, April 17, 2010, https://www.ajc.com/travel/newsmedleystory1296876/6eDOFyNNypx6Qn9PSq8uHN/.

Hamilton, Emory L. "The Killing of William Parks in Powell Valley." From the unpublished manuscript *Indian Atrocities Along the Clinch, Powell, and Holston Rivers*.

Kellner, Esther. *Moonshine: Its History and Folklore*. New York: Weathervane Books, 1971.

Miller, Zell. *The Mountains Within Me*. Toccoa, GA: Commercial Printing Company, 1976.

O'Donnell, Kevin. "Climate Change in Appalachia: A Study Shows That Appalachia May Provide a 'Stronghold' of Natural Resilience—But Don't Get Complacent; Or, What Happens When the Chickadees Run Out of Mountain." Now and Then FUTURE, East Tennessee State University.

Shores, John, as told to Stephen Tyler. *A Hostel on the Nolichucky*. Erwin, TN: Trailside Books, 2016.

Williams, David. *The Georgia Gold Rush: Twenty-Niners, Cherokees, and Gold Fever*. Columbia: University of South Carolina Press, 1993.

Index